The Cultural Turn in Translation Studies

Applying the latest Western translation theories to the situation in China, this book redefines translation from an interdisciplinary and intercultural perspective, bringing intercultural semiotic translation into the sight of translation researchers.

This book systematically expounds on the cultural turn in translation studies and contributes to the escape of translation studies from the "cage of language". It focuses on discussing the deconstructive, postmodernist, and cultural translation theories that have motivated and promoted the cultural turn, especially Benjamin's translation theory, Derrida's deconstructive view of translation, and postcolonial translation theory. It also discusses in detail the theories of major international translation theorists, including Hillis Miller, Wolfgang Iser, Edward Said, Gayatri Spivak, Homi Bhabha, André Lefevere, Susan Bassnett, and Lawrence Venuti. These theories are mostly based on examples from Western or English-language texts, leaving a wide gap in the discourse of the field. This book seeks to fill that gap. For example, intercultural semiotic translation is defined and explained through the successful experiences of the Chinese translator Fu Lei. The role of translation during the Chinese revolution and the relocation of Chinese culture in the global cultural landscape through translation are also discussed.

This book will be an essential read to students and scholars of translation studies and Chinese studies. It will also be a useful resource for translators and researchers of comparative literature and cultural studies.

Professor Wang Ning is currently Dean of the School of Humanities and Distinguished University Professor of Humanities and Social Sciences at Shanghai Jiao Tong University, China. He has been a Changjiang Distinguished Professor in the Foreign Languages and Literature Department of Tsinghua University, China, where he was also a member of the Academic Committee of the University and Head of the Academic Committee of the Department. His academic titles also include past President of the Chinese Comparative Literature Association, Vice President of the Chinese Association of Chinese and Foreign Literary Theory, and Vice President of the Chinese Association for Theory of Literature and Art. Professor Wang is the author of more than 20 books in Chinese, and 3 in English, including *After Postmodernism* (2023) by Routledge.

China Perspectives

The *China Perspectives* series focuses on translating and publishing works by leading Chinese scholars, writing about both global topics and China-related themes. It covers Humanities & Social Sciences, Education, Media and Psychology, as well as many interdisciplinary themes.

This is the first time any of these books have been published in English for international readers. The series aims to put forward a Chinese perspective, give insights into cutting-edge academic thinking in China, and inspire researchers globally.

To submit proposals, please contact the Taylor & Francis Publisher for the China Publishing Programme, Lian Sun (Lian.Sun@informa.com)

Titles in linguistics currently include:

Singapore Mandarin Grammar I
Lu Jianming

Cognitive Neural Mechanism of Semantic Rhetoric
Qiaoyun Liao, Lijun Meng

Singapore Mandarin Grammar II
Lu Jianming

Automated Written Corrective Feedback in Research Paper Revision
The Good, The Bad, and The Missing
Qian Guo, Ruiling Feng, and Yuanfang Hua

The Chinese Rhyme Tables
Volume II
Pan Wenguo

The Cultural Turn in Translation Studies
Wang Ning

For more information, please visit https://www.routledge.com/China-Perspectives/book-series/CPH

The Cultural Turn in Translation Studies

Wang Ning

Taylor & Francis Group
LONDON AND NEW YORK

This work is published with financial support from Chinese Fund for the Humanities and Social Sciences [Grant Number: 20WWWB001].

First published 2024
by Routledge
4 Park Square, Milton Park, Abingdon, Oxon OX14 4RN

and by Routledge
605 Third Avenue, New York, NY 10158

Routledge is an imprint of the Taylor & Francis Group, an informa business

© 2024 Wang Ning

Translated by Deng Xiangjun and Audrey J. Heijns

The right of Wang Ning to be identified as author of this work has been asserted in accordance with sections 77 and 78 of the Copyright, Designs and Patents Act 1988.

All rights reserved. No part of this book may be reprinted or reproduced or utilised in any form or by any electronic, mechanical, or other means, now known or hereafter invented, including photocopying and recording, or in any information storage or retrieval system, without permission in writing from the publishers.

Trademark notice: Product or corporate names may be trademarks or registered trademarks, and are used only for identification and explanation without intent to infringe.

English version by permission of Tsinghua University Press.

British Library Cataloguing-in-Publication Data
A catalogue record for this book is available from the British Library

ISBN: 978-1-032-63819-5 (hbk)
ISBN: 978-1-032-64293-2 (pbk)
ISBN: 978-1-032-64276-5 (ebk)

DOI: 10.4324/9781032642765

Typeset in Times New Roman
by codeMantra

Contents

Acknowledgments	*vii*
Preface	*ix*

1	Introduction: the cultural turn in translation and the turn to translation studies in cultural studies	1
2	Theorizing translation studies: an interdisciplinary perspective	15
3	The cultural turn of deconstruction: Benjamin and Derrida	29
4	Deconstruction and cultural criticism: domestication and foreignization in translation	54
5	The theory and practice of postcolonial translation	81
6	The intervention of comparative literature and cultural studies	106
7	Intersemiotic translation and the "visual turn" in cultural studies	135
8	Translation and the relocation of cultures	165
9	The role of translation in the Chinese revolution	178
10	The future of translation studies in the age of globalization	192

Bibliography	*211*
Index	*221*

Acknowledgments

This book was originally written in Chinese and published by Tsinghua University Press in 2009. Before the publication of the English version, I would like to thank the translators, Deng Xiangjun and Audrey J. Heijns, as well as the reviewers of the translation, Tan Zaixi and Bradley C. Phillips, for the great efforts they have made in rendering this book into English faithfully and reliably. The first draft of their translation was sent to me for careful review, and I found their understanding of the views of this book accurate and their expression in English smooth and faithful. Of course, any errors or infelicities that may remain are my sole responsibility.

Preface

Before the English version of this book is about to be delivered to the publishing house for publication, I feel it necessary to explain the context of my writing of this book and the process of revision, and also to thank the institutions and individuals who have supported this book project all along.

First of all, I would like to speak a little about my linkage to translation. Readers familiar with my academic career may probably know that my major at university was English language and literature. Initially, my ideal was to be able to translate and introduce to China masterpieces of foreign literature, mainly those from English-speaking countries. Backed by such a motive, after graduating from college, I began to translate short stories and became one of the first in the 1980s to translate the works by some of my favorite authors, including O. Henry's "After 20 Years"; Jack London's "The Law of Life", "The Heathen", and "A Piece of Steak"; Hemingway's "A Clean, Well-lighted Place", "The Killers", and "Hills Like White Elephants"; and Saul Bellow's novella *Leaving the Yellow House*. I had been so deeply attracted by these works that I often forgot meal times and spent sleepless nights translating them into Chinese. I then sent them out to different literary magazines, but like all novice translators, most of those translations got rejected by the magazines, for various reasons. Some of them were not published until I established my name in academic circles many years later, while some were not submitted to any place at all because seemingly better versions had been found published and I did not want to produce repeated publications. There was no doubt, however, that, whether or not those early efforts had turned out well, they had laid the foundation for me in producing more translations in subsequent years. It was around the mid-1980s that I put my hand to translating full-length works. By that time, that is, after going through those prior practices, I had well grasped some of the skills and techniques of literary translation and began to publish translations in magazines quite frequently. Therefore, I was fortunate enough to receive the invitation to translate or edit four full-length works all at once. Liu Yawei, Editor of the Shaanxi People's Publishing House, invited me to cooperate with my friends Xu Xin and Ming Dong Gu to translate the novel *Tender Is the Night* by modern American novelist Francis Scott Fitzgerald. After its publication in 1987, the translation was purchased by two other publishing houses for its copyright and was reprinted again and again, and it can still be seen in bookstores today. Zhang Xuecheng, Editor of the Jiangsu Art Publishing House, invited me and Sun Jin to translate *A History of Western Art* by British art historian Michael Levy. The translation was also published in 1987, but it was reprinted only once, because the publishing house failed to purchase the copyright of the original book. Qian Zhongwen, a research fellow at the Institute of Literature of the Chinese Academy of Social Sciences, invited me and two other colleagues to translate the American literary critic Frederick John Hoffman's theoretical work *Freudianism and the Literary Mind* for the "Foreign Literature and Art Translation Series" that he edited. The translation was published by SDX Joint Publishing Company in 1987, but it was also not reprinted due to the copyright issue. Jiang Rong, Senior Editor of the Peking University Press, invited Ming Dong Gu and me to compile a book *On Literary Creation by Nobel Prize Laureates*, which was published in 1987. It can be said that 1987 was a very fruitful year for me in the field of translation and people think of it as my time of rising in the field. Although I had accumulated experience for several years before that, it was nonetheless surprising that my full-length translated books appeared in print all together in the same year. At the same time, because of those book-length translations, I suddenly received attention from domestic translation and theoretical circles. Since then, more publishers began to invite me to compile, translate, and write books, but I was busy writing my doctoral dissertation and had to concentrate on my research work, so I completed the writing and defense of my doctoral thesis on time at Peking University in 1989. Probably not long after that, I gradually drifted away from translation practice, to eventually land in the field of literary theory and criticism and comparative literature. Nevertheless, I still have not completely left translation practice. Whenever I read a book that has theoretical depth and can contribute to my academic research, I can't help but feel the itch to either write a book review recommending it to relevant publishers, or invite friends to translate it with me. In this way, I translated and published some theoretical works from time to time, including Dutch scholars Douwe Fokkema and Hans Bertens' edited volume *Approaching Postmodernism*, American scholar Arif Dirlik's two monographs *The Post-Revolutionary Aura* and *Postcolonial Criticism in the Era of Transnational Capitalism*, and *The Routledge Encyclopedia of Globalization*, which I co-edited. These translated or edited works are not only of great help to my own research but also laid a necessary practical foundation for me to engage in the study of translation theory.

Presumably, my embarking on the road of translation studies hinges on the following four factors: first, at an international conference, I had the privilege of meeting the famous American translation theorist André Lefevere. Since we were both involved in translation studies from the perspectives of comparative literature and cultural studies, we felt like old friends at first sight and soon became real friends. He immediately invited me to edit a collection of English articles entitled *Chinese Translation Studies* for the "Translation Studies Series" co-edited by him and

Susan Bassnett. After I returned home, I immediately invited some senior scholars and peers to write some articles from their own perspectives. In the summer of 1993, I flew from Toronto, Canada, to the University of Texas in Austin, and stayed at Lefevere's house for a month to discuss with him the draft papers and how to modify and edit them. Later, because he got cancer and died soon, my manuscript that had not yet been entered into the computer got misplaced. Despite this, many of our conversations are still fresh in my memory, and I can say that he led me to the door of international translation studies. Second, at an international conference on literature and psychoanalysis, I met the Danish scholar of translation studies Cay Dollerup. From our conversation, I learned that his main professional interest is not psychoanalysis, but translation studies. He had founded the international journal of translation studies *Perspectives: Studies in Translatology* just a few years before.[1] Although he himself did not know Chinese, he was very interested in Chinese culture and literature. Through many conversations with me, he decided to invite me to edit a special issue on Chinese translation studies for the journal. So, I retrieved part of the photocopy of the old manuscript of the collection of papers that I had originally edited for Lefevere and invited some other scholars to write a few more. Together, they were compiled into the special issue "Chinese Translation Studies", published as Issue 1 of Volume 4 (1996) of *Perspectives: Studies in Translatology*. Upon publication, it had a certain impact on the circle of international translation studies, and as a result, I have been frequently invited to attend international conferences and give speeches at universities in some European, American, Australian, and Asian countries. Third, an important factor that directly prompted me to enter the international translation studies circle is that I accepted the invitation of Dollerup and served as one of the co-editors of *Perspectives: Studies in Translatology* in 2001. Since then, I have had a closer relationship with translation studies. I deeply understand that in order to make China's translation studies go global and make our voice heard in the international academic community, it is important to join in editing an international academic journal and publish articles in English. Therefore, I made full use of this position, publishing more than 30 papers by Chinese scholars and editing three special issues for the journal, so that China's strategy for its humanities and social sciences to go international seemed to have made a breakthrough first in the field of translation studies. The fourth factor is that after I came to Tsinghua University at the beginning of this century, I offered two compulsory and elective courses on translation theory and practice in the Department of Foreign Languages and Literature, which allowed me to apply my academic research findings directly to my teaching practice. This book originally came from my lecture notes prepared for the course "Introduction to Translation Studies" for senior undergraduate students there. Later, in 2004, I applied and got a grant from the National Social Sciences Fund, which gave me the opportunity to transform the lecture notes into a theoretical monograph. Some scholars suggest that this book be used as a textbook for translation and comparative literature majors in universities, but I think it might as well be used as a teaching reference book for graduates first, and then get revised and enriched after a period of trial.

Of course, the writing of this book is inseparable from the help and support of colleagues and friends both at home and abroad. Some chapters of this book have been published in some domestic journals in the form of articles. Some chapters have been delivered as English speeches in the following overseas universities or at international conferences held there. I would now like to take this opportunity to thank the scholars who invited me to give those speeches: Professor Robert Hegel of Washington University in St. Louis in the United States, Professor Mary Jacobus of Cambridge University, Professor Susan Bassnett and Dr. Red Chan of Warwick University, Professor Guosheng Chen of RMIT in Australia, Professor Laurence Wong of the Chinese University of Hong Kong, and Professor Sun Yifeng and Professor Li Defeng of the University of Macao. Their warm invitations and careful arrangements gave me the opportunity to listen to the opinions of peer experts while interacting with international academic circles, so as to modify parts of this book.

The eventual publication of the book as a monograph was also made possible by the funding and support from the following institutions: A grant from the National Philosophy and Social Sciences Planning Office allowed me to have sufficient funds and time to write up the book; a generous grant from the Humanities Center of Washington University in St. Louis enabled me to take four months off work to consult materials and concentrate on the revision of the book draft; and the encouragement and urging by my colleague Professor Luo Xuanmin, editor of the series in which this book was originally published, also accelerated my pace of compiling and finally submitting the manuscript to Tsinghua University Press for publication. Here, I would also like to express my sincere thanks to Gong Li, then director of the foreign language branch of Tsinghua University Press, and editor Qu Haiyan. Without their hard work and careful editing, the first edition of this book could not have been published successfully.

After its first publication, the book has been well received by domestic academic circles. Comparative literature and translation majors in some colleges and universities use it as a teaching reference book for postgraduates. The publisher has reprinted it once. During this period, the editor urged me from time to time to revise and supplement it in order to publish a hardcover edition. I have always had such a plan to do so, but my busy schedule of teaching, research, and administrative duties kept delaying my revision plan until the book luckily won inclusion in the Chinese academic translation projects funded by China's National Social Sciences Fund, and several translators asked to translate it into different languages. Only then did I realize that in the face of international readers, I must revise and supplement it to reflect the current situation of translation studies more comprehensively, and communicate and have dialogues with international counterparts from the perspective of China. So, I revised the book, by adding two chapters, supplementing the last chapter with an extra section, and updating the references. Here, I sincerely thank Hao Jianhua, current director of the foreign language branch of Tsinghua University Press, and Liu Xizhen, director of the business department, for their strong support and encouragement.

Lastly, a team from Shenzhen University translated my book into English. Upon its publication, I earnestly welcome criticism and suggestions from those in the profession and general readers, so that it may be improved in future editions.

Wang Ning
Shanghai, China
June 2023

Note

1 Translators' note: The journal is now renamed *Perspectives: Studies in Translation Practice and Theory.*

1 Introduction

The cultural turn in translation and the turn to translation studies in cultural studies

In the current international academic circles of the humanities and social sciences, examining translation issues from the perspectives of comparative literature and cultural studies is nothing new. However, it has been at least since the 1990s that translation studies has really been examined in the context of comparative cultural studies between East and West. In this respect, the ground-breaking work done by comparative literature and translation studies scholars Susan Bassnett and André Lefevere cannot be ignored.[1] Both scholars studied translation from the perspectives of comparative literature and cultural studies, so their theoretical starting point of translation studies was, as a matter of course, comparative literature. Moreover, compared with traditional European comparatists, they were even more concerned with the development of cultural studies and attempted to expand the narrow scope of comparative literature to the broader field of comparative culture. In addition, both of them were the main advocates and promoters of the "cultural turn" in contemporary translation studies, so by having such important figures to jointly promote it, the cultural turn in translation studies in the early 1990s became very powerful. With the passage of time, after the cultural turn in translation studies continued for about a decade, the two scholars published a volume together: *Constructing Cultures: Essays on Literary Translation* (1998),[2] in which they introduced a new view of the translation turn in cultural studies. This in fact contributed to the reversal of the Anglocentric model of cultural studies and became the first attempt to expand cultural studies to the more encompassing discourse of cross-cultural studies through the entry point of translation studies. Unfortunately, they did not further elucidate their position, and probably also because of the limitations of their knowledge, they were unable to engage with the theoretical issues of East-West cross-cultural comparisons which are even broader in scope. We are now in an era of globalization. In this era, with the expansion of the translation field and a re-emergence of translation studies, coupled with a setback in cultural studies, the "translation turn" in cultural studies has proved imminent and will have promising prospects of development. Therefore, this introduction tentatively borrows the original intention of the "translation turn", extends it to the Chinese and comparative contexts, and sets off discussions surrounding translation and culture, with the two types of "turns" interacting with each other.

1.1 Cultural translation, or the reconstruction of translation based on cultural studies

Undoubtedly, in the current era of globalization, English as a hegemonic language has constantly penetrated weaker nations and countries; some Third World countries and even people in developed European countries have no choice but to spend a lot of energy to learn English to communicate and "connect" with the world. Therefore, perhaps some people might well wonder whether there is a need for translation in the future considering that the whole world is learning English and communicating directly in English in mutual exchange. Will the function of translation disappear naturally in the era of globalization? Our answer to this seemingly simple yet in fact very complicated question is that the function of translation has not diminished and will not diminish even if the present situation looks like such. On the contrary, translation has already shown and will continue to show its increasing importance. This is not unlike what happened to the influence of globalization on culture. Instead of making different cultures converge, globalization has accelerated the pace at which cultures have become more diversified, and as a result translation research that is carried out from the perspective of cultural studies has become a cutting-edge disciplinary theoretical subject among contemporary international academic communities. In this respect, such scholars and theorists as Jacques Derrida, Cay Dollerup, José Lambert, Wolfgang Iser, Horst Turk, Susan Bassnett, Theo Hermans, J. Hillis Miller, Gayatri Spivak, Homi Bhabha, André Lefevere, Eugene Chen Eoyang, and Thomas Beebee have all conducted in-depth research, and published important works, in which they put forward many insights that are instructive for our research today. Scholars who study translation theory often call those who do translation studies from cultural perspectives collectively the "Cultural School". In fact, they are not a "school", at least not in the sense of a close-knit group with a common program, but a developing direction or a trend. Centered on this direction or trend, a group of generally like-minded scholars carry out discussions and learn from each other by exchanging views, giving the impression that they have formed an invisible research group. Of course, it is impossible to give a fixed name list of all the scholars involved in this trend, especially since it is continuously expanding. In an era of globalization where "culture" is all-encompassing and pervasive, it is even more difficult for translation to break away from the influence of "culture". As it is increasingly attracting the attention of so-called "outsiders",[3] the boundaries of translation studies continue to expand. We can hardly find the terminology that traditional translation scholars conventionally used in the writing of these "outsiders", but constantly see new terms closely related to culture. As a result, some translation researchers who abide by traditional concepts pound the table and jump to their feet to express objection, attempting to defend the "purity" and seriousness of traditional translation studies. Such charitable intention is perhaps understandable but in our intercultural and interdisciplinary information age, even the definition of translation is constantly changing. To keep a discipline vibrant and dynamic, it must constantly innovate its methods and concepts to meet the needs of the ever-changing era. In this view, if translation studies only attracts the attention of a small number of experts like in the past, it will never transcend its "marginalized" position. What used to be considered "pseudo-translation" or "adaptation" or "rewriting" have perhaps overtly entered the vision of today's translation scholars. Is this actually a good or bad thing for the discipline? It is probably too early to draw a conclusion now. Perhaps readers will naturally draw convincing conclusions through reading this book.

Admittedly, the research findings of the above-mentioned Western scholars have indeed provided methodological insight for Chinese scholars to conduct in-depth research from an East-West cross-cultural theoretical perspective, and at the same time also laid the necessary foundation for us to further examine translation problems and translation phenomena in a broader cross-cultural context. However, except for Eugene Chen Eoyang, a sinologist born in China who is proficient in the Chinese language and culture, all the works and case studies by the above-mentioned scholars are based on their own cultural context, or rely on the medium of translation in their research work, so it is difficult to say if the conclusions that they draw are comprehensive and flawless. Of course, many of them have an interest in Eastern culture, including Chinese language and culture, with some even having spent much time studying Chinese, but the fact remains that even for Chinese scholars who are born and raised in China, it requires long-term arduous study to master the true meaning of traditional Chinese culture. Thus, compared with the development in the international academic circles of the last four decades, one can say that translation studies in China is still in its infancy. The majority of translation scholars are unable to go beyond the superficial level in discussing Yan Fu's three principles of *xin* [faithfulness], *da* [expressiveness], and *ya* [elegance], or stay at the level of introducing Western translation theories and fail to consciously include translation studies in the context of intercultural research in the age of globalization. Therefore, there are only very few solid research works and perhaps at most only some articles scattered in journals or edited volumes in China that can engage in dialogue on equal footing with the international academic world.[4] Of course, the advent of the globalization era has greatly accelerated our exchanges with the international academic community. On the large platform of globalization, it is an indisputable fact that the dialogue between Chinese and Western scholars has reached an equal level. Moreover, an increasing number of Western scholars have realized that engagement in Chinese and Western translation studies or cultural studies will not be complete without knowledge of Chinese culture or Chinese language. Considering current translation studies still adheres to the narrow linguistic dilemma to a considerable degree, it is undoubtedly essential to reflect on the issues of translation studies from a broad global context. On the one hand, this can make up for the shortcomings of Chinese scholarship in this area; on the other hand, it can also encourage us to use Chinese scholars' research achievements to have fruitful academic discussions with foreign scholars in the same field, and from this, we can achieve equal dialogue with international academic circles.[5] Ultimately, after these discussions and dialogues, we can question or even reconstruct the kind of translation theory that has been abstracted from the Western cultural context, which I think is the historical mission of Chinese translation researchers.

Since we uphold our views on cultural translation,[6] I believe that when we examine the impact and purpose of globalization within the domain of translation from a cultural dimension, we should regard language as a vehicle to disseminate culture. The act of examining translation is an effective attempt to combine empirical studies of linguistics, humanistic interpretation of cultural studies, and case analysis of translation texts, with the ultimate goal to achieve a theoretical construction of translation studies, a new immature marginalized discipline. As mentioned above, in the present context of globalization, the function of translation has not been weakened, but has become more important, and along with it the definition of translation should also undergo change. Translation studies, as a discipline that lies in the marginal area between the humanities, social sciences, and natural sciences, should have its own means of existence. In this regard, many colleagues in academia both in the East and West and I have all along been calling for the inception and development of translation studies as an academic discipline. The next chapter of this book will discuss this issue, so I will not elaborate on it here. I think that in the era of globalization since the dissemination of information and the rise of mass media have made the connection between globalization and culture even more inextricably linked, translation undoubtedly serves as a tool for the dissemination of information. Hence the study of translation should also be free from the narrow linguistic constraints on text level and placed in the broader intercultural context, so that the conclusions drawn can have general methodological guidance for other disciplines. In view of this, one of our urgent tasks on hand is to give a new interpretation and explanation to the existing definition of translation: from the translation (conversion) of texts gradually expanding to the translation of cultural connotation (conversion in form and the dynamic interpretation and reproduction of connotation). As a result, the study of translation in itself is a cultural issue, especially if it involves an interactive relationship and comparative study of two cultures. In this respect, the view that "translation is a cultural construction" put forward by Bassnett and Lefevere is quite insightful, and their regarding translation as an interaction between two cultures also paves the way for translation studies and cultural studies to mutually infiltrate and complement each other. Indeed, there is no doubt that the rise and fall of translation studies is closely related to the status of cultural studies. Especially when cultural studies shows signs of "crises", it is imperative to call for the "translation studies turn" in cultural studies. Given the fact that translation involves at least two languages and cultures, this fundamentally breaks down the constraints and limitations of the Anglocentrism existing in cultural studies and lays the foundation for the coming of a truly multicultural pattern. Furthermore, intercultural translation studies brings the intercultural perspective to scholars in cultural studies and enables them to go beyond the narrow mode of "Anglocentrism" to enter a broader cross-cultural context.

Indeed, as Chinese practitioners of translation studies and cultural studies, we must first firmly establish ourselves in Chinese cultural soil, and examine the major function that translation has for the construction of new culture and new literature in China. Anyone familiar with modern Chinese history knows that cultural translation has a long and far-reaching history in China, which started from the large-scale translation and introduction of foreign cultures at the end of the Qing dynasty and the beginning of the early years of the Republic of China,[7] or even earlier. Therefore, in the discussion about the relation between translation and culture in the Chinese context, it is inevitable to think about the irreplaceable role that translation plays in promoting the formation and development of Chinese cultural modernity and constructing the theoretical discourse of Chinese literary criticism. As we all know, Chinese literature has in the past century been influenced largely by Western culture and literature, so much so that many Chinese scholars who uphold traditional concepts believe that a history of modern Chinese literature is in fact a history of Western culture colonizing Chinese culture, or in other words, a history of translating foreign literature. They are particularly opposed to the May Fourth movement because it started a sort of new Chinese literature, and at the same time also started China's cultural modernity. An especially important phenomenon during the May Fourth movement is that a large number of foreign literary works, especially Western literary works and cultural trends and theories, were translated into Chinese, making Chinese language "Europeanized" and no longer pure. Considering the contemporary view of "faithfulness", it is entirely reasonable to criticize the May Fourth pioneers, for many of them were clearly unfaithful and some even based their translations on source texts which were themselves translations from another language, but the objective effect and influence of these "translated" texts cannot be denied. Of course, one of the consequences was the "Europeanization" of the Chinese language and the "loss" of Chinese literary discourse. In all fairness, the concept of "grabbism" put forward by Lu Xun back then indeed promoted this kind of Western learning spreading to the East.[8] As we all know, when Lu Xun spoke about the inspiration for his own fiction writing, he once said without reservation that his writing "relied on nothing but the hundreds of foreign works he had read and a little knowledge of medical science", with no other preparation whatsoever.[9] Because of this statement, Lu Xun, viewed as a representative of this "Westernization", later became the target of attack by conservative forces. There were other May Fourth leading figures including Hu Shi and Guo Moruo, who effectively deconstructed the traditional Chinese literary discourse by translating and introducing Western literary works on a large scale. As a result, a "translated", "hybrid" discourse system of modern Chinese literature, or a canon of modern Chinese literature, was formed. Due to the great difference from its predecessors, as well as the natural distinction from Western literature, this discursive system could carry out dialogue with classical Chinese literature, as well as with Western cultural modernity. Seen from another angle it actually dispels the myth of a singular modernity, which paved the way for an "alternative" modernity with Chinese characteristics, or another form of modernity.[10] Therefore, it can be said that translation had an important position in the history of modern Chinese literature. We can further infer that translated literature should be considered an inseparable part of modern Chinese literary history. If seen from the perspective of comparative literature, a history of modern Chinese literature is to a certain extent a history of translated literature, and the study of translation is also an important aspect of cultural studies. In other words, from the angle of culture, translation is in the end a kind of cultural phenomenon, even more so if it involves literary translation because the concept of translation as we understand it nowadays is no longer a purely technical rendition from one language into another, but also a transformation, interpretation, and representation from one form into another, and from one culture into another. This kind of transformation and representation is achieved precisely through the main medium of language.

1.2 The dilemma of cultural studies and the way out

Although cultural studies was introduced to China two decades ago, and the discussions and controversies evoked in the Chinese mainland, Hong Kong and Taiwan have attracted the attention of the academic communities worldwide,[11] to this day the meaning and definition of "cultural studies" remain very vague among many scholars. Therefore, I think it is necessary to define it before discussing the future trend of cultural studies and its interaction with translation studies. The cultural studies that I discuss in this introduction refers to "Cultural Studies", both words starting with a capital letter, implying that it is no longer the elite cultural studies in the traditional sense, but a discursive mode crossing disciplinary boundaries, fields of aesthetic expression and academic research methods that are currently popular in academic fields in the West. It emerged from literary studies in the UK, its rise marked by the establishment of the Centre for Contemporary Cultural Studies (CCCS), at the University of Birmingham in 1964, but if you trace its earlier roots, then you will find the seeds in F. R. Leavis' elite cultural studies, dating to the 1940s.[12] If you apply the narrow definition set by Bassnett and Lefevere, then it originated in 1976 at the Translation Studies Colloquium in Leuven. In this view, cultural studies appeared much earlier than translation studies; therefore, it goes without saying that its methodology was more mature than that of translation studies. As a result, early translation studies theorists called for the cultural turn in translation studies, which has certain guiding effects in terms of theory and methodology. In fact, the target of the "cultural studies" discussed here is not at all the sophisticated cultural products that are written on the pages of a book—literature—but is the ongoing, vivid cultural phenomena right now, for example, our community culture, consumer culture, popular culture, fashion and film culture, media culture, even Internet culture and online writing. These are all cultural phenomena that occur in our daily lives and inevitably affect us. Although early researchers of culture failed to include translation studies in their vision, as translation studies evolved and its interaction with cultural studies became more and more prominent, translation studies had inadvertently joined the area of media studies in cultural studies by the 1990s and drawn the attention of many scholars in cultural studies. In particular, since the advent of the era of globalization, when translation of culture has become increasingly important, studying translation from the perspective of cultural studies has naturally formed a basic consensus among scholars of translation studies, especially for literary translation and the interpretation and representation of cultural phenomena.

We say that there is a close inseparable relation between translation studies and cultural studies, which is based on the following fact: cultural studies emerged as a non-elite academic discourse and research method, with its main characteristics being "anti-institutional" and "critical". This, though with a different object of research, is similar to translation studies' marginality, the rebellion against the traditional discipline, and the "creative treason" against the original. It cannot be denied that Western Marxism played an irreplaceable role in the contemporary development of cultural studies. For example, Marxist theorists, such as Raymond Williams and Terry Eagleton in the UK, and Fredric Jameson in the US, had a leading role in the development and prosperity of cultural studies and cultural criticism in the English-speaking or Anglophone world. Given the "anti-elite" and "mass-oriented" characteristics of cultural studies, it posed a great challenge and had an impact on literary studies, causing many scholars who adhere to conventional concepts, out of concern for the fate of literary studies, to bear a natural hostility to cultural studies. They believe that the rise of cultural studies and the prosperity of cultural criticism will cause or signal the end of literary studies and literary criticism, especially because the latter tends to focus on form and aesthetics which is the exact opposite of the "anti-aesthetic" nature of cultural studies. Of course, there are also scholars who attempt to communicate and coordinate between cultural and literary studies or try to place literary studies in the broader (cross-)cultural context for investigation and research. This is of course feasible, and it has already achieved some effect. Today an increasingly large number of researchers in literary studies have realized this fact: cultural studies is not completely in opposition to literary studies, but they kind of complement each other.[13] This will be discussed in more detail in Chapter 6.

Let us now turn to the current situation of translation studies. Similar to cultural studies, translation studies has been a marginal field since its inception. This is its weakness as well as its strength: it is not tied to whatever the established discipline approves, but it can move between many disciplines. For a long time, it did not exist in the most prestigious universities in Europe and the US, while it was once demoted to a research direction under a tertiary or secondary discipline in China's educational system.[14] However, its interdisciplinary and marginal nature enabled it to enter into dialogue with natural sciences, social sciences, and the humanities. In other words, scholars from natural sciences, social sciences and the humanities could all in their own discipline be involved in translation studies. It was entirely possible for them to step beyond the boundaries of their own discipline and address a wider range of cultural phenomena. In addition, as in the situation in cultural studies, over the past two decades, a group of world-class researchers in literary and cultural studies, including Jacques Derrida, Wolfgang Iser, Hillis Miller, Gayatri Spivak, and Homi Bhabha have become aware of the importance of translation in disseminating culture. Each of them in their own research fields has become involved in translation studies and wrote works that have had great theoretical impact and insight, and to some extent guide the research direction of translation studies scholars. In addition, the late American deconstructionist critic

Paul de Man's interpretation of German modern thinker Walter Benjamin's cultural translation theory has further contributed to the marriage of translation studies with cultural studies. If translation studies needed a "cultural turn" when it was in its infancy, then cultural studies, which is in a crisis at this moment, should also call for a "translation turn".

It is beyond doubt that cultural studies has occupied an important position in the contemporary field of the humanities for more than two decades. Some people think it has reached its zenith and is about to decline, after which literary studies will resume its leading role. Although I beg to differ, I am also aware of its latent "crisis". Indeed, the current globalization is beneficial to the development of cultural studies focusing on non-elitist culture. So, what direction has cultural studies developed since the start of the twenty-first century? This is of course an issue that concerns scholars. I believe that in the context of globalization, cultural studies will develop in the following three directions. First, it will advance beyond the "Western-centric" and "English-centric" research mode, and take the cultural phenomena of different languages, nations, and cultural traditions as the object of research, to contribute to the construction of cultural theory. This extended cultural theory, which is developed from its core of literature and art, can be abstracted into a theory that, on the one hand, is self-sufficient and, on the other, can be used to guide the study of all cultural phenomena, including literature and art. Second, while following the earlier elitist literary route, with literature (aesthetic culture) as its main object of study, it will expand its research scope to ultimately realize a cultural study of literature with expanded boundaries. Third, it will completely turn away from the purpose of elite literature, and move instead in the direction of mass media and all the phenomena that have aesthetic and cultural meaning in daily life, or it will investigate these phenomena from the perspectives of anthropology or sociology, and finally set up a "quasi-discipline" separated from literature and art. For literary scholars, focusing on the second direction may perhaps be the most suitable, because it can retain their "elite" status of literary scholars, and at the same time can also broaden their research perspectives to ultimately achieve transcendence in interdisciplinary and intercultural literary research. For translation researchers, directions (1) and (2) are very suitable. As for the first direction, the hegemony of cultural studies' "English-centrism" has already been disrupted by cultural diversity as a result of globalization. In future cultural exchanges, other major languages, in addition to English as the main medium, will play an increasingly irreplaceable role. In this regard, the popularity of the Chinese language will be confirmed as China's comprehensive national power grows stronger and the value of Chinese culture becomes more prominent. As for the second direction, through cultural translation with more "interpretive" meaning, elite culture will become more popular, and culture will become more diverse and "hybrid". As a result, the "coordinating" and "interactive" role of translation between different cultures will become increasingly indispensable. It can even to a certain extent help cultural studies to get out of the increasingly closed field of "English-centrism", and achieve intercultural purpose. I will go into further detail on this in the last section of the introduction.

1.3 The "translation studies turn" as an approach to cultural studies

In view of the situation in cultural studies, some scholars in the West believe that if there was a "cultural turn" in translation studies in the early 1990s, then at the current stage, should we call for a "translation turn" in cultural studies? Since no research between two or more cultures and literatures can be done without the medium of translation, or rather, since translation in itself is a sort of cultural translation that transcends the confines of language and text, it is only a matter of course to call for the translation turn in cultural studies. As cultural studies is increasingly becoming a discipline and the awareness of translation as a discipline should accordingly also gain strength, I change "translation turn" into "translation studies turn", with the intention of discussing the issue from a theoretical perspective. Undoubtedly, from the cultural perspective, translation has actually become a kind of cultural dissemination and interpretation. In particular, the translation of literary works is so complicated and sophisticated, that even in the globalization era, machine translation and the newly rising Artificial Intelligence (AI) translation cannot convey their profound aesthetic connotations and beautiful literary styles. In order to achieve the ideal literary translation, a kind of equilibrium between the translator and the author has to be achieved: (1) if the translator's literary level is higher than the original author's, then the translator can "embellish" or modify the work as he likes; (2) if the translator's level is lower than the original author's then the translator will often encounter some insolvable translation problems, and produce a "pseudo-translation" full of flaws; (3) the most ideal situation is when the level of the translator and that of the author are similar or almost similar. In case the translator is temporarily unable to reach the level of the author, he should acquire an adequate understanding and carry out an in-depth study of the author and the author's other works through a careful reading of the original or through other means. That is the only way a translator can produce a translation that achieves the level equivalent to the original, and only then will readers be able to read excellent literary translations. When Spivak translated Derrida's *Of Grammatology*, she was just embarking on her academic career but she had diligently read almost every theoretical work related to the book and made detailed notes. These notes eventually formed the more than 80 pages long "Translator's Preface" and are considered by the academic community to be of equal value as Derrida's original work. Presented to the Anglophone world, the foreword and the successful translation paved the way for the theory of deconstruction to move from the periphery to the center and to become a universal theory of cultural interpretation.[15] By comparison, in the current Chinese context, very few translations reach the first level, not many reach the third level, and a great number of translations merely remain at the second level. What about the translation of Chinese literature or academic works in the English context? The situation is even less optimistic. Besides the "demonizing" descriptions and influence of Western mainstream ideology and media on China, there are also restrictions imposed on us by the publishing industry and the book market, so there has always been a "deficit" in our import and export of culture, unlike the "surplus" situation of China's foreign trade. This does not match our status as a major cultural power at all. Undoubtedly, we all realize that in the current globalization context, our literary and cultural translations should transform their inherent functions. In the past, we translated large quantities of foreign literature into Chinese; now that many readers are able to read the original work in foreign languages (mainly English), we should shift the focus from translating foreign works into Chinese to translating Chinese works into foreign languages. In other words, it is time to translate Chinese cultural classics and Chinese literary classics into the world's major language—English—to attract a wider readership in the world. In my view, this is yet another direction of cultural translation in the era of globalization. But what is the current state of China's cultural academic circles? People may often wonder, with the history of Chinese culture being so long, and there being so many masterpieces in the history of Chinese literature, why so few works are known to the world. I think the absence and weakness of translation is an important factor, especially in terms of the extreme shortage of advanced literary translation and cultural translation. Therefore, those engaged in comparative cultural studies across Eastern and Western traditions need the support of translation.

In the field of cultural scholarship, I have always advocated that on the one hand, we should make every effort to import and introduce the accomplishments in international academic circles, while on the other hand, we should spare no effort to introduce the research output of Chinese scholars to the international academic world, in order to make the voice of China's humanities scholars heard. This is the reason why we continue to encourage Chinese scholars in translation studies to go abroad, to improve their English writing skills while writing in Chinese at the same time, and to break down the existing "weak" situation of Chinese humanities through publishing research output in international academic journals. However, in the current literary theoretical circles in China, there is a concern that Chinese literary criticism and cultural criticism "lose their voice", and Chinese academia suffer from a sort of "aphasia". In other words, few scholars in China are able to make their voices heard in international forums. In the field of international humanities and social sciences, China's voices are almost inaudible, or even if occasionally heard, their voices are extremely weak. So, what exactly is it that caused this situation? Of course, many people may think it is because the language we use is not a world language, but I don't think it is merely a language problem. The first problem is whether we have posed cutting-edge topics in current international academic circles in the humanities and social sciences. The second problem is whether we are able to express ourselves accurately and fluently or just engage in dialogue with the international academic community on only part of the topics? If we engage in dialogue with our foreign counterparts at a different level, then it will not achieve the desired effect. Finally, of course, the medium of dialogue–the issue of language is involved. If we compare the international level of Chinese cultural studies with that of translation studies, there is no doubt that the latter is of a higher level than the former, mainly because the cultural awareness of translation researchers is much stronger than the translation awareness of cultural researchers. From the perspective of literature, truly outstanding literary works, even if written in Chinese, are translated, adapted, or expressed in English by Western sinologists, or they can take the initiative to enter into dialogue with you. Therefore, on the other hand, we cannot deny that the phenomenon of aphasia in Chinese culture to a certain extent does exist, and as a result, China's long cultural history and rich heritage of literary theory and criticism are still largely unknown to people around the world, except for a few sinologists of course. As we know, the status of sinology in the international academic world is extremely marginal: not many universities in Europe offer Chinese language and literature majors, while in the US only some major universities have East Asian Departments, only some colleges offer Chinese language courses, and only very few universities offer Chinese literature and culture courses. Of course, the situation has changed in recent years as a result of the rapid development of the Chinese economy, but for many foreigners, it is unclear why they should learn Chinese. In fact, for many people, the purpose of learning the Chinese language is not to better understand Chinese literature and culture, but rather for doing business with China, so after they learn some Chinese, they immediately turn to the economic, trade, and commercial fields, and very few continue their studies in the field of language and literature. Therefore, if we fail to actively engage in dialogue with scholars at the international academic frontiers and only passively wait for Western sinologists to discover the outstanding works of Chinese culture and literature, we will always lag behind and this is bound to cause aphasia.

Therefore, in terms of cultural studies (including translation studies), connecting internationally does not mean merely joining with the West, but also means engaging in dialogue with the West. Through dialogue we can gradually achieve two-way theoretical and academic exchange, and only through the process of this exchange can Chinese scholars exert a subtle influence on Western scholars. Indeed, in the age of globalization, almost everybody in China is learning English, in an attempt to make our voices heard in this world language, so what role will Chinese scholars in the humanities and social sciences play? We all know that in the field of natural sciences, Chinese scientists have consciously published their scientific research results in English, in international authoritative journals, and in terms of the number of articles published in international English journals, China has ranked second in the world.[16] However, in the humanities and social sciences, there are quite a large number of scholars who are unable to communicate directly with international scholars, so to a large extent, they still rely on translation as a medium. We know that some highly culturally loaded issues are untranslatable, not only in terms of the literal meaning they carry but even more so in terms of their deep meaning. Translation implies "loss". For example, classical Chinese poetry and some allusive writing that requires great poetic skill will lose these things in the process of translation.[17] Therefore, in order to speed up the inclusion of Chinese humanities and social sciences in international frontier research, we have to resort to the medium of English temporarily. Hence, I believe that when communicating with the international academic community, even if we sometimes use the language that is commonly used all over the world (English), the content and argument of the topic are Chinese, in other words "local", so it does in no way mean that Chinese culture will be colonized by Western culture. On the contrary, it will more effectively enable us to gradually introduce some views of Chinese cultural scholarship to the world, so that it will on the one hand strengthen the voice of Chinese scholars in the humanities in international forums, and on the other hand help more and more people to know China and the broadness and profoundness of Chinese culture. In this regard, the efforts and achievements of Chinese scholars in cultural studies and translation studies should be recognized in a factual manner.

As insightfully pointed out by Susan Bassnett in Chapter 8 "The Translation Turn in Cultural Studies", in the book *Constructing Cultures: Essays on Literary Translation* which she co-authored with the late André Lefevere:

> In short, cultural studies has moved from its very English beginnings towards increased internationalisation, and has discovered the comparative dimension necessary for what we might call 'intercultural analysis'. Translation studies has moved away from an anthropological notion of culture [...] towards a notion of cultures in the plural. In terms of methodology, cultural studies has abandoned its evangelical phase as an oppositional force to traditional literary studies and is looking more closely at questions of hegemonic relations in text production. Similarly, translation studies has moved on from endless debates about "equivalence" to discussion of factors involved in text production across linguistic boundaries. The processes that both these interdisciplinary fields have been passing through over the past two or three decades have been remarkably similar, and have led in the same direction, towards a greater awareness of the international context and the need to balance local with global discourses.[18]

This passage shows that it is natural to draw the conclusion of "the translation turn of cultural studies". However, Bassnett and her co-author Lefevere are after all intellectuals in the humanities cultivated in a Western cultural context. Even though they sympathize with and understand Eastern cultures, and paid attention to Eastern cultures including Chinese culture to different extents,[19] they are, after all, still quite unfamiliar with it. Whatever little knowledge of Eastern culture they have was indirectly acquired and cannot in any way satisfy their engagement in translation studies that cross languages and cultural traditions, let alone meet their ambitious goal of promoting the "translation studies turn" in cultural studies. Therefore, this important historical task will undoubtedly fall on the shoulders of Chinese scholars, and we should be confident to make our own efforts. This book presents the first step in this direction.

Notes

1 In general, translation studies has two meanings: in the broad sense, it refers to "translation study" or "translation research", while in the narrow sense it means "translation studies". It is obvious that the discussion in this introduction is about the latter. Universal consensus among international translation theorist circles is the fact that the rise of translation studies as a discipline happened at a colloquium in KU Leuven, Belgium in 1976. Among its representatives besides the two mentioned above, are José Lambert

from Belgium, Theo Hermans and Mona Baker from the UK, Cay Dollerup from Denmark and Edwin Gentzler from the US.
2. Bassnett, S. & Lefevere, A. 1998. *Constructing Cultures: Essays on Literary Translation*. Clevedon & London: Multilingual Matters Ltd.
3. Translators' note: Here "outsiders" refer to scholars outside the field of translation studies.
4. In the Chinese context, possibly because of the status of translation studies, the majority of translation researchers publish their articles in Chinese in *Zhongguo Fanyi* [Chinese Translators Journal] and some journals dedicated to the research of foreign languages. The good thing is that some specialized academic journals in the humanities and social sciences, including *Zhongguo Bijiao Wenxue* [Comparative Literature in China] and *Wenyi Yanjiu* [Literature & Art Studies], have also started publishing papers on translation studies in recent years, though most of them are articles about cultural translation in the broad sense.
5. Although the first edition of this book was published in the first decade of the century, the role of Chinese scholars in present-day international academic circles of translation studies is quite surprising, which is easy to see from the articles written by Chinese scholars published in top international journals in translation studies, including *Perspectives: Studies in Translation Theory and Practice, Babel, Target, META, Translation Studies*, sometimes even a whole issue was edited by one Chinese scholar, including myself, as guest editor. This is proof that Chinese researchers in translation studies have already started to focus on equal dialogue with the international academic community.
6. For a study on cultural translation in English, see Wang, N. 2004. *Globalization and Cultural Translation*. Singapore: Marshall Cavendish Academic.
7. Translators' note: The Qing Dynasty was the last imperial dynasty in China, which lasted from 1636 to 1911. It was followed by the Republic of China from 1911 till 1949.
8. Translators' note: Lu Xun (1881–1936) is considered the "Father of modern Chinese literature" and he introduced the term "grabbism" meaning to adopt foreign models for local use.
9. Lu Xun. 1981. How I first came to write fiction. *The Complete Works of Lu Xun*. Vol. 4. Beijing: Renmin Wenxue Chubanshe [People's Literature Publishing House], 512.
10. For a detailed discussion of the "Alternative Modernity", see Liu, K. 1998. Is there an alternative to (capitalist) globalization? The debate about modernity in China. In F. Jameson & M. Miyoshi (eds.), *The Cultures of Globalization*. Durham, NC: Duke University Press, 164–188. For a recent article on the topic translated in Chinese, see Derek, A. 2007. The Critique of Modernity in Contemporary Perspective. *Journal of Nanjing University*, (6): 50–59.
11. There is little academic writing about this available in English, but the following two titles may serve as references: Wang, N. 2003. Cultural studies in China: Towards closing the gap between elite culture and popular culture. *European Review, 11*(2): 183–191; Tao, D. & Jin, Y. (eds.). 2005. *Cultural Studies in China*. Singapore: Marshall Cavendish Academic.
12. About the emergence of cultural studies in the UK, and its dissemination and development in other countries in the world including China, see Lu, Y. (ed.). 2008. *An Introduction to Cultural Studies*. Shanghai: Fudan University Press.
13. It should be pointed out that some scholars, such as the Dutch scholar Douwe Fokkema, even introduced a new term, "Cultural Sciences", in an attempt to make up for cultural studies' limitation in disciplinary significance. See Fokkema's lecture on "Cultural Studies and Cultural Sciences" delivered at Tsinghua University on 10 June 2005.
14. Indeed, for a long time translation studies had no foothold at all at world-class universities including Oxford, Cambridge, Harvard and Yale, while in Chinese universities, translation studies was either under the second-level discipline of foreign language and literature—"Foreign Linguistics and Applied Linguistics", or under the second-level

discipline of Chinese language and literature—"Comparative Literature and World Literature". At best, it could only be counted as a third-level discipline similar to research directions like "Stylistics", "Modern British Drama", and "Study of Southern American Literature". However, in the past ten years, there has been some favorable development. Cambridge University, Yale University and Tsinghua University jointly initiated and conducted a large-scale project of international collaboration—"Translating Modernism, Translating Theory, and Translating Culture" and hosted a series of conferences. The first time it was held in Cambridge in May 2008, the second time in Yale in September 2009, and the third in Beijing in November 2011. In fact, the meaning of translation here was greatly expanded to a type of "cultural transmission" and "cultural transformation". The Academic Degree Evaluation Committee of the State Council of China in 2007 also established an appraisal group for the professional degree of translation and interpreting, and the Master's degree that they approved is equivalent to an MBA degree. Some universities have also set up schools or departments of translation.
15 In October 2015, when I gave a lecture at Sorbonne University in Paris, there was a Frenchman in the audience who told me that when he read the original text of *Of Grammatology*, he would consult Spivak's English translation for the passage that he didn't understand, and then it was immediately clear for him. Therefore, there is also a need for a dynamic interpretation and representation for the translation of theory.
16 According to the statistics released in December 2008 by the Institute of Scientific and Technical Information of China, the statistics of the Engineering Citation Index (EI) show that the number of scientific and technological articles published in 2007 by Chinese scientists ranked first in the world ahead of the US for the first time. According to another more authoritative database Science Citation Index (SCI), the number of scientific papers published in 2007 by Chinese scientists ranked third in the world after the US and the UK. According to the data in recent years, the number of papers published by Chinese scientists as recorded in the SCI database is second only to the US in the world.
17 Translators' note: "These things" refer to the beauty in form, the deep meaning of the original, and the cultural elements loaded in the original as discussed above.
18 Bassnett, S. & Lefevere, A. 1998. *Constructing Cultures: Essays on Literary Translation*. Clevedon & London: Multilingual Matters, 133.
19 It is worth noting that these two scholars' attention to Chinese culture and literature is also uncommon among Western scholars. Special mention should be made that these two scholars have supervised doctoral dissertations of translation researchers from the mainland of China and Hong Kong which should have been of benefit to them.

2 Theorizing translation studies
An interdisciplinary perspective

As stated in the Introduction, with the cultural turn emerging in the 1990s, the field of translation studies seems to have become increasingly appealing to scholars of literature and cultural studies in the current international academic circles of the humanities and social sciences.[1] Some consider this a welcomed change, as translatology or translation studies has become more independent and influential, whereas those who are more conservative fear that with the expansion of this discipline and researchers from fields other than translation studies joining the club, the bar will be significantly lowered and the identity of translation as a highly specialized field of study threatened. This fear is not unfounded. Nevertheless, generally speaking, only those works that have true scholarly merit and profound theoretical significance will be retained over time and remembered in the history of translation studies, while those lacking insight will be unmercifully forgotten by history, eliminated from the market, and dismissed by the academic audience. Translation studies or translatology emerged as an academic field at the international translation symposium in Leuven, Belgium in 1976. More than 40 years have passed since then. One may thus ask if translation studies has become a mature branch of the social sciences or the humanities. Has it distinguished itself from contrastive linguistics and comparative literature, fields under which it was once subsumed, and gained independence? In the age of globalization, facing the impact of various theoretical positions across disciplines and the challenges posed to the humanities and social sciences, one cannot help asking such questions: what is the status quo of translation studies? What is its future? There are even more questions to ask. To answer them satisfactorily, we should have at least two premises: first, we must have a global view, namely, we must overcome the stereotype of Eurocentrism or Western-centrism; second, we must adopt an interdisciplinary and theoretical perspective. For a long time, translation studies has been viewed as a field without theory. Whoever has a little command of a foreign language or has translated one or two works can identify himself or herself as a researcher in translation studies. Any published personal experience or critiques of translation phenomena can be considered translation studies. As a result, the status of translation and translation studies remains very low. In the evaluation of professional titles and the promotion of academic staff in universities in the Chinese mainland, works of translation (including translations of academic monographs) are not counted as research output, while those books that are only adaptations of foreign originals have entered the ranks of "monographs". This is almost absurd. In this light, we must guide our investigation and analysis of various translation phenomena with theory and make necessary theorization efforts on the term and discipline of translatology or translation studies.[2]

2.1 Legitimizing translation studies

In the past decades, with the joint efforts of researchers in the field, translation studies has been developing in the direction of becoming an independent and mature discipline of the humanities and social sciences. Even though Cay Dollerup and the journal *Perspectives: Studies in Translatology*,[3] for which he served as editor-in-chief for years, have been dedicated to promoting the growth of this discipline since the early 1990s, the term "translatology" is still not widely accepted in the international field of translation studies.[4] The Chinese facsimile reprint of this journal made great contributions to the dissemination of this term and the discipline, but to make people recognize the rightful status of the discipline, a theoretical approach is needed.[5] The aim of this chapter is to provide theoretical (re)construction of this controversial concept from the perspective of culture. In fact, some scholars have realized that the position of translation studies or translatology on the academic map should be redefined. Although the term translation studies has not yet been as widely recognized in university curricula as other disciplines, it has indeed been widely used by translation scholars, especially in Europe and China, where it has been used frequently from the beginning, thus making the disciplinary status of translation studies at least tentatively recognized.

Unquestionably, every mature discipline must have its unique research objects and basic methodology, so, as an independent discipline, translation studies should also have its own objects of study, research territory, and basic methodology. Since translation studies views the practice and theory of all translation and interpretation as its objects of study, it is actually qualified as a mature discipline. As a result, its methodology should be pluralistic: it should be aesthetic and critical (when literary translation is involved), and it should also be empirical and scientific (when the translation of scientific works is concerned). It can be investigated in an interdisciplinary manner within three related disciplines—contrastive linguistics, comparative literature, and cultural studies. It, however, belongs to none of the three disciplines under which it was once subsumed. With the increasingly rapid pace of globalization, the function of translation studies becomes even more prominent.

Although translation studies has developed rapidly throughout China, with a lot of universities in the mainland of China and Hong Kong establishing schools or departments of translation one after another,[6] and some universities offering Master of Translation and Interpreting programs, a considerable number of college students and teachers are still confused about the relationship between translation and translation studies. Therefore, it is necessary to restate the relation between translation studies and the practice of translation. As we all know, translation, as a communication skill, has been in existence as long as human beings have had social interaction. Westerners' interest in translation can be dated back to Marcus Tullius Cicero in the century before the Common Era. In Eastern countries like China, the history of translation is even longer. The translation of the Buddhist Scriptures in China was historically influential and has always been one of the topics of the international translation community. In terms of traditional linguistics, we might say that translation means conversion from one language into another, or the transfer of meaning from one form into another through the medium of language. Since most researchers believe that there are different kinds of translation, the investigation of translation can also be conducted at different levels. According to Shuttleworth and Cowie, "[t]ranslation is frequently characterized metaphorically, and has—amongst many other things—been compared to playing a GAME or making a MAP".[7] Their description makes some sense, but is not particularly comprehensive or thorough, especially in describing the function of translation in this day and age. Contemporary scholars' research on translation was mainly conducted within the framework of contrastive linguistics or comparative literature, but in recent years, there has been a radical shake-up. With the birth of translation studies, translation is attracting more and more attention and examination from scholars who work on literary theories and cultural studies. It brings in new theories and methods from structuralism, poststructuralism, postcolonialism, hermeneutics, cultural anthropology, feminism, and cultural studies, and great progress is being made.

Undoubtedly, translation studies has made a lot of remarkable achievements, attracting the attention of many philosophers, linguists, literary theorists, and cultural studies scholars, and even anthropologists, sociologists, and political scholars have begun to heed it. More and more scholars have called for the birth of an independent discipline of translation in the past decades, hoping that it can be independent from both contrastive linguistics and comparative literature. Yet translation studies has consistently been challenged, or even relentlessly suppressed, by the traditional "orthodox" disciplines in the humanities and social sciences. Many translators, especially literary translators, have always advocated that translation is an art, or an art of re-creation, so it is natural that translation theory should be based on the experience gained from such an artistic practice. As a corollary, translation studies is at best a summary of some scattered experiences of translation practice, and as such, there is no theory. Other scholars, on the other hand, hope to maintain the proper status of translation studies as a discipline and believe it should be respected like other disciplines such as cultural studies and art history. Now that literary creation needs its theory, why can't translation, as a form of re-creation, have its own theory? Since literary theory has been more and more associated with philosophy, psychology, anthropology, and many other disciplines in the humanities and has become increasingly self-sufficient, why does translation theory have to be dependent on translation practice? Couldn't it be an independent meta-critical discourse like literary theory? Of course, it is not possible to answer the complicated questions above in only a few sentences.

Another trend is that in today's context of globalization, translation studies is getting closer to cultural studies, which is especially reflected in the study of literary translation. In fact, as I see it, if we investigate translation from a cultural perspective, translation studies should first become a branch in the broad domain of cultural studies. Hence, we should distinguish the concept of translation and that of translation studies in the first place: the former is a practical skill, based on comprehensive knowledge and frequent practice; while the latter is a discipline, or a branch of the humanities on the basis of in-depth theoretical exploration and empirical research. Even though translation theory may guide the practice of translation, with the gradual maturity of this discipline, it has become more and more autonomous, diverging from the practice of translation and converging with other theories in the humanities. Presumably, translation theory should be able to guide the practice of translation, but the guidance often lies not at the technical level, but more at the level of ideas and principles. Imagine how Benjamin's "The Task of the Translator" could have had such a lasting and far-reaching impact on contemporary translation studies if it had only given limited guidance from a specific text or sentence. We can understand it in this way: when a translation theory is put forward, it can alter people's view toward some old translation standards and give birth to a new mode of doing translation. Translation theories should be concerned about the topics closely related to translation and having cultural significance, such as translatability and untranslatability, the relationship between the original and the translation, the criteria and methods of good translation, the status of the translator, reconstruction, re-creation, interpretation, and adaptation. Many people view translation as useless in the increasingly evident cultural globalization, because world cultures are becoming more and more homogeneous, and people can easily access information in English from the Internet. On the other hand, we must face the fact that as long as people communicate or write in different languages, translation cannot be done away with. Therefore, some scholars, Susan Bassnett and André Lefevere in particular, have appealed for a cultural turn in translation studies and, correspondingly, a translation turn in cultural studies. They believe that translation will continue to occupy an important position in the realm of knowledge in globalization and will continue to play a significant role in the upcoming years. Therefore, the traditional definition of translation based on contrastive linguistics must be abandoned and the intension of translation must be expanded, i.e., from purely a literal paraphrase to a cultural translation and interpretation. Thus, the historical task of translation has not become lighter, but heavier. Accordingly, the tasks for translation studies also become more significant and essential.

2.2 Redefining translation and the construction of translation studies

Though different translation theorists have different views on the definition and function of translation, in my opinion, translation is after all indispensable in people's daily life and communication. The biblical story of the Tower of Babel points to the importance of language in communication. Without translation, people from different nationalities or cultures will be isolated from each other. This is especially true in this globalized information age as they will be increasingly isolated from the world. Of the various means of communication, language is always of primary importance, and translation, first and foremost, is a way to transfer meaning from one language to another. How can translation researchers put forward their ideal and most relevant translation? This question has been discussed ever since the emergence of translation. Almost all translators try to approach the meaning of the original in the translation process, and all theorists want to develop a universally applicable theory that can guide the practice of translation, but almost all find it extremely difficult, if not impossible, to achieve faithfulness. For various reasons, the meaning from the source language cannot be expressed absolutely faithfully in the target language. Any faithfulness is only relative. One of the outstanding reasons is the cultural factor. Any communication between different cultures is far more complicated than the simple transformation from one language to another. Due to cultural factors, the untranslatability inherent in the original is in fact more serious than it looks. To overcome the difficulties in reconstruction resulting from untranslatability, the translator has to coordinate two or more cultures and make necessary sacrifices in order to find translatable elements to complete the translation. Therefore, some translation scholars grope for a compromise solution to the problem of "faithfulness" or "equivalence". A famous example in the last decades is "dynamic equivalence", proposed by the American translation scholar Eugene Nida. From the perspective of linguistics, he observed that the translator "aims at complete naturalness of expression, and tries to relate the receptor to modes of behavior relevant within the context of his own culture".[8] Obviously, Nida believed that complete equivalence cannot be attained due to a variety of factors, including culture, and furthermore that it is not necessary to pursue this type of equivalence. Therefore, he tried to find a comparatively appropriate method to reconstruct the meaning of the source language text so that the meaning expressed in the target language actually achieves the effect of "dynamic equivalence". He knew that the effect was the result of the translator's own dynamic role. Here, Nida attempted to resolve the contradictions between his dual roles: as a linguist, he must be faithful to the original, but as a translator of the Bible, he also had the religious duty to disseminate and popularize the gospel. Therefore, he had to interpret the profound meaning of the Bible, and the resulting faithfulness or equivalence was only relative or "dynamic"—imprinted with a distinct element of the translator's subjective interpretation. Walter Benjamin, and later Jacques Derrida, went even further in this direction. They attached great importance to the translator's subjective interpretation, namely, to cultural factors. Indeed, most of the translation studies of the contemporary cultural translation school have been influenced by them. If we acknowledge that Benjamin's article exploring the challenges of the translator's task heralded the deconstructive perspective and methods in contemporary translation studies, Derrida's attempt paved the way for the theoretical and practical legitimacy of translation with deconstructive ideas and purposes.

I will discuss Benjamin's and Derrida's translation theories in detail in the next chapter. What I want to point out here is that their major contribution to translation studies is deconstructing the myth of "faithfulness", or the so-called cultural authenticity. In Derrida's view, no translator can be certain that he has grasped the truth (faithfulness), and at best what he can do is to approximate the truth (faithfulness). In the Marxist view, any truth is relative, and it takes the sum of countless relative truths to become absolute truth.[9] Following Derrida's deconstructive study on translation, other theorists of cultural translation, such as Gayatri Spivak, Homi Bhabha, and Lawrence Venuti, all proposed their own deconstructive strategies in their respective translation studies. Edwin Gentzler even endeavored to broaden the interdisciplinary theoretical view of contemporary translation studies and greatly expanded the narrow territory of traditional translation studies. The promotional contribution of the theorists above lies in the following: Spivak's long translator's preface for Derrida's *De la grammatologie* opens up a new approach to translating and interpreting theoretical works from a poststructuralist perspective; Bhabha's "cultural translation" foreshadows a broad multi-disciplinary and multi-perspective approach to translation and reconstructs and redefines (national) culture from a postcolonial theoretical perspective; Venuti's emphasis on foreignization and domestication indicates that the two opposing directions of literary and cultural translation have always been present in the history of translation in the West, and promotes the translator's subjectivity and dynamic function. In the following chapters, we will discuss in detail the historical contributions of these theorists to translation and translation studies. In my view, the highest "faithfulness" lies in reconstructing the original work's cultural spirit, as every generation of translators endeavors to approach this ideal. This is perhaps the reason why translators of different eras have always spent so much time retranslating literary masterpieces in order to meet the basic needs of readers of different eras. In terms of culture and hermeneutics, translation, especially literary translation, can also be viewed as a means for interpretation and reconstruction.

Since cultural translation is more controversial in our theoretical debates, let's start with Nida's translation theory, since Nida and his translation theory were once very influential in the Chinese context and were often cited. As stated above, Nida's dual roles determined his heed to the cultural factors in translation. As a linguist, he was inspired and influenced by Noam Chomsky's transformational-generative grammar, but as a professional translator with the mission of preaching, he was not satisfied with merely conveying in the translation the basic information of the original. Of course, from the modern perspective, it is easy to see that his theory resides at the level of structural linguistics, and although he more or less touched upon some aspects of culture, he is no longer influential in our discussion of translation under the context of cultural studies. The latest example in discussing "relevant translation" can be found in one speech given by Derrida in 1998, in which translation is no longer a word-for-word rendition at the traditional linguistic level, but a sense-for-sense translation or interpretation at the cultural level. Being a poststructuralist theorist who aimed at deconstruction, Derrida, like some other poststructuralists, did not believe in the legitimacy and authenticity of any absolutely relevant translation, because in his eyes, any entity only exists in relation to other entities. Therefore, he and those who interpreted him believed that the so-called "relevant translation" is by no means "new in translation theory, even if it has been subject to varying formulations, particularly over the last three centuries".[10] Although it is impossible to achieve an absolutely "relevant translation", translators can still attain a relatively "relevant translation" if they work really hard. In his theoretical exploration, people actually have seen the shift of the translation focus, from literal translation at the linguistic level to dynamic cultural interpretation and reconstruction. Therefore, Derrida held that translation functions at both the linguistic level and the cultural level,[11] and the latter is more appealing to contemporary translation researchers.

Generally speaking, a purely literal translation is absolutely necessary to faithfully reproduce the content and meaning of scientific literature, but in this day and age, this task can be replaced to some extent by computer-updated machine translation as well as artificially intelligent translation. Nevertheless, the resulting faithfulness is not absolute, as many difficulties still need to be solved through manual translation and proofreading in the end. However, there is nothing more difficult and controversial in literary translation than reproducing the meanings hidden between the lines or even behind the lines, especially those of metaphors and symbolic meanings. Literary works usually contain rich and varied cultural and aesthetic connotations, which cannot be translated at all if the translator only sticks to the superficial faithfulness of the literal language. Therefore, for excellent translators, being spiritually and stylistically faithful to the original is much better than being literally and syntactically faithful. When talking about the role of translation in the construction and reconstruction of literary classics, we can easily find that excellent translation will greatly help to construct new classics, whereas bad translation will reduce classics in the source language to non-classics in the target language. Thus, we hold that it is necessary to redefine translation in a new context, as with the progress of cultural studies, more and more scholars recognize that translation and culture are inextricably linked. It is entirely possible to conduct translation studies in the broad context of cultural studies, since translation involves at least two languages and cultures, as well as their reconstruction.

Next, let us turn back to Derrida's translation theory. In accordance with an ideal translation standard, Derrida points out:

> No translation strategy can be linked deterministically to a textual effect, theme, cultural discourse, ideology, or institution. Such linkages are contingent upon the cultural and political situation in which the translation is produced. Literalizing strategies have actually been put to contrary uses in the history of translation.[12]

Hence in today's global cultural exchange, what people need most is understanding the subtle meanings in exotic cultures, so that they can communicate with people from those cultural traditions in the most efficient way. For Derrida,

> A relevant translation would therefore be, quite simply, a 'good' translation, a translation that does what one expects of it, in short, a version that performs its mission, honors its debt and does its job or its duty while inscribing in the receiving language the most *relevant* equivalent for an original, the language

that is *the most* right, appropriate, pertinent, adequate, opportune, pointed, univocal, idiomatic, and so on.[13]

Here, even though Derrida tries to propose an ideal standard for what is relevant or the best translation, he actually discloses that such a standard is itself indeterminate, and there is room for further discussion. We will discuss this in detail in the next chapter.

When discussing the different aspects of translation, we immediately think of the famous three-way classification propounded by the formal-structural linguist and literary critic Roman Jakobson: interlingual, intralingual, and intersemiotic translation.[14] The formal and structural orientation that he proposed in defining the three aspects of translation above is quite obvious. According to his classification, from a linguistic point of view, intralingual translation and intersemiotic translation are not real translation, and only interlingual translation between two languages is the real object of translation studies. Jakobson's formal linguistic classification impacted a whole generation of (contrastive linguistics) translation researchers. Of course, his classification remains controversial, especially with regard to how to explain cross-cultural intersemiotic translation. We will discuss this in detail in Chapter 7. Even so, in the current context of globalization, we find another deficiency in the three aspects—intercultural translation, or translation between two cultures mediated by language, which has played an increasingly important role in the research of globalization. Now that globalization has made ethnic and cultural identity fuzzy and sophisticated, it has also made the status of translation studies fuzzy and sophisticated, and has turned it into a "marginal" discipline which lies at the border of many disciplines and thus has interdisciplinary features. Scholars in this field all realize that the significance of translation today consists not only in paraphrasing the content at the linguistic level, but also in interpretation and reconstruction at the cultural level, and the significance of the latter is being increasingly emphasized. The function of translation should be altered today—from the simple explanation of literal meaning to the interpretation and reconstruction of cultural significance. Here, culture does not refer exclusively to literary culture, but also denotes visual culture. Translation at the linguistic level may be replaced by machine translation to a certain degree, but interpretation and reconstruction of meaning at the cultural level must be done by human beings, because only humans are in the position to grasp the subtle meanings in culture, and express and reconstruct them most appropriately.

2.3 More on the "translation studies turn" in cultural studies

In the Introduction of this book, we have mentioned the translation turn in cultural studies, or the translation studies turn from the perspective of the discipline, and I will elaborate on this point further here. In the age of globalization, as described by Martin, in an "electronic global village where, through the mediation of information and communication technologies, new patterns of social and cultural organization are emerging".[15] This information society telescopes the traditional concepts of time and space, and makes people communicate in a more straightforward and convenient way. A direct impact of globalization on culture is a remapping of global language systems and cultural landscapes: those widely used languages will become more popular, and those dominant cultures will become even more powerful; while those less popular languages will become extinct or endangered, and those vulnerable cultures will become even weaker and more "colonized". To take English as an example, the function of English is becoming more and more prominent in globalization: to be recognized by international peers, all scientific papers must be written in English and published in international journals; and people from all around the world prefer communicating with the outside world in their own language through translation. In such a way, English is playing an increasingly essential role in a global information society.[16] In view of this, one can't help asking what the use of translation is, given that all people are learning English. The real situation is just the opposite: translation seems increasingly necessary in this era of globalization, even though many people are learning English and communicating directly in English. People need more efficient communication without misunderstanding, so the requirements for translation are even higher. Meanwhile, scientists do not want their discoveries distorted or expressed inappropriately, so they need people with a high command of English to polish their articles. Scholars of the humanities have an even more urgent need of outstanding translators who can help them to create faithful and appropriate translation—not only conveying the gist of their works precisely but also elucidating and expressing the profound and subtle cultural implications.

Evidently, the laws of globalization have marginalized the majority of the world's population, and only 20% of the population nowadays can be said to benefit directly from globalization. Economic globalization also gives rise to cultural globalization. During this process, Western cultures, especially American culture, are imposing their values on Third World countries. Therefore, people from some non-English speaking countries worry about their languages and cultures being colonized. Translation thus plays a critical part in this respect. To take China as an example, in the twentieth century, large-scale literary and cultural translation introduced advanced Western cultural and academic ideas to China and accelerated the modernization of Chinese culture. By the end of the twentieth century, however, with the rapid development of China's economy, the Chinese government realized that being an economic power alone is not enough and China also needs to show its political and cultural power in the international community, so it decided to project an image of cultural power. That is, China's peaceful rise does not pose any threat to its neighbors, and China itself is going through a process of de-povertizing and de-third-worldizing. In order to popularize Chinese language and culture, the government has invested heavily in establishing hundreds of Confucius Institutes worldwide. Against such a background, the practical, functional, and cultural aspects of translation have been highlighted at once. It is recognized that in today's China, the focus of translation is no longer on foreign-to-Chinese translation but should be more on Chinese-to-foreign translation, especially using the powerful means of cultural translation to translate the classic works of Chinese culture and literature into the major languages in the world, English in particular. This will make the rich and profound spirit of Chinese culture known throughout the world. Thus, translation here again displays its prominent practical and political functions, far beyond the function of communication at the linguistic level.

One may ask what the function of translation is, given that world cultures are converging in globalization. In fact, the influence of globalization is manifested in two extremes: as a traveling concept, it travels from the West to the East, and from the East to the West at the same time. Dialectically speaking, globalization has deconstructed the natural boundaries between the "center" and the "periphery", leading to closer links between different socio-cultural phenomena, such as identities, social relations, and even institutions, and these links have to be placed in a specific historical context.[17] Therefore, in the age of globalization, "all identities are irreducibly hybrid, inevitably instituted by the representation of performance as statement",[18] but new identities can also be constructed and reconstructed in a new cultural context. In this respect, translation can make great contributions to the reconstruction of cultural identity or identities. Besides, the communication between different societies, cultures, and ethnic groups relies more and more on information exchange, in the process of which, language, or more specifically, English, plays a key role. Hence, translation appears even more essential: it has the function of communication, as well as the function of promoting cultural exchange and implementing political strategies. It has gone far beyond the surface of relaying literal meanings, so in the study of translation, one should give closer attention to its cultural aspect.

Since cultural communication is realized, to a large extent, through the mediation of translation in today's "global village", translation will continue to occupy an important position in people's cultural life and daily communication, despite the impact of the market economy and the decline of literature and other elite cultural forms. The territory of translation has been gradually expanding, and has gone far beyond the linguistic level of conversion, which will be discussed in detail in the following chapters.

In consideration of the factors above, we translation scholars have been more and more aware of the need to seize this favorable opportunity to redefine translation studies as a scientific discipline. Although translation studies is not yet as commonly recognized in university curricula as other independent humanities and social sciences disciplines, the term has been widely used among translation researchers, especially in Europe and China, where it is used more frequently to describe the aesthetic or empirical study of translation phenomena. It is formed on the basis of translation practice but is not necessarily used to guide specific translation practice, because it is an autonomous academic discipline with its own independent territory, object of study, and methodology. It not only contributes to the practice of translation, but more importantly, it will also contribute to the overall construction of knowledge in the humanities and social sciences.

Since its birth as a discipline, translation studies has witnessed growth for more than 30 years. We can't help thinking about the necessity of theorizing it, because that is the basic requirement of a mature discipline. More than two decades ago, when calling for the independence of translation studies from comparative literature, Susan Bassnett asserted with a firm, or even radical, tone:

> Comparative literature as a discipline has had its day. Cross-cultural work in women's studies, in post-colonial theory, in cultural studies has changed the face of literary studies generally. We should look upon translation studies as the principal discipline from now on, with comparative literature as a valued but subsidiary subject area.[19]

Bassnett is both a comparatist and a translation scholar. Her assertion aroused dissatisfaction, or even anger, from those who worked in comparative literature, but her emphasis on translation studies won recognition from those scholars of translation studies. We do not have to agree with Bassnett's act of favoring one over another, but we have to admit that dramatic changes have occurred in the realm of translation studies in the past 20 years. Translation studies is now understood to "refer to the academic discipline concerned with the study of translation at large, including literary and non-literary translation, various forms of oral interpreting, as well as DUBBING and SUBTITLING",[20] even including intersemiotic translation oriented toward visual culture. However, up to this day, scholars in this field are still focusing on discussing the legitimacy and theoretical framework of translation studies. I contend that translation studies should be viewed as an autonomous discipline, independent of contrastive linguistics, comparative literature, and any other disciplines. Now the field boasts numerous academic journals and publications as its basis and college curricula have included translation courses, therefore, translation studies is becoming more and more mature. Likewise, it has its own unique characteristics, so if we take into account its linguistic aspect, its aesthetic and cultural implications, and the empirical nature of its study, we cannot classify it only in the humanities, and certainly not in the social sciences, because it also has the function of cultural interpretation and reproduction, and translation should be first and foremost a cultural issue. Thus, translation studies should be viewed as an interdisciplinary subject like semiotics, anthropology, or even psychology, as it has a lot of connections with the natural sciences (e.g., machine translation, the development of new translation software, and computer language), social sciences (e.g., the empirical research of translation texts, and corpus-based linguistic analysis of different translations) and humanities (e.g., the aesthetic appreciation of literary translation, and the comparative study of different translations of the same classic). All of these connections comprise the necessary foundation for building an independent discipline.

As an independent discipline that has been in a marginal position for a long time, translation studies should have its own object of study, territory, and methodology. To put it specifically, translation studies should be carried out in three dimensions.

First is research in the dimension of comparative literature. When translation studies was suppressed to the periphery in the past decades, a lot of comparatists, such as André Lefevere, Susan Bassnett, José Lambert, Edwin Gentzler, Eugene Chen Eoyang, and Thomas Beebee, took the lead in studying translation issues from the angle of comparative literature. They often went beyond the comparison between European and American literature and culture, and pursued the high-level intercultural comparison between Eastern and Western literature. Translation was just the stepping stone in their study of comparative literature and comparative culture, but, as a result, their influence on translation studies was much larger than their influence on comparative literature. This at least indicates that there is much room for development in translation studies, a virgin land newly explored. Their exploration in practice and theory paved the way for translation studies to move from the periphery to the center and for getting rid of the monolithic center, and their final goal was to separate translation studies from comparative literature and make it an independent discipline.

Second is the comparison and analysis of translated texts in the linguistic dimension. If the first dimension is characterized by the researchers' dynamic interpretation and aesthetic reconstruction, in the second dimension, researchers emphasize the empirical and scientific nature of translation and are characterized by the construction of corpora and the meticulousness in data analysis. Researchers who adopt this approach endeavor to prove the scientific nature of this discipline through corpus-based analysis and other empirical evidence. This approach is close to the empirical studies in the social sciences and seldom carries out the judgment of aesthetic values on the translation. The task that concerns these researchers, as Benjamin stated, is to prove the need to return to the original text which determines the translation rules and involves translatability, because translation is only a mode.

Third is research in the intercultural dimension, or in the broad context of cultural studies. Here, culture refers not only to textual culture, but also to visual culture. Translation studies is actually a part of media studies under the broad umbrella of cultural studies, because language is a crucial medium in cultural transmission, and thus the transmission function of translation cannot be overlooked. In this broad context, translation studies is both theoretical and marked with scholars' critical and interpretive views. Indeed, cultural studies is known for being anti-institutional, anti-theoretical, or even anti-interpretive, but the practice of cultural studies scholars actually proves that this type of research is supported by various postmodern theories. It is these postmodern theories that liberate discourses, sub-cultures, and sub-literary and artistic genres that have long been repressed to the margins. Therefore, translation studies can be subsumed under cultural studies in the broad sense and draw on its methods.

In the early 1990s, when translation studies was still in a crisis situation and in the "cage of language", Bassnett and Lefevere boldly appealed for the "cultural turn" in translation studies. This not only helped this emergent discipline out of a difficult position but also pointed out a new theoretical perspective for the researchers. Translation studies has developed in this cultural direction ever since then. As summarized by Gentzler in discussing early translation studies,

> Translation studies began with a call to suspend temporarily the attempts to define a theory of translation, trying first to learn more about translation procedures. Instead of trying to solve the philosophic problem of the nature of

meaning, translation studies scholars became concerned with how meaning travels. Most characteristic about the new field was its insistence on openness to interdisciplinary approaches: having literary scholars work together with logicians, linguists together with philosophers.[21]

This statement was true for the emerging translation studies then, but after more than 30 years, this discipline is burgeoning, and it is no longer acceptable if it is still not theorized. Currently, the once prosperous cultural studies is in a crisis of monologue, and some visionary Western scholars, such as Hillis Miller, Gayatri Spivak, and Cay Dollerup, have tried very hard to dismantle the Anglocentric mindset of contemporary cultural studies.[22] Bassnett and Lefevere called for the "translational turn" in cultural studies, but Bassnett lacked the background knowledge of Eastern culture, and Lefevere, though concerned with Chinese culture and translation studies, did not know Chinese, and died young. Therefore, the theoretical construction has not been completed. In view of the increasing maturity of translation studies, its rapid development first in China, and the fact that many Chinese translation scholars have frequently published their works in international academic circles, we are in a position to announce that the translation turn in cultural studies is being undertaken by Chinese scholars.[23] After 40 years of reform and opening up, we have been introduced to almost all Western cultural theories, and have always been indulged in consuming these theories. Now, it is time for our country with its rich cultural heritage to gradually change direction—from a theory-consuming country to a theory-producing country. Can't we take the lead in making breakthroughs in translation studies?

Notes

1 Even though Edwin Gentzler observed that translation studies in the United States developed extremely slowly and lagged behind Europe and China, some literary and cultural researchers including Gayatri Spivak and David Damrosch have started to devote themselves with great enthusiasm to this burgeoning discipline in recent years. They have hosted two international symposiums on translation and world literature at Columbia University since September 2005.
2 In fact, translation also attracts intense interest from researchers outside translation. For example, researchers in sociology and international politics are concerned about cultural translation. Roland Robertson and Jan Aart Scholte, in compiling the *Encyclopedia of Globalization*, invited me to join the editorial board. I contributed an extended entry of "translation", and highlighted the role of translation in the age of globalization. This encyclopedia (four volumes) was published by Routledge in late 2006. The Chinese version was published by Yilin Press in 2010.
3 The journal has been renamed *Perspectives: Studies in Translation Theory and Practice*, which covers a wider and more diverse range of translation studies.
4 *Perspectives: Studies in Translatology* was once the only international journal of translation studies with the title of "translatology".
5 Tsinghua University Press began to publish one volume of the photocopy of the renowned international journal *Perspectives: Studies in Translatology* each year starting in 2003 in order to keep Chinese readers posted on the latest developments in the international field of translation studies. Now three volumes have been published, with the

number of copies for each volume exceeding 4,000. After the chief editor Dollerup's retirement in 2007, however, this cooperation was suspended.
6 Beijing Foreign Studies University, Shanghai International Studies University, Guangdong University of Foreign Studies, and Sun Yat-sen University among others have schools of translation. Sichuan University, Hebei University, Lingnan University in Hong Kong, the Chinese University of Hong Kong and so forth have departments of translation.
7 Shuttleworth, M. & Cowie, M. 1997. *Dictionary of Translation Studies*. Manchester: St. Jerome, 181.
8 Nida, E. 1964. *Towards a Science of Translating, with Special Reference to Principles and Procedures Involved in Bible Translating*. Leiden: E. J. Brill, 159.
9 For more information about the relation between deconstruction and Marxism, see Wang, N. 2007. Marxism and the theory of deconstruction. *Xueshu Yuekan* [Academic Monthly], (9): 5–12.
10 See Venuti, L. 2001. Introduction to Derrida's "What is a 'relevant' translation?" *Critical Inquiry*, 27(2): 170.
11 Ibid., p. 175.
12 Ibid., p. 172.
13 Derrida, J. 2001. What is a "relevant" translation? *Critical Inquiry*, 27(2): 177.
14 For the three aspects proposed by Jakobson from the perspective of linguistics, see Jakobson, R. 1992. On linguistic aspects of translation. In R. Schulte & J. Biguenet (eds.), *Theories of Translation: An Anthology of Essays from Dryden to Derrida*. Chicago, IL & London: The University of Chicago Press, 144–151.
15 Martin, W. J. 1995. *The Global Information Society*. Hampshire: Aslib Gower, 11–12.
16 Even though English is obviously dominant in today's world, some have noticed the underlying crisis, and predicted that Chinese could become one of the most influential languages in remapping world languages in the new century. Please refer to David Graddol, *English Next*, British Council, 2006. To disseminate this radical view, he gave a public speech in Beijing in early 2006.
17 Cf. Jameson, F. 1998. Notes on globalization as a philosophical issue. In F. Jameson & M. Miyoshi (eds.), *The Cultures of Globalization*. Durham, NC: Duke University Press, 54–77.
18 Spivak, G. C. 1999. *A Critique of Postcolonial Reason: Toward a History of the Vanishing Present*. Cambridge, MA: Harvard University Press, 155.
19 Bassnett, S. 1993. *Comparative Literature: A Critical Introduction*. Oxford: Wiley-Blackwell, 161.
20 Baker, M. 1998. *Routledge Encyclopedia of Translation Studies*. London & New York: Routledge, 277.
21 Gentzler, E. 2001. *Contemporary Translation Theories* (2nd ed.). Clevedon: Multilingual Matters, 78.
22 Admittedly, these Western scholars are really interested in, and know something about, Chinese culture and language. For instance, Miller, over 80, declared that "if I were 20 years younger, I would start from the very beginning to learn the Chinese language". Spivak has attended Chinese classes just as an ordinary student in the department of East Asian Studies in Columbia University since 2002 and can communicate in simple Chinese. Dollerup is one of the few editors-in-chief of international journals that are very keen on Chinese translation studies. When he was the editor-in-chief for *Perspectives: Studies in Translatology*, the journal published many articles by Chinese scholars, so he made special contributions to the development and maturity of Chinese translation studies and helped Chinese translation studies to be recognized by the world.
23 See the Introduction of this book.

3 The cultural turn of deconstruction
Benjamin and Derrida

Deconstruction in relation to translation issues is nothing new in the discussion of contemporary translation studies. For or against the theory of deconstruction, one cannot deny its influence. In describing various translation theories, American translation theorist Edwin Gentzler admitted that most of the theories prior to the deconstructive translation theory centered on the issue of equivalence and resulted in no major breakthrough in culture. In mentioning the attack from deconstruction, he pointed out with keen insight, "[y]et deconstructionists are undertaking a radical redrawing of the question upon which translation theory is founded".[1] Admittedly, deconstruction's great contribution to the cultural turn in translation is obvious to all, and as time goes on, this contribution and impact will become more and more evident. According to Gentzler,

> Deconstructionists not only raise questions challenging fundamental notions prevalent in all the theories discussed above but also question the very nature of the act of raising such questions ... Deconstructionists go so far as to suggest that perhaps the *translated text writes us* and not we the translated text.[2]

In particular, the insights of Jacques Derrida, founder of deconstruction, though not systematic, are an invaluable legacy for contemporary translation theories. Nonetheless, in discussing the deconstructive translation theory, we tend to begin with Martin Heidegger, pass by Walter Benjamin, the most important theorist after Heidegger, and finally reach the summit of Derrida. Later deconstructive translation theorists drew their inspiration mainly from the latter two masters. Though Heidegger's hermeneutic theory influenced Derrida in terms of linguistic and philosophical theories, it did not directly affect the cultural turn in translation studies.[3] Therefore, this chapter starts from Benjamin's translation theory and focuses on Derrida's theoretical contributions to contemporary cultural translation and translation studies.

3.1 Benjamin: the forerunner of deconstructive translation

Undoubtedly, deconstructive translation benefits largely from the theory of German thinker and literary critic Walter Benjamin, so it is only natural to regard Benjamin as a pioneer of deconstructive translation and its study. Although Benjamin

DOI: 10.4324/9781032642765-3

expressed his views on literary translation sporadically in his own translation practice, his essays devoted to translation are mainly found in his translator's prefaces, in particular in his widely cited and discussed article "The Task of the Translator". It is this insightful article and the translation of a series of literary works before or after this article that laid the foundation of Benjamin's fame as the forerunner and spiritual leader of deconstructive translation theory and practice.

Walter Benjamin (1892–1940) was born to a well-to-do Jewish family in Berlin on July 15, 1892. He began his college life at Albert Ludwig University of Freiburg in 1912, but it was not until 1919 that he, under the supervision of Professor Richard Herberts at the University of Bern, Switzerland, completed his doctoral dissertation *Der Begriff der Kunstkritik in der deutschen Romantik* [The Concept of Art Criticism in German Romanticism] and received his PhD. After that, he lived in Berlin, Frankfurt, Switzerland, Italy, France, and Denmark for a long time and published a large number of works and translations, including *Goethes Wahlverwandtschaften* [Goethe's *Elective Affinities*] (1924–25), *Einbahnstrasse* [One-Way Street] (1928), *Ursprung des deutschen Trauerspiels* [The Origin of German Tragic Drama] (1928), *Das Kunstwerk im Zeitalter Seiner Technischen Reproduzierbarkeit* [The Work of Art in the Age of Mechanical Reproduction] (1936). He offered seminars on the origin of German tragedies at the University of Frankfurt in 1932 but was exiled to France and lived in Paris the next year due to the Nazis coming to power and their merciless persecution of Jews. When he learned that he was on the death list of German fascists, he chose to commit suicide to end his life on September 26, 1940. Even though he was not an official member at the University of Frankfurt, he took active part in the activities and publications of the Frankfurt School, influenced an important figure in this school, Theodor W. Adorno, and made great contributions to the theoretical construction of the Frankfurt School. Scholars of the Frankfurt School thus tend to consider him also as one of its full members. Due to the originality of his work and his farsightedness in modern and postmodern literary and art criticism, Benjamin was unanimously viewed as one of Germany's greatest philosophers and literary and art critics in the first half of the twentieth century.

As an outstanding literary translator, he translated many famous French literary works during his lifetime, especially the works of Charles Baudelaire and Marcel Proust, two masters of modernism. One is a poet and the other a novelist; one is the originator of modernist poetry with his own unique aesthetic ideas, and the other is one of the pioneers of modern stream-of-consciousness novels, whose style influenced the development of French and Western modernist novels throughout the twentieth century. Therefore, Benjamin's translation theory is abstracted from his direct experience in the practice of translating poetry and novels, which is not only theoretically and methodologically enlightening, but also provides concrete guidance for the practice of translating literary works. "Die Aufgabe des Übersetzers" [The Task of the Translator] was first written in 1923 as the translator's preface to Baudelaire's collection of poems *Le Spleen de Paris* [Paris Spleen], and was selected to be included in his posthumous collection of papers *Illuminationen* [Illuminations] (1961) that discussed issues on literary translation. In this preface, Benjamin first deconstructed the hierarchical differences between the original author and the translator. He believed that the great writers in history were exceptional translators, and so was Baudelaire:

> Benjamin's Baudelaire translations are primarily the aesthetic evocation and revocation of a man whom, for the whole of his life, he not only considered a great poet and translator, but in addition to whom he remained highly indebted for a long time on numerous accounts: in questions of literary taste and aesthetic judgement, indeed in his entire bearing as a writer. As such, these translations were a move to free himself from a man whose influence on his thought and creative output cannot be overestimated.[4]

Even though many similar translations had been published in the German-speaking world prior to his translation of Baudelaire's poetry, Benjamin's unique understanding of modernist poetics and the faithfulness of his translations gave Baudelaire more of a voice among German readers.

Since this essay focused on the task of the translator, it necessarily dealt with the relationship between the translation and the original, which was precisely the issue Benjamin first addressed. He asked:

> Is a translation meant for readers who do not understand the original? This would seem to explain adequately the divergence of their standing in the realm of art... Yet any translation which intends to perform a transmitting function cannot transmit anything but information—hence, something inessential. This is the hallmark of bad translations.[5]

What is a good translation then? Or, in other words, how to make translation go beyond the function of simply transmitting information? That is what Benjamin was about to investigate.

Benjamin contended that translation, in comparison with the original, is a mode. We have to, however, face this fact:

> To comprehend it as mode one must go back to the original, for that contains the law governing the translation: its translatability. The question of whether a work is translatable has a dual meaning. Either: Will an adequate translator ever be found among the totality of its readers? Or, more pertinently: Does its nature lend itself to translation and, therefore, in view of the significance of the mode, call for it? In principle, the first question can be decided only contingently; the second, however, apodictically.[6]

In other words, whether one can find a suitable translator among numerous readers is only an external factor, while the inherent feature of the text, namely the so-called translatability is the factor that determines whether a work is suitable to be translated, and whether a translation is equivalent to, or even better than, the original. Some works are the special production of some special linguistic and cultural background, and can only be read, understood, and appreciated in that linguistic and cultural background. Once translated into another language, these works either are themselves deformed or become something else of equal value. To Chinese translation scholars today, these examples can be easily found in the literary history at home and abroad. How does Benjamin solve this problem?

When discussing translatability, he notes directly:

> Translatability is an essential quality of certain works, which is not to say that it is essential that they be translated; it means rather that a specific significance inherent in the original manifests itself in its translatability. It is plausible that no translation, however good it may be, can have any significance as regards the original. Yet, by virtue of its translatability the original is closely connected with the translation; in fact, this connection is all the closer since it is no longer of importance to the original. We may call this connection a natural one, or, more specifically, a vital connection. Just as the manifestations of life are intimately connected with the phenomenon of life without being of importance to it, a translation issues from the original—not so much from its life as from its afterlife. For a translation comes later than the original, and since the important works of world literature never find their chosen translators at the time of their origin, their translation marks their stage of continued life. The idea of life and afterlife in works of art should be regarded with an entirely unmetaphorical objectivity.[7]

Obviously, Benjamin emphasizes the important role that translation plays in extending the life of the original. He does not emphasize the linguistic faithfulness of the translation to the original work, because such superficial faithfulness can at best convey some of the information in the original, but cannot reach a higher level of artistic creation, especially for literary translation. The translation of a literary work should first consider its quality as a literary work, and it is impossible for a poor translator to reproduce the literary taste of the original work. Therefore, Benjamin holds that it is the unparalleled translation of the good translator that makes the original, which has already died, take on an "afterlife". His view not only emphasizes the important role of the translator but also prefigures the idea of reception aesthetics that will emerge in German literary theories years later. In reception aesthetics, the author of a work does not complete all the creation of the work. Once he publishes it, he can no longer exert any influence on it. If this work is not read by the reader or recipient-interpreter, its significance may end there. Only if it is read and received by the reader can its intrinsic significance be revealed by the reader-interpreter and the process of creation completed. Undoubtedly, translation is reading and interpreting between two languages and cultures. An excellent translator is first and foremost a reader-interpreter. He must have a deep understanding of the original before he can translate it. In this process of translation, a certain synergy or interaction occurs between the inherent significance of the original and the translator, which finally gives rise to the translation. Admittedly, Benjamin's translation of Baudelaire's and Proust's works is such a process. Many years later,

American deconstructive theorist Paul de Man goes further in this respect in interpreting Benjamin's theory of translation.[8]

Given that translation is a mode, its value cannot be equal to that of the artwork itself. Benjamin notes,

> Although translation, unlike art, cannot claim permanence for its products, its goal is undeniably a final, conclusive, decisive stage of all linguistic creation. In translation the original rises into a higher and purer linguistic air, as it were. It cannot live there permanently, to be sure, and it certainly does not reach it in its entirety.[9]

To put it differently, via translation, the original displays its unrevealed intrinsic values to the fullest, and its unfinished part is brought to a culmination in the process of translation. Of course, a single translation of the original cannot exhaust all of its intrinsic values, but at least in some way it will approach that ultimate value and meaning. Thus, translation is always an open process. This open view has important implications for later deconstructive translation theorists such as Derrida and has been elaborated in detail by them.

Since translation is so significant, what is the specific task of the translator? Benjamin states:

> The task of the translator consists in finding that intended effect [*Intention*] upon the language into which he is translating which produces in it the echo of the original. This is a feature of translation which basically differentiates it from the poet's work, because the effort of the latter is never directed at the language as such, as its totality, but solely and immediately at specific linguistic contextual aspects.[10]

In other words, only by finding the special meaning implied in the original work can the translator create some kind of resonance with the original, but of course this resonance is not a passive resonance dependent on the original, but more with the translator's own understanding and creative interpretation. Some form of communication and interaction actually happens between the translator and the author. In this interactive relationship, the translator takes on considerable initiative, in contrast to the passive situation of the past, and his role is no less than that of the original author. In this sense, an excellent translation results from the joint efforts and close cooperation of the translator and the author. Without either party, the translation cannot be completed. Here Benjamin clearly raised the status of translators, who had long been "invisible", and predicted the "visibility" of translators and the awakening of their subjectivity in contemporary translation circles.

Given that translation itself has independent value just as the original, what is its relationship with the original? Benjamin did not avoid this question. As he saw it, "[a] real translation is transparent; it does not cover the original, does not block its light, but allows the pure language, as though reinforced by its own medium, to shine upon the original all the more fully".[11] All great works are open to translation and the translator should be the best reader, recipient and interpreter of the original. Therefore,

> [j]ust as, in the original, language and revelation are one without any tension, so the translation must be one with the original in the form of the interlinear version, in which literalness and freedom are united. For to some degree all great texts contain their potential translation between the lines; this is true to the highest degree of sacred writings.[12]

In fact, it is through continuous translation and interpretation by translators from different linguistic backgrounds that the Bible became so widespread around the globe today. Benjamin's requirements for translation go far beyond the simple division between literal and free translation, and ultimately deconstruct the dichotomy between the two.

Therefore, the relationship between the translation and the original is much more than that of master and servant in the traditional sense, but an equal relationship and interaction. The translation not only digs out the potential significance and value of the original and completes the unfinished part but also gives new life or afterlife to the original. In this way, Benjamin, like all deconstructionists, reverses the hierarchy between the author and the translator, and attaches greater importance to the translator. By extension, good translation can facilitate the canonization of a literary work in different languages and cultures, while bad translation may make an excellent work that is canonical in its original language lose its attraction and not be considered canonical in another language. In exploring the great influence of translation on the original, Benjamin further points out:

> Translations that are more than transmissions of subject matter come into being when in the course of its survival a work has reached the age of its fame. Contrary, therefore, to the claims of bad translators, such translations do not so much serve the work as owe their existence to it. The life of the originals attains in them to its ever-renewed latest and most abundant flowering.[13]

Therefore, Benjamin completely deconstructs the supreme authority of the original, overthrows the master-servant hierarchy between the translation and the original, and makes the strongest case for the rightful place of translators and the value that translations should have. In addition, he lists examples of some writers and translators of Western literary history to show that some writers attain their fame in history not so much because they are great writers but because they are great translators. Their own works may have long been forgotten by people, but the works that they translate are immortal. This view of his is somewhat radical but profound. We can definitely find corresponding examples in Western literary history and modern and contemporary Chinese literature.

Lu Xun, as a deconstructionist of traditional Chinese culture and literary language, was also very thorough in his subversion and deconstruction of traditional stereotypes. He tried to reform Chinese literary language through translation. When talking about the influence of foreign works on his fiction writing, he admitted quite frankly:

> I wrote fiction, not because I considered myself gifted in writing fiction, but because I lived in a guild hall in Beijing at that time. I had no reference books to write academic articles and no original works to translate. Therefore, I had to write something like fiction. That was *Kuangren Riji* [A madman's diary]. What I relied on were just the one hundred or so foreign works and a little knowledge of medicine. I had no other preparation.[14]

Of course, anyone that is familiar with Lu Xun's literary life will not forget that he had extensive knowledge of traditional Chinese culture and literature. Therefore, his statement is certainly radical, but it does reflect his deep loathing of the traditional Chinese culture with which he was familiar. As a destroyer of the old cultural tradition, he would rather admit that he was more influenced by foreign literature than mention that his inspiration had also come from classical Chinese literature. If Lu Xun's acknowledgment of being influenced by translated works is indirect, contemporary writer Yu Hua, in talking about the (translated foreign literary) works that influenced his writing, said directly:

> When our generation of writers begin to write, we are most influenced by translated fiction, less so by classic Chinese literature, and least so by modern Chinese literature; I have always thought that the contribution to the construction and development of new Chinese in China should be credited first and foremost to the group of translators who found a middle way between Chinese and foreign languages.[15]

From the statements of the two modern or contemporary writers above, we can see that Lu Xun had a solid foundation of Chinese culture, but he emphasized the major influence of foreign literature on his fiction writing, because he wanted to separate himself from traditional Chinese culture to create a brand-new literary form and literary language. What Yu Hua said is a fact: he and many of his contemporary avant-garde novelists voraciously read translated foreign literary works from the day they developed a passion for literature. What influenced their literary language is the style of the original (conveyed by those excellent translators), rather than the idea of the original. Some of those translators may also be literary creators, but it is highly possible that they will be remembered by later generations due to their outstanding translations. It is beyond doubt that translated literature plays a major role in influencing contemporary Chinese writers. It is in this respect that writers and critics in the German-speaking world today can also draw insights from Benjamin's translations of French literary works. The renowned German literary critic Friedrich Burschell once wrote an impassioned letter to the editor of the journal *Die literarische Welt*, and highly praised Proust's novel *À la recherche du temps perdu* [Remembrance of Things Past] co-translated by Benjamin and Hessel:

What makes this new translation so special is the happy fact that it is the successful collaboration of two authors, each of whom is more suited than any other to translating Proust—the most cultivated and demanding of all modern authors—as a result of their linguistic knowledge, education and taste. Yet they have exchanged their ideas, merged together and amalgamated to produce—even where their individual contributions can be clearly distinguished from one another—an astonishing approximation (for even the perfect translation can be no more than an approximation) of not only the original, but also of that which the author had intended to underlie his words. The elements which they each contribute from their individual personalities and scholarly backgrounds seem to have been predestined to blend within the great medium of Proust's ingenuity… Walter Benjamin represents the subtle, exact, unremittingly probing, critically transcending side which is never satisfied with a single solution, and that corresponds with the other aspect of Proust's talent: the passionate compulsion not to leave anything untouched and to retain in the depths of memory and knowledge all that has been experienced. Naturally, Proust cannot be dissected into parts: almost every sentence of this gigantic work is a miracle of modulation and nuance, and nor are the two translators rigid or inflexible; Hessel is sufficiently thoughtful, and Benjamin has shown not only here, but also in his Baudelaire translations, just what strong emotions and powers of expression he can summon to convey poetic virtues and resonances. Consequently this new translation is built on the best of possible foundations. It would have been difficult to entrust this work to more solid, skillfully interlocked hands. The German version of Proust that matches up to the original is at last emerging.[16]

The comments above by Burschell is the best praise an excellent literary translator can get. In fact, this is the crystallization of the concrete practice from which Benjamin's theory of translation is extracted and abstracted. Today, the German translation by Benjamin may have been surpassed by a new generation of translators, but his translation thoughts, as part of deconstructive translation theory, go down in history, and "travel" around the globe through the mediation of his English translators to exert an increasingly profound and lasting impact on subsequent translation practice and theory. We will see the factor of such influence in analyzing Derrida's translation theory in the next section.

3.2 Derrida's intervention and influence

No matter in deconstructive philosophy or deconstructive criticism, Jacques Derrida (1930-2004) is the most representative and influential thinker and theorist. This is also true in contemporary translation studies. Derrida is a renowned French philosopher, thinker, and a contemporary master of deconstructive theory. On July 15th, 1930, when Benjamin was exactly 38 years old, Derrida was born in a Sephardic Jew family in Algiers, Algeria. He served as a soldier in youth and paid a one-year visit to Harvard University in the United States. Coincidentally, these two thinkers, both of whom came from Jewish families, also share the same birthday. What is even more coincidental is that Benjamin translated from French to German, and when Derrida started his translation, he translated from German to French. Derrida graduated from École Normale Supérieure (ENS). He taught philosophy at Paris IV (the Sorbonne) from 1960 to 1964 and served as a professor of philosophy at ENS from 1965. He founded Collège International de Philosophie and was elected as its first president, and was a long-term researcher at École des Hautes Études en Sciences Sociales before his death. His great reputation in the theoretical circles of Western culture in the second half of the twentieth century is due in large part to his scholarly activities in the United States and to the translation and introduction of his writings by American critics of literary theory. His influence on the circles of American literary theories was even greater than his influence on French philosophical circles, which was evident from the reverberation caused by his death. Derrida taught at Johns Hopkins University in the 1960s and was a visiting professor at Yale University from 1975 to 1985. After deconstruction was out of fashion in North America he was then appointed as a research fellow at the Critical Theory Institute at the University of California, Irvine, and meanwhile he served as visiting professor at many renowned universities such as Cornell University, Duke University, and New York University. In September 2001, he was invited to visit China, delivered lectures, and talked to academics at universities and research institutions in Beijing and Shanghai. His first and only visit to China brought a Derrida whirlwind in the academic circles of China, and the impact on every field of the arts and humanities was huge.[17] Derrida died of cancer in Paris on October 8th, 2004.

Undoubtedly, Derrida is first of all a philosopher. His great academic reputation and widespread influence in various fields of the humanities internationally today are largely linked to his deconstructive philosophy. This philosophy is also called "post-philosophy" which powerfully challenges and deconstructs traditional philosophy of reason. The penetrating power and the radiation of Derrida's post-philosophy deconstruct the boundary between philosophy and literature, accelerate the "end of philosophy" and the "liberation of literature", and pave the way for the birth of an emerging human science. Even though Derrida argued repeatedly that deconstruction is not a theory, and is even to some extent an anti-theory strategy for reading and criticism, but its results serve as an important theoretical basis for the deconstructive criticism that was once popular in the United States, and greatly influenced subsequent critical theories. This chapter focuses on Derrida's views on translation and translation studies but leaves out his theory of cultural criticism.

In his early years, Derrida translated Edmund Husserl's *Origin of Geometry* and wrote a long translator's preface to introduce and comment on this book. Apart from that, he rarely translated. Even if he sometimes published on translation on different occasions, his purpose was to apply his theory of deconstruction to the work of cultural translation in its broad sense. However, his influence on contemporary cultural theories, translation theories, and literary critical theories is manifested in many respects. First, he was always concerned with language issues and was once obsessed with Ferdinand de Saussure's structural linguistics and Claude

Lévi-Strauss' structural anthropology. He rejected the one-sided linguistic view of structuralism that appeals to a single structure and believed that words have many dimensions and multiple meanings. Therefore, the interpretation of literary texts composed of words should be many-faceted. All these were scattered in some of his views on translation, which served as a kind of guide for us to clearly see the hidden features of deconstruction and pluralism. Obviously, his view poses a potent challenge for the view that language is the direct form of communication while countering the idea that the author of a text is the master of meaning. His view plays an important deconstructive role in reducing the authority of the author and the original in the process of translation. Under the tireless efforts and advancement of the purveyors of deconstruction led by Derrida, written language was freed from the shackles of linguistic structure, which paves the way for the multiplicity of meaning and interpretation. This is one of the reasons why his theory inspired translation studies in many ways.

Unlike scholars who are confined by the academy, Derrida has written extensively on all areas of the humanities, and his works have distinct interdisciplinary characteristics. Being a prolific creative theorist, he viewed his works as something between philosophy and literature, or as a kind of literary philosophical work. He published a lot, and nearly all his works were quickly introduced to the English-speaking world upon publication and had a significant impact on the critical theory community in North America. Here is a list of his publications after 1967: *De la grammatologie* (On Grammatology, 1967), *L'écriture et la différence* (Writing and Difference, 1967), *La voix et le phénomène* (Speech and Phenomenon, 1967), *La Dissémination* (Dissemination, 1972), *Marges de la philosophie* (Margins of Philosophy, 1972), *Glas* (Glas, 1974), *La Carte postale* (The Post Card, 1980), *L'Oreille de l'autre* (The Ear of the Other, 1982), *Du Droit a la philosophie* (The Law of Philosophy, 1990), *Spectres de Marx* (Specters of Marx, 1993), *Le monolingualisme de l'autre: ou la prothèse d'origine* (Monolingualism of the Other; or, the Prosthesis of Origin, 1998), etc. In these works, he systematically expounded his deconstructive theory. His philosophical thoughts are not restricted to traditional philosophy, but incorporate elements from anthropology, linguistics, literature and psychoanalysis to develop a kind of critical theory with a wider range, so his status in the conservative circles of scholasticism has always been questioned. However, the English translators of his works have brought these works, originally written in French, a much broader and far-reaching impact and "afterlife". It may, therefore, not be an accident that Derrida paid attention and attached great importance to translation.

Derrida could not have such a big influence on English-speaking academic circles without the efforts of three American critics: Gayatri Spivak, Jonathan Culler and Hillis Miller. Among them, Spivak's contribution lies in translating Derrida's early representative work *De la grammatologie* into English with great precision and explaining Derrida's abstract and obscure theory of deconstruction systematically in the translator's preface which runs to more than 80 pages. Spivak's efforts paved the way for promoting and popularizing Derrida among American critics, and through this creative work and expository introduction, she also established herself as a translation theorist with a self-conscious sense of interpretation. Culler's book *On Deconstruction: Theory and Criticism after Structuralism* (1983) is the clearest literary theoretic work that introduced Derrida's early theories in a comprehensive way. It played an important role in introducing deconstruction into the college campus and applying it to the practice of literary criticism. Miller's contribution is mainly in the timely materialization of Derrida's academic ideas and critical constructions in various periods in literary criticism and reading, and in setting up a workable paradigm for deconstructive literary criticism and text reading.

In the traditional field of translation studies, Derrida has not been considered a translation theorist, and some believed that he did not know translation (in its traditional sense), because his theory cannot be used to guide specific translation practice. However, on a higher theoretical level, his theories, including those on the issue of being faithful to the original, the authority of the original, the absence of the author and the presence of the translator, translatability and untranslatability, the standard of translation, and the multiple orientations of meaning, have always influenced the practice of translation. Even though these issues had been touched upon in Benjamin's articles on translation studies, they received theoretical explanation and discussion in Derrida's works. Because of the significant impact his theories have had on contemporary translation studies, those engaged in translation theory or practice cannot ignore Derrida's presence. In 1992, two American translation scholars Rainer Schulte and John Biguenet compiled a textbook on translation theories, which was entitled *Theories of Translation: An Anthology of Essays from Dryden to Derrida*.[18] The book has been reprinted several times since its publication and is widely used as a textbook for translation and related courses in European and American universities, which shows the popularity and wide influence of Derrida's translation theory in the English-speaking world. Besides his works on philosophy and literature, he also took part in some theoretical discussions on translation. One of his most influential concepts for contemporary translation studies is his creation of the French word "différance", which does not mean the presence (of language), but rather its absence.[19] His translation theory is always articulated around the game of difference and deferral. According to Derrida, meaning is characterized by both difference and deferral, and certainty and finality can never be achieved. This naturally influenced his view on the indeterminacy of translation standards, and it can be said that his translation theory is mainly based on this baseline. To a large extent, it is thanks to Derrida's intervention in translation theory and translation studies that contemporary translation studies has gained a conscious interdisciplinary theoretical awareness, and has raised the discussion originally confined to language issues to the metaphysical height and cultural breadth of language philosophy. Apart from his views scattered in his philosophical works, his major works on translation are two articles—"Des Tours de Babel" [The Tower of Babel] and "What Is a 'Relevant' Translation?" In this chapter, we discuss Derrida's theory of deconstructive cultural translation based on these two articles.

3.3 The tower of babel: the issue of untranslatability in translation

In discussing deconstructive translation theory, one cannot help but refer to Derrida's long article "Des Tours de Babel" (The Tower of Babel) and be fascinated by, and even argue endlessly over, this figurative metaphor. In this article, Derrida compared the difficulty of translation to climbing "the tower of Babel" (also translated in Chinese as "the tower leading to the sky"). Babel is a city name in the Christian Bible. Legend has it that Noah's posterity tried to build a tower leading to the sky. God was unsatisfied with their arrogant ambition and was enraged, so he deliberately made the people who built the tower to use different languages, causing difficulties in communicating with each other. Finally, this tower was not completed. The tower of Babel can thus be likened to an unrealizable utopian plan. The use of the metaphor to refer to translation is clearly meaningful. At the beginning of the article, Derrida first pointed out, "The 'tower of Babel' does not merely figure the irreducible multiplicity of tongues; it exhibits an incompletion, the impossibility of finishing, of totalizing, of saturating, of completing something on the order of edification, architectural construction, system and architectonics".[20] Since the tower of Babel is given by God as a proper name, people cannot change or translate it freely. No paraphrase, reproduction, or translation of it can accurately reproduce its original form. Here, the story of the tower of Babel shows that since language is in chaos at the very beginning, the multiple meanings of those idioms in different languages cannot be reproduced, so communication between human beings is difficult and inconvenient, and "[t]ranslation then becomes necessary and impossible".[21] This obviously is a paradox: people cannot go without translation in work and life, and they need translation to communicate with each other, but translation itself is an impossible mission. To solve this paradox, people need to answer why translation is an impossible mission. Derrida stated:

> Now, in general one pays little attention to this fact: it is in translation that we most often read this narrative. And in this translation, the proper name retains a singular destiny, since it is not translated in its appearance as proper name. Now, a proper name as such remains forever untranslatable, a fact that may lead one to conclude that it does not strictly belong, for the same reason as the other words, to the language, to the system of the language, be it translated or translating.[22]

Just like the effect of fighting hard to seize a name, the gap between two absolute proper names seems to be both a necessity and impossibility. Since this type of proper names are given by God, they are "untranslatable". Any translation of them would be a betrayal. With this tone set by Derrida, the first thing that deconstructive translation theory has to emphasize is linguistic difference and untranslatability.

After using examples to illustrate the untranslatability of proper names, Derrida explained and discussed the three types of translation proposed by the formalist-structuralist linguist and literary critic Roman Jakobson one by one: intralingual translation, interlingual translation, and intersemiotic translation. He stated that intralingual translation "interprets linguistic signs by means of other signs of the same language"; interlingual translation can be called translation "proper", because it "interprets linguistic signs by means of some other language"; as for intersemiotic translation, he considered it a transmutation, "which interprets linguistic signs by means of systems of nonlinguistic signs". To Jakobson, only the second type is true translation, because it is "post-Babelian".[23] Therefore, Derrida made the following binary distinction about translation

> There would thus be a translation in the proper sense and a translation in the figurative sense. And in order to translate the one into the other, within the same tongue or from one tongue to another, in the figurative or in the proper sense, one would engage upon a course that would quickly reveal how this reassuring tripartition can be problematic.[24]

Since all names are given by God, they have translatability and untranslatability at the same time. To facilitate communication, people feel the need to translate the names into other languages, but it is impossible to translate the original works (precisely) into other languages. This is the so-called paradox of translation proposed by Derrida. He then inferred:

> Translation becomes law, duty and debt, but the debt one can no longer discharge. Such insolvency is found marked in the very name of Babel: which at once translates and does not translate itself, belongs without belonging to a language and indebts itself to itself for an insolvent debt, to itself as if other. Such would be the Babelian performance.[25]

Since the name was given by God, "Babel is untranslatable". What revelation did Derrida make here? For him, firstly, the original work is given, and the translator, in translating it into another language, is on a "road of no return" that requires the payment of a debt, and it is impossible for him to reproduce the original meaning in his translation. Second, since this debt cannot be paid by one translator, many, or even generations of, translators need to pay the debt together. In this way, translation can never come to an end, and it will always be an incomplete job. Next, as the meaning of the original cannot be reproduced, it is not possible to judge whether the translator is faithful to the original. Even if he himself wants to be faithful to the original, the faithfulness is unreliable due to the principle of the tower of Babel. Here we see that Derrida's deconstruction is incremental, finally shaking the myth of the so-called "faithfulness" of translation from its roots and deconstructing it.

It is impossible to be absolutely faithful in the process of translation, but it is possible for an excellent translator to be relatively faithful. Here Derrida fell back into the relativism of deconstruction. As he saw it, the translator cannot make himself invisible, because he is also a person with his own choices and preferences. He was enlightened by Benjamin in this regard, and further expounded and promoted the subjectivity and active role of the translator. In reading Benjamin's "The task of the translator", he stated that Benjamin inspired him with the view that the so-called authenticity of the original work is absolutely non-existent, and that the translator, through his translation of the original work, defers and keeps alive the value of the original, hence the importance of the translator being equal to that of the author. In the process of translation, what role does the translator play? From his theory of "debt", he inferred that "the translator is indebted, he appears to himself as translator in a situation of debt; and his task is to render, to render that which must have been given".[26] "To render" means to understand and interpret the original actively, and "to be given" means to acquire a new significance that exceeds the original through one's creative interpretation. Here he emphasized the creativity of the translator. The translation and explanation of Derrida's *Of Grammatology* by Spivak is such a case. The later deconstructive translation school followed the theories of Benjamin and Derrida, and made translation an active cultural interpretation and creative reconstruction.

Based on Derrida's understanding and interpretation, the task of the translator mainly falls into the following four areas

1 The task of the translator does not announce itself or follow from a *reception*. The theory of translation does not depend for the essential on any theory of reception, even though it can inversely contribute to the elaboration and explanation of such a theory.
2 Translation does not have as essential mission any *communication*.
3 If there is indeed between the translated text and the translating text a relation of "original" to version, it could not be *representative* or *reproductive*. Translation is neither an image nor a copy.
4 If the debt of the translator commits him neither with regard to the author... nor with regard to a model which must be reproduced or represented, to what or to whom is he committed?[27]

That is to say that in the process of translation, the translator is never just a passive paraphraser of the meaning of the original work; he should assume his own obligations, because he has his own unique understanding of the original, his own trade-offs, his own choice of words and ways of expression. All these factors add up to the situation where he cannot just paraphrase the original meaning immutably and passively, but has to add his own creative understanding and subjective interpretation to the paraphrasing process. In this light, the translator is not only confined by the original, but creatively reconstructs the original in a larger sense, and in some ways makes the "dead" original work come to life again. Without a doubt, here Derrida followed Benjamin, and his deconstruction is even more thorough than Benjamin's, so the subjectivity of the translator is greatly manifested and promoted in deconstructive translation theories. This point was further explained and extended by Lawrence Venuti.

Derrida continued to point out that "if the translator neither restitutes nor copies an original, it is because the original lives on and transforms itself. The translation will truly be a moment in the growth of the original, which will complete itself in enlarging itself".[28] This tells us: in fact, no matter how the translator exerts his subjective initiative and subjective interpretation or creativity, he cannot do everything he wants unfettered by the bounds of the original; he must always keep in mind that he is translating or reproducing something that already exists in the original work. However, different translators obviously have different attitudes toward the original. The traditional view of translation holds that the first task of translation is to be faithful to the original work, that is, to submit to the original. However, what standards should we use to measure whether the translator is faithful to the original? It depends on different translators' levels. Generally speaking, there are three situations in literary or philosophical translation: (1) the translator's level and knowledge are superior to the author; (2) the translator's level and knowledge are equal to the author; (3) the translator's level and knowledge are inferior to the author. We should admit that the most frequent situation found in the contemporary Chinese translation community is the third one, especially when the works that the translator tries to translate are famous authors' masterpieces, and excellent translators are lacking or they have other translation tasks to perform first. Many novice translators rush into the field without training, which will obviously greatly undermine the quality of the translation. That's why many readers who have some foreign language knowledge complain that they would rather read the original than read some difficult theoretical works through Chinese translation, because many sentences that cannot be read through the translation are not so complicated in the original, and some are even readily comprehensible in the original. However, if the translator has a solid foreign language foundation and the necessary expertise that is close to the original, and he reads extensively to make up for the knowledge gap, it is possible to produce a fairly good translation. The first situation is extremely rare in this era, because few contemporary scholars can be well versed in both ancient and modern matters, and both Chinese and Western cultures. However, we can see an example of this in the unique case of Lin Shu's translation in the history of modern Chinese translation.[29]

It is well known that Lin Shu did not know foreign languages, but he translated a large amount of Western literary works with the help of his collaborators. He created a myth of "translated literature" in the history of modern and contemporary Chinese literature. This is indeed a wonder. Viewed from traditional translation theories, Lin's translation is not true translation. It is more like adaptation or rewriting, but if translation is considered a form of rewriting by cultural translation theorists, then Lin's translation certainly belongs to such a form of translation. According to Qian Zhongshu,[30] one of the greatest successes of Lin's translation lies in his "domestication" of the foreign text into Chinese cultural tradition, thus creating a new, slightly "Europeanized" modern Chinese literary discourse that has both similarities and greater differences from the original:

> Lin Shu held that there were flies in the ointment in the original, so he supplemented something here, and polish something there. Therefore, his language is more concrete, vivid, and descriptive. We are reminded of the embellishments or additions to the biographies of the past by Sima Qian, whom he admired, in *Shiji* [The Historical Records]...[31] When (Lin Shu) encountered

sentences which he considered weak or faulty parts of the original in translation, he couldn't help but write anew for the author. Seen from the angle of translation, it was an "error". Well modified as the translation was, it still changed the meaning of the original...[32]

This comment on the merits and demerits of Lin's translation is appropriate. Many contemporary Chinese writers and scholars, including Qian Zhongshu, were influenced by Western literature, to a large extent through the intermediary of Lin. Qian's love for Lin's translations even exceeded his love for the original texts. As for the external influences on their writing style, these writers were more directly influenced by the translation style of Lin and other translators than by foreign writers themselves. Therefore, the translation made by excellent translators should have the same status as the original. Sometimes, an excellent work of translation even helps the original to gain popularity in a larger audience and to become a classic in the target language. Derrida's academic thoughts could be disseminated and practiced in the English-speaking world, largely because they were translated into English. It is through the English translators' dynamic interpretation and creative translation that his deconstructive theory combined with the principles of American New Criticism to form a unique Americanized deconstructive criticism. Derrida himself recognized the new meanings and new schools of criticism that emerged from this mutation and offered great help to his English translators. Even though there were some misinterpretations in the translations, under the permission of Derrida himself these misinterpretations eventually led to another form of innovation in the target language. How did Derrida view being faithful to the original?

In reading Benjamin, he found:

The word "truth" appears more than once in "The Task of the Translator". We must not rush to lay hold of it. It is not a matter of truth for a translation in so far as it might conform or be faithful to its model, the original. Nor any more a matter, either for the original or even for the translation, of some adequation of the language to meaning or to reality, nor indeed of the representation to something. Then what is it that goes under the name of truth? And will it be that new?[33]

Here, "truth" is never ultimate, but is always relative. This is the common proposition of deconstructive philosophy and Marxist philosophy: truth is first and foremost relative. Countless relative truths add up to form the absolute truth. It is just that deconstruction sometimes over-emphasizes the relative nature of truth at the expense of its absolute nature. In specific translation practice, it means that since translation is constrained by the principle of the tower of Babel, faithfulness can only be relative and absolute faithfulness cannot be reached. A good translator can only try to approach truth (the original), but cannot achieve it. This is precisely the value of a good translation that has the potential to surpass the original and give it a new life, because

The cultural turn of deconstruction: Benjamin and Derrida 45

[t]ranslation promises a kingdom to the reconciliation of languages... Not to a language that is true, adequate to some exterior content, but to a true tongue, to a language whose truth would be referred only to itself. It would be a matter of truth as authenticity, truth of act or event which would belong to the original rather than to translation, even if the original is already in a position of demand or debt.[34]

Since Derrida's article is rather metaphysical and abstract, the English translator was not sure in some aspects, so he confided in the "Translator's Note" the following frank statement:

Translation is an art of compromise, if only because the problems of translation have no one solution and none that is fully satisfactory. The best translation is merely better than the worst to some extent, more or less. Compromise also precludes consistency.[35]

Here the English translator of Derrida's work cannot find a better solution in view of the complexity and plurality of translation.

From the analyses above, we find it probably easy to see that the principle of the tower of Babel is reflected in the paradox of the necessity and impossibility of translation, a central concept that runs throughout Derrida's deconstructive translation theory. Later deconstructive translation theorists and practitioners carried out his principle in their own research and translation practice. Derrida further discussed these views in another article that he published at the end of the 1990s.

3.4   What is a "relevant" translation?

"What Is a 'Relevant' Translation?" is originally a lecture that Derrida delivered in 1998 at an academic conference. It was then rewritten by the author and translated into English by Lawrence Venuti, and published in the 27th volume (2nd issue) of *Critical Inquiry*, a prestigious journal of international literary theories and cultural criticism. Invited by the editor of the journal, Venuti wrote an introduction to this article, making a brief review of its core ideas and main points.[36] It is said that when the paper was presented at the conference, like Derrida's other papers, there were many listeners, but very few really understood it. Some thought that Derrida indeed formulated a number of guiding theoretical principles for contemporary translation studies at a high level, which greatly inspired the audience. Some held that he played some mysterious word tricks in proposing the standards of translation but what he said amounted to nothing in the end. Still many believed that his idealized relevant translation is too far away from translation practice, and cannot be carried out in practice. In fact, this is the brilliant part of Derrida's deconstructive theoretical interpretation: he always left an open end for the readers, and his final conclusion is there for them to experience and figure out.

In that article, Derrida further developed the concept of untranslatability proposed earlier. He defined in detail "what is a relevant translation"[37] or "what is a good translation" from the perspective of different modes of thinking, and expressed his views on issues such as the standard of translation and its ultimate significance. In fact, as what he held on to all along, the "translation" he referred to here has gone beyond the narrow scope of "word-by-word" translation, but was raised to the "literal translation" or "interpretation" of the meaning hidden behind words at the cultural level. He did not believe the legitimacy and authenticity of certain absolutely relevant translation. In his view, the existence of anything is relative to that of something else. Therefore, a "relevant" translation does not mean anything "new in translation theory, even if it has been subject to varying formulations, particularly over the last three centuries".[38] Derrida did not forget at any time the important meaning of deconstruction: the relativity and unattainability of truth. Therefore, he believed that absolutely "relevant" translation cannot be reached, but if the translator tries his best, it is possible to reach relatively "relevant" translation, and countless translators' relatively "relevant" translations add up to absolute "relevance". Here we have already seen a shift in the focus on the reference to (relevant) translation: from translation in the purely linguistic sense to the realm of dynamic cultural interpretation and creative reconstruction. In this sense, Derrida can thus be considered more of a theoretical and cultural interpreter-translator than a translator in the traditional literal sense.

It is well known that Derrida liked word, and was good at playing with words, but here "word" refers to "Word" with a capitalized "W" (meaning Tao or Logos) instead of word in its literal sense. It has both linguistic and cultural meanings:

> As for the word (for the word will be my theme)—neither grammar nor lexicon hold an interest for me—I believe I can say that if I love the word, it is only in the body of its idiomatic singularity, that is, where a passion for translation comes to lick it as a flame or an amorous tongue might: approaching as closely as possible while refusing at the last moment to threaten or to reduce, to consume or to consummate, leaving the other body interact but not without causing the other to appear—on the very brink of this refusal or withdrawal.[39]

This vivid and abstract metaphor beautifully reproduces Derrida's love of words, and inspires translation theory and practice profoundly at a higher spiritual level.

Starting from the established mindset of the indeterminacy of deconstruction and the inconclusiveness of meaning, Derrida also described and shed new light on the issue of criteria for translation in his paper. Based on these ideal translation standards, people generally hold:

> No translation strategy can be linked deterministically to a textual effect, theme, cultural discourse, ideology, or institution. Such linkages are contingent upon the cultural and political situation in which the translation is produced. Literalizing strategies have actually been put to contrary uses in the history of translation.[40]

Therefore, Derrida proposed what he conceived as "relevant" translation. To him:

> A relevant translation would therefore be, quite simply, a "good" translation, a translation that does what one expects of it, in short, a version that performs its mission, honors its debt and does its job or its duty while inscribing in the receiving language the most *relevant* equivalent for an original, the language that is *the most* right, appropriate, pertinent, adequate, opportune, pointed, univocal, idiomatic, and so on.[41]

This series of the superlative forms of adjectives show that there is no absolute standard for this "relevant" translation. It is still in an unfinished process and there is still room for improvement, so the standard is comparatively open-ended. It is obvious that Derrida did not oppose a standard of translation. The above standard he set is obviously a high or even an idealized standard, but this standard is difficult for the average translator to reach, thus leaving room for later practitioners to try to reach it. The use of this series of adjectives in their superlative forms appeals to the translator's subjective volition, without any objective criteria to measure, so the final results depend on different translators' abilities and achievements. Indeed, truth is not accessible according to the principles of deconstruction. You can definitely say that you are close to truth, but you cannot claim that you have already grasped the absolute truth. This also applies to translation: every translator claims that his translation is the closest to the original, but no one dares to say he has grasped 100% of the original's meaning and been absolutely faithful in reconstructing the original. This principle of the relativity of truth also paves the way for the irreproducibility of the original and the constant revision and updating of the translation, and at a higher level makes it legitimate and reasonable to constantly retranslate famous literary works.

It seems contradictory to say that something is both translatable and untranslatable, and Derrida himself recognized this, but he still raised such a question:

> How can one dare say that nothing is translatable and, by the same token, that nothing is untranslatable? To what concept of translation must one appeal to prevent this axiom from seeming simply unintelligible and contradictory: "nothing is translatable; nothing is untranslatable"? To the condition of a certain *economy* that relates the translatable to the untranslatable, not as the same to the other, but as same to same or other to other.[42]

He fell into relativism again: nothing can be translated into another language exactly, but for the convenience of communication, everything must be translated into another language, otherwise the communication between people from different linguistic and cultural backgrounds will stop. It is only that different translators' translations produce different effects of relevance.

To discuss translatability and untranslatability, one has to start with the definition of translation. Derrida acknowledged that different people use the word translation from different perspectives and thus interpret it differently:

> To make legitimate use of the word *translation* (*traduction*, *Übersetzung*, *traducción*, *translaciôn*, and so forth), in the rigorous sense conferred on it over several centuries by a long and complex history in a given cultural situation (more precisely, more narrowly, in Abrahamic and post-Lutheran Europe), the translation must be *quantitatively* equivalent to the original, apart from any paraphrase, explication, explicitation, analysis, and the like.[43]

Here Derrida distinguished between translation on the one hand and paraphrase, explication, explicitation, and analysis on the other: in the latter, the interpreter can add his own understanding and subjective explanation, and the number of words may far outnumber the original; in translation, however, the translator cannot add things that do not belong to the original, and the original is used to judge whether the translation is relevant, so the number of words should be kept roughly constant from the original to the translation, as he held that "[t]his quantitative unit of measurement is not in itself quantitative; it is rather qualitative in a certain sense".[44] This clearly indicates the precision and relevance that translation must achieve: even if it is impossible to achieve full parity in purely quantitative terms, translations should achieve parity with the original in terms of quality. He also acknowledged that it is impossible to translate the same text in different languages with the same number of words, especially outside the Western linguistic and cultural system, so he specifically used "word" to illustrate the quantitative correspondence that should be achieved in the translation. On another occasion, to explicitly distinguish translation and transformation, he also pointed out:

> In the limits to which it is possible, or at least *appears* possible, translation practices the difference between signified and signifier. But if this difference is never pure, no more so is translation, and for the notion of translation we would have to substitute a notion of *transformation*: a regulated transformation of one language by another, of one text by another.[45]

In fact, the transformation Derrida referred to here includes both linguistic and (textual) formal transformation, and thus is what we call cultural translation today in a broader context. This is the characteristic feature of Derrida's philosophy of language, and this point also becomes the logical starting point for his discussion of the philosophy of translation.

As a philosopher, Derrida was not content to ask questions on the basis of facts. He would rather start with the essence of things in particular, so he finally answered the question "what is translation":

> On the one hand, it extends and announces the accomplishment of an ambitious response to the question of the essence of translation. (What is a translation?) To know what a relevant translation can mean and be, it is necessary to know what the essence of translation, its mission, its ultimate goal, its vocation is.

On the other hand, a relevant translation is assumed, rightly or wrongly, to be better than a translation that is not relevant. A relevant translation is held, rightly or wrongly, to be the best translation possible. The teleological definition of translation, the definition of the essence that is realized in translation, is therefore implicated in the definition of a relevant translation. The question, What is a relevant translation? would return to the question, What is translation? or, What should a translation be? And the question, What should a translation be? implies, as if synonymously, What should the best possible translation be?[46]

Such questions can naturally be pursued in an infinite loop, and the final conclusion will never be reached, but this type of trace-to-its-source question ultimately goes back to the question "what is relevant translation". Although such a deduction is rather roundabout, the explanation implicit in it has actually partially answered this series of questions, thus making people have a general understanding of his translation theory full of relativistic implications. Just as pointed out by Spivak, a major English translator of Derrida's works:

Yet, if we respect Derrida's discourse, we cannot catch him out so easily. What does it show but that he is after all caught and held by the metaphysical enclosure even as he questions it, that his text, as all others, is open to an interpretation that he has done a great deal to describe? He does not succeed in applying his own theory perfectly, for the successful application is forever deferred. Differance/writing/trace as a structure is no less than a prudent articulation of the Nietzschean play of knowledge and forgetfulness.[47]

We should say that Spivak's comment was to the point. She affirmed the revolutionary and deconstructive nature of Derrida's theory on the one hand but pointed out its inevitable self-deconstructive/constructive nature on the other hand. As the translator and interpreter of Derrida's works, Spivak also had similar experiences. If she was still on the side of deconstruction when saying the above, then we can also look at what Edwin Gentzler, whose main object of study was translation, said about Derrida:

Derrida's translation "theory" is not a theory in a traditional sense—it is not prescriptive nor does it propose a better model of transporting. Instead, it suggests that one thinks less in terms of copying or reproducing and more in terms of how languages relate to each other. Marks, traces, affinities with other languages are present simultaneously with the presentation of whatever the text purports to be about. For in translation languages do touch, in whatever minuscule or tangential way, before they again separate; possibilities present themselves before the act of naming and identifying stops the interactive play. Fleeting moments of what Heidegger refers to as the ungraspable situation perhaps can be uncannily sensed by the translator during the activity of translation. Derrida's interest in translation is in the process before the naming takes place, while the "thing" still is not. Thus the process of translation deconstructs texts and returns to a point before a thing has been named, thereby making visible a path by which meaning has been rerouted or diverted.[48]

Indeed, Derrida's theory of translation is merely descriptive and not prescriptive, leaving open space for translators to fully display their creative talents. After deconstructing the pre-existing logos center with the strategy of différance, the late and absent meaning hidden behind it actually constitutes a new center, so that such deconstruction will never end. From the statement above we can easily see that deconstructive translation theorists, be it Benjamin or Derrida, do not treat various issues in translation theory and practice in a vain manner. Rather, they constantly challenged and deconstructed existing traditional rules and translation principles, making the core principles in the traditional sense, such as faithfulness, standard, the original, translatability, and untranslatability, lose their original meaning, so as to re-establish a new set of rules and principles in the process of deconstruction, the most important of which is the irreproducibility of the original work's authenticity and the incompleteness or unfinishedness of the translation. Besides, the intervention of deconstruction in the discussion of translation issues also activates some topics that were considered conclusive to be open for discussion again. Moreover, deconstruction, after breaking the scientific, rigid, and stereotypical model of structuralism, makes the role of the translator, who has long been invisible, much more visible. This is the greatest contribution that deconstructive translation theory has made to the cultural turn. As some learned scholars in the field of Western translation studies realized, the intervention of deconstruction in translation studies has undoubtedly brought a new wind of culture to this closed field long held by linguists:

> the shift to a more philosophic stance from which the entire problematic of translation can be better viewed may not only be beneficial for translation theory, but that after such a confrontation, the discourse which has limited the development of translation theory will invariably undergo a transformation, allowing new insights and fresh interdisciplinary approaches, breaking, if you will, a logjam of stagnated terms and notions.[49]

Thanks to the translation and dissemination of Derrida's works in the English-speaking world, and thanks to American deconstructive criticism, especially the critical practice by the "Yale School", deconstruction first gained momentum in American literary theory and criticism, quickly replacing the earlier dominance of New Criticism and turning the "structuralist turn" into a "deconstructive turn" in American criticism. In translation studies, deconstruction also flourished. Some of its basic principles attracted a batch of leading translation researchers, and were soon further elaborated and brought into play in their translation practice and translation studies, especially by postcolonial translation theorists, which we will discuss in a separate chapter. Traditional translation researchers have been skeptical of Derrida's theory and the subsequent deconstructive turn in translation studies. They even argue that long-time translation researcher and Israeli scholar Gideon Toury's polysystem theory is at least parallel to, and even predates Derrida in time, so Derrida's theory does not count as a new linguistic theory, but an old and "very prescriptive" theory: deconstruction appreciates only the kind of norms that turn out to occupy only an insignificant place in the classical opposition today.[50] Though such comments are caustic and extreme, it proves a fact from the opposite side: When polysystem theory was applied to translation studies, it had at best only a limited impact in a relatively narrow coterie and did not revolutionize the cultural turn in translation studies. Once Derrida stepped in to intervene in translation studies, these theories of translation were overshadowed by his immense shadow. Therefore, we can think this way: no matter what one may say about the efforts of deconstruction, objectively speaking, this cultural turn in translation studies has been pushed forward significantly and will be taken to new extremes in the translation theory and practice of Spivak, Venuti, and others.

Notes

1 Gentzler, E. 2001. *Contemporary Translation Theories* (2nd ed.). Clevedon: Multilingual Matters, 145.
2 Ibid., pp. 145–146.
3 To know more about the influence of Heidegger's hermeneutic theory on contemporary deconstructive translation theories, please refer to Gentzler, E. 2001. *Contemporary Translation Theories* (2nd ed.). Clevedon: Multilingual Matters, 153–157.
4 Brodsen, M. 2000. *Walter Benjamin: A Biography*. R. Guo, Y. Tang & Z. Song (trans.). Lanzhou: Dunhuang Literature and Art Publishing House, 139. Translators' note: In translating this passage from the Chinese original, we have consulted the English version rendered by Malcolm R. Green and Ingrida Ligers and published by Verso in 1996.
5 Benjamin, W. 1968. The task of the translator. In R. Schulte & J. Biguenet (eds.), *Theories of Translation: An Anthology of Essays from Dryden to Derrida*. Chicago, IL & London: The University of Chicago Press, 71. The original Chinese citation refers to the translation of Chen Yongguo, with some changes.
6 Ibid., p. 72.
7 Ibid., pp. 72–73.
8 Cf. De Man, P. 1986. Conclusions: Walter Benjamin's "The task of the translator". In *The Resistance to Theory*. Minneapolis: University of Minnesota Press, 73–105.
9 Benjamin, W. The task of the translator. In R. Schulte & J. Biguenet (eds.), *Theories of Translation: An Anthology of Essays from Dryden to Derrida*. Chicago, IL & London: The University of Chicago Press, 76.
10 Ibid., p. 77.
11 Ibid., pp. 79–80.
12 Ibid., p. 82.
13 Ibid., p. 73.
14 Lu Xun 1981. How I first came to write fiction. *The Complete Works of Lu Xun*. Vol. 4. Beijing: Renmin Wenxue Chubanshe [People's Literature Publishing House], 512.
15 See Yu, H. & Pan, K. 1996. Dialogue on the first day of the New Year. *Writer*, (3): 6.
16 Brodsen, M. 2000. *Walter Benjamin: A Biography*. R. Guo, Y. Tang & Z. Song (trans.) Lanzhou: Dunhuang Literature and Art Publishing House, 208–209. Translators' note: In translating this passage from the Chinese original, we have consulted the English

version rendered by Malcolm R. Green and Ingrida Ligers and published by Verso in 1996.
17 For more information about Derrida's travel to China and the introduction and acceptance of his works in China, please refer to my work: Wang, N. 2018. Specters of Derrida: Toward a cosmopolitan humanities. *Derrida Today, 11*(1): 72–80.
18 Cf. Schulte, R. & Biguenet, J. (eds.). 1992. *Theories of Translation: An Anthology of Essays from Dryden to Derrida*. Chicago, IL & London: The University of Chicago Press.
19 Cf. Gentzler, E. 2001. *Contemporary Translation Theories* (2nd ed.). Clevedon: Multilingual Matters, 157.
20 Derrida, J. 1985. Des Tours de Babel. J. F. Graham (trans.). In J. F. Graham (ed.), *Difference in Translation*. Ithaca, NY & New York: Cornell University Press, 165.
21 Ibid., p. 170.
22 Ibid., p. 171.
23 Ibid., p. 173.
24 Ibid., p. 174.
25 Ibid., pp. 174-175.
26 Ibid., p. 176.
27 Ibid., pp. 179-183.
28 Ibid., p. 188.
29 Translators' note: Lin Shu (1852–1924) was a Chinese man of letters, renowned especially for introducing Western literature to a whole generation of Chinese readers, despite the fact that he did not speak any foreign language at all. Collaborating with others, he translated more than 180 works, mostly novels, from English and French into Chinese by using the classical literary style.
30 Translators' note: Qian Zhongshu (1910–1998) is a renowned twentieth century Chinese literary scholar and writer, famous for his literary wit and erudition. He is best known for his satirical novel *Fortress Besieged*.
31 Translators' note: Sima Qian (c. 145 BCE–c. 86 BCE) was a Chinese historian of the early Han Dynasty (206 BCE–220 CE). He is considered father of Chinese historiography for his *Historical Records*, a general history of China covering more than two thousand years beginning from the rise of the legendary Yellow Emperor and the formation of the first Chinese polity (2717 BCE–2599 BCE) to the reigning sovereign of Emperor Wu of Han (156 BCE–87 BCE).
32 Qian, Z. 1981. *Lin Shu's Translation*. Beijing: The Commercial Press, 26.
33 Derrida, J. 1985. Des Tours de Babel. J. F. Graham (trans.). In J. F. Graham (ed.), *Difference in Translation*. Ithaca, NY & New York: Cornell University Press, 190.
34 Ibid., p. 200.
35 Ibid., p. 205.
36 Cf. Venuti, L. 2001. Introduction to Derrida's "What is a 'relevant' translation?" *Critical Inquiry, 27*(2): 169–173.
37 Some Chinese scholars, such as Cai Xinle, translated the title of the article as *Shenme Shi Xiangguan de Fanyi* [What is a relevant translation]. Although the English word "relevant" has the meaning of *xiangguan* (Translators' note: This Chinese term can be back-translated into English either as "relevant" or "related"), we should realize that Derrida, a master of playing word games, often uses a word with different meanings. In the autumn of 2001, after reading this article, I happened to meet Derrida in Beijing, so I asked him whether "relevant" here means "close to the original" or "best" or "most pointed to", etc. He replied with a smile: "That's it". Obviously, what the word means is "appropriate" first and then "relevant". For more information, see Cai, X. 2007. *The Relevance of Relevance: Derrida's Ideas on "Relevant" Translation and beyond*. Beijing: China Social Sciences Press. See also the Chinese translation of this article in Chen, Y. (ed.). 2005. *Translation and Postmodernity*. Beijing: China Renmin University Press.

38 Venuti, L. 2001. Introduction to Derrida's "What is a 'relevant' translation?" *Critical Inquiry*, *27*(2): 170.
39 Derrida, J. 2001. What is a "relevant" translation? *Critical Inquiry*, *27*(2): 175.
40 Venuti, L. 2001. Introduction to Derrida's "What is a 'relevant' translation?" *Critical Inquiry*, *27*(2): 172.
41 Derrida, J. 2001. What is a "relevant" translation? *Critical Inquiry*, *27*(2): 177.
42 Ibid., p. 178.
43 Ibid., p. 179.
44 Ibid., p. 180.
45 Derrida, J. 1972. *Positions*. Paris: Minuit, 31. Translators' note: In translating this passage from the Chinese original, we consulted the English version published by The University of Chicago Press in 1981, p. 20.
46 Derrida, J. 2001. What is a "relevant" translation? *Critical Inquiry*, *27*(2): 182.
47 Spivak, G. C. 1974. Translator's preface. In J. Derrida *of Grammatology*. Baltimore, MD: The Johns Hopkins University Press, xlv.
48 Gentzler, E. 2001. *Contemporary Translation Theories* (2nd ed.). Clevedon: Multilingual Matters, 165.
49 Ibid., p. 146.
50 Van den Broeck, R. 1988. Translation Theory after Deconstruction. *Linguistica Antverpiensia*, 22: 281.

4 Deconstruction and cultural criticism
Domestication and foreignization in translation

Thanks to the important role of translation, Derrida's theory on deconstruction rapidly spread and was practiced widely and persistently in the Anglophone world. In particular, in the United States in the 1970s–1980s, an influential school of deconstructive criticism was formed with Yale University as its center: The New Criticism base camp turned into the center of deconstructive criticism. The four most important members of the "Yale School" were Paul de Man, Geoffrey Hartman, J. Hillis Miller, and Harold Bloom, while Derrida was their spiritual leader and key member. Of course, contrary to the impression that they gave, the critical theories of the members of the Yale School were not consistent at all: De Man and Miller have always been staunch deconstructionists and close friends with Derrida, whereas Hartman was only a deconstructive "fellow" who was influenced by him and tried to apply deconstructive methods to the practice of criticism. It is only Bloom who, though influenced by Derrida and his deconstructive theory, was very critical of deconstruction from the start and ultimately parted ways with Derrida. Therefore, some scholars prefer to call them the "Yale Critics" to avoid unnecessary controversy. Even so, in their own critical practices these four Yale critics each have a clear tendency toward deconstruction, though their ideas on translation are very different. Hartman pays little attention to translation issues; he mainly conducts research into British Romantic poetry, and has only written about the theoretical analysis and interpretation of literary texts. Bloom is knowledgeable, and although he has not published any books on translation studies, his theory of "misreading" has a certain impact on translation practice. Only de Man and Miller paid attention to translation to a certain extent and wrote some articles about it.[1] De Man passed away in the early 1980s and his influence on translation studies diminished gradually, so in this chapter, we will first discuss some views by Miller who was very active before his death in 2021.

There is no doubt that without the vigorous practice and promotion of scholars in the field of professional translation, deconstructive translation theory could not have such a lasting impact in the Anglophone world. In this regard, Lawrence Venuti has also made outstanding contributions. As a professional translator and a cultural translation scholar with a clear deconstructive tendency, he has also written and translated prolifically and is considered one of the main representatives of deconstructive translation in the United States and even in the entire Anglophone world.² However, in fact, he himself stresses foreignization strategy and cultural differences, and therefore his translation theory comes closer to a kind of deconstructive postcolonial cultural translation. Chinese and foreign scholars have engaged in preliminary discussions about this complicated phenomenon. Hence, this chapter will discuss in more detail his ideas on translation and his contribution to the cultural turn of translation studies in the Anglophone world.

4.1 The translation and transformation of theory

Among European and American theorists of literary criticism nowadays, J. Hillis Miller (1928–2021) has long-lasting influence, which is confirmed not only by the important role that he played in the early Geneva School of phenomenology but also by his even greater influence as a major representative of the Yale School of deconstructive criticism in North America in the 1970s. Indeed, what distinguished him from the general critics "at large" is that Miller's status was not only recognized by his own professional academic circles, but also valued and respected by colleagues in the much broader areas of literary theory and comparative literature, in the East and the West. Although he is known for being radical in terms of academic theories, his gentle and generous elderly demeanor makes him easily approachable to people from all walks of life.

Born in Virginia, the eastern part of the United States, Miller first studied at Oberlin College and then Harvard University,³ and obtained his PhD from Harvard University in 1952. He has taught at Johns Hopkins University, and later joined Yale University where he served as chair of the English Department and director of Postgraduate Studies.⁴ He trained a number of outstanding scholars of literature for American universities. Since 1986, he has been a distinguished professor of English and Comparative Literature at the University of California, Irvine, and before his death, although retired, he was still active in academia as a distinguished research professor of the Critical Theory Institute at this university. He once served as the president of the prestigious Modern Language Association of America and was elected to the American Academy of Arts and Sciences.

Miller has been an influential figure among American literary theorists and critics from the time he emerged among literary critics in European and American criticism in the 1960s. He has written extensively about a broad range of topics, which is seldom seen in American academic circles of literary theory and comparative literature. His representative works include *Charles Dickens: The World of His Novels* (1958), *The Disappearance of God: Five Nineteenth-Century Writers* (1963), *Poets of Reality: Six Twentieth-Century Writers* (1965), *Fiction and Repetition: Seven English Novels* (1982), *The Ethics of Reading: Kant, de Man, Eliot, Trollope, James, and Benjamin* (1986), *Versions of Pygmalion* (1990), *Hawthorne and History: Defacing It* (1991), *Victorian Subjects* (1991), *Topographies* (1994), *Reading Narrative* (1998), *Black Holes* (co-authored with Manuel Asensi, 1999), *Speech Acts in Literature* (2001), *Others* (2001), and *On Literature* (2002). Furthermore, he has also published more than 100 academic articles and critical essays, many of which have been translated into foreign languages, including Chinese.

All these works are a testimony to Miller's long yet complicated and colorful critical path and academic career.

Similar to the paths taken by other major literary theorists and critics in the history of twentieth-century world literature, Miller's career in criticism was not smooth. However, what made him distinct from some of his colleagues is that he was a scholarly critic who was never satisfied with his status quo, in the sense that his critical thinking was constantly changing to adapt to the trend of the times. Yet he was not that kind of critic who simply followed suit either; he had his own unique critical view. As a critic mainly engaged in the study of British and American literature and comparative literature, he started from language in his criticism, which may have been the reason why he paid attention to translation issues. Although Miller kept an eye on social issues and popular topics in other disciplines as a scholar of literary studies, he claims his first and foremost field is in literary studies and his research can never do away with reading and analyzing literary texts. In his view, every reader who has read foreign literary works has in fact experienced a kind of translation, even when reading the original through the source text. He consistently holds the view that great literary works have some inherent elements that can be read and experimented with in a deconstructive way, and therefore the meaning of the literary text can have multiple interpretations. The relation between one text and another is in fact intertextual and there is no fixed interpretation. The deconstruction of a text is always a fundamental way of thinking in reading the text and observing the world. Miller's multi-disciplinary knowledge is extremely broad and he is fluent in multiple European languages including English, French, and German, and at the age of 75 he even wanted to learn Chinese. He is very passionate about Chinese literature and once wrote an essay calling for the Chinese classic novel *Dream of the Red Chamber* to be included in the required reading list of world literature courses taught at American universities and saying that even reading through translation is better than not reading. In the past two decades, he visited China many times, lectured at more than a dozen universities and research institutions in the mainland and Taiwan, and gave keynote speeches at several international conferences. In recent years, though he mainly stayed at home, he was still concerned with literary critical debates in China and conducted a highly effective dialogue with Chinese scholar Zhang Jiang through the medium of translation, which contributed to mutual understanding between Chinese and Western literary theorists.[5] Although Miller has addressed the issues of literary translation and theoretical interpretation on various occasions, his only article that discusses the issue of theoretical translation is "Border Crossings: Translating Theory". This article is a revised version of the lecture that he gave at Academia Sinica in Taipei and is included in the edited volume of lectures *New Starts: Performative Topographies in Literature and Criticism*.

In this article, Miller mainly discusses an issue similar to Said's well-known concept of "traveling theory". The difference is that Said does not specifically mention the mediating and interpretative role of translation in the transmission of theories, while Miller emphasizes that a transformation happens when theories travel from one country to another, from one era to another, and from one linguistic and cultural context to another. He believes that translation is an important factor that causes this transformation. As the title of his edited volume shows, the theory mediated through translation may lose its original inner spirit but it may also create a "new start". The emphasis on the revival of the theory, as a "new start", is the central point of this volume. In his foreword, he starts with these questions:

> What happens when theoretical work is translated into another language or transposed to another culture and becomes effective there? What is the function of landscape descriptions in poems or novels? How is it that such descriptions make an ethical demand on the reader or force him or her to incur an ethical obligation? In what sense may works of literature be said to provide new starts for their readers or communities of readers? As can easily be seen, these four questions are closely related. They are all versions of the question of how literature or theory can be productive, initiatory, in the culture of its readers, as opposed to merely reflecting or describing that culture.[6]

Here, Miller reiterates on the one hand the principle of deconstructive translation, that is translation itself is impossible, but in real life translation is absolutely necessary, especially when it comes to the translation of literary and theoretical works because they contain profound and complicated cultural factors. Therefore, in order to reconstruct them in another language and culture, translators have to take into account the new aspects that they bring. In fact, this is the inevitable outcome of all successful literary and cultural translations. In the text that follows, Miller starts discussing new effects that translation such as the translation of theory can bring forth.

First, Miller writes about the start and development of his own academic career. He was one of the important members of the Geneva School of Georges Poulet's phenomenological criticism. Later, he was the main practitioner of Derrida's deconstructive theory in literary reading and criticism. Even though he read the work of these two French theorists directly in French, the factor of translation could not be avoided in this process. Hence, in his view:

> A work is, in a sense, "translated", that is, displaced, transported, carried across, even if it is read in its original language by someone who belongs to another country and another culture. In my own case, what I made, when I first read it, of Georges Poulet's work and, later on, of Jacques Derrida's work [when I first read it] was no doubt something that would have seemed more than a little strange to them, even though I could read them in French. Though I read them in their original language I nevertheless "translated" Poulet and Derrida into my own idiom.[7]

Clearly, the translation experience Miller mentions is different from that of ordinary people: ordinary people read the translation because they are unable to understand the source text, and therefore have to resort to the medium of translation. In Miller's view, the role of translation is almost omnipresent in reading: even if a theoretical work is read in the original source language, readers will still experience some medium of translation. Because Miller himself, as a reader, does not belong to the linguistic and cultural context (of the French world) in the original, he quickly converts it into the expressions of his own mother tongue during the reading process, using the cultural theories stored in his brain. When he taught students, he would convey these theoretical ideas in the form of his native English; similarly, when he wrote articles or books on the basis of this, these theoretical ideas, together with his own experience and feelings, would be expressed between the lines in his native language of English. Hence this is also a kind of translation, and a kind of transformational-generative translation at a deep level, which results in a new product. This must be Miller's expectation of a translation of theory, and this explains why Derrida's theory was translated and received in the United States.

Are theories, then, as untranslatable as some of the most complex and elaborate works of literature? If so, how can theories be said to "travel" to another country or language and culture to play a universal role? Miller argues,

> It is conceivable that true literary theory, the real right thing, may be impossible to teach or to use in practical criticism. Theory may be impossible to translate in all senses of that word, that is, impossible to transfer to another context, for example another language. [...] To translate theory is to traduce it, to betray it. Nevertheless, something called theory is now being translated from the United States all over the world. How does this happen?[8]

If we carefully think over Miller's ironic and paradoxical words, it is probably not difficult to understand his real intention. In his view, the true form of a theory cannot be translated, not even be paraphrased, because even if a teacher relays it to the students in the same language, it is likely that it deviates from the original meaning of the theorist, let alone translating it to another language. Nowadays, academic theorists from all over the world spare no effort to translate some of the latest theories from the United States, the majority of which in fact come from Europe. However, to have a wider impact, these theories must go through the intermediary of the United States and the English-speaking world, and therefore, they are translated at least twice or more. As Benjamin points out, without the intermediary of translation, a work, including theoretical writing, will reach the end of its life early. Only after being translated, more than once, can it be full of vitality. It is possible that every time a work is translated into another language it loses something or goes through the process of being misunderstood or misread, but eventually in another cultural context it may generate something new that the author of the original had not thought about. This must be the inevitable outcome when theories travel. An excellent example is what happened when Derrida's philosophical ideas on deconstruction quickly evolved into a powerful deconstructive literary criticism in the United States after being translated. Even though Derrida's admirers in the French-speaking world might accuse Americans of misunderstanding and misinterpreting his theory, Derrida himself is very pleased with the popularization and spread of his theory in the United States, because his theory eventually fulfills the aim of moving from the periphery to the center and spreading around the world, and ultimately became a relatively universal philosophical thought, reading strategy and method of literary criticism. He never expected this and his French colleagues who enjoy similar fame and status in France cannot match this.

Miller is familiar with the laws of natural science because he first studied physics before deciding to turn to literary studies. In many of his works, he has consciously used some of the latest discoveries of natural science in the analysis of literary phenomena. After conducting a comparative study, he pointed out in his article,

> Though theory might seem to be as impersonal and universal as any technological innovation, in fact it grows from one particular place, time, culture, and language. It remains tied to that place and language. Theory, when it is translated or transported, when it crosses a border, comes bringing the culture of its originator with it. Quite extraordinary feats of translation are necessary to disentangle a given theoretical formulation from its linguistic and cultural roots, assuming anyone should wish to do that.[9]

The reason why Miller compares theory with technological innovation here is to emphasize its universality and applicability. Once a new technology is invented, it can be used by people from different countries and eventually becomes universal. Even though this is also true of theories, the difference with pure technological innovations is that they are conceived by the human brain at a certain time and place, carry highly ideological and cultural connotations, and are subject to specific linguistic and cultural contexts. Wherever theories travel, these cultural elements are bound to follow. After these cultural connotations, which are distinctly local, are mediated by the universality of globalization and then settle in another cultural soil with its local color, they will inevitably clash and come into contact with the new cultural soil. Part of it will integrate and produce something new after this interaction, while the rest does not survive the journey and gets lost in translation. This is probably what we often call the loss and gain in translation.

As mentioned above, the way Miller proposes a theoretical view is always based on his careful reading of a text, therefore it gives the impression that it is not only inspiring in terms of theoretical principle, but also practical at the level of concrete operations, a feature also reflected in his lecture. After discussing the general principles of theoretical translation, he then points out the inevitable loss in translating the story of Ruth in the Bible: "No translation can carry over all the subtleties of alliteration, anagrammatic echo, and repetition of words, motifs, and episodes, that organize this text in itself and also tie it by allusion to other parts of the Bible".[10] However, if a translation can bring something new to the target culture, it can be considered successful. Indeed, stories from the Bible have been translated into dozens of different languages, and in each different linguistic and cultural context its function is not quite the same. Scholars who specialize in the reception history of the Bible can find a new lead for further study in these numerous translations: translation of the Bible, travel, reception, and reproduction. Perhaps that is why the interest in the Bible never wanes. In this respect, translation undoubtedly plays an indispensable role.

According to the principles of deconstruction, there is no end to the interpretation of a text, and it is always open for future re-interpretation. For a theory to gain universal value and significance, it must be open to interpretation and application in different languages, and its vitality gains strength as the number of interpretations and applications increases. In the same vein, as the number of translations into different languages increases, its afterlife is prolonged, because in Miller's view:

> Theory's openness to translation is a result of the fact that a theory, in spite of appearances, is a performative, not a cognitive, use of language. [...] In those new contexts they enable, or perhaps distort, new acts of reading, even readings of works in languages the originator of the theory did not know. At the new site, giving an impetus to a new start, the theory will be radically transformed, even though the same form of words may still be used, translated as accurately as possible into the new language. If the theory is transformed by translation, it also to some degree transforms the culture it enters. The vitality of theory is to be open to such unforeseeable transformations and to bring them about as it crosses borders and is carried into new idioms.[11]

Here "translation" in fact plays the role of "transformation", and cultural translation also becomes cultural transformation. Similarly, the translation of a theory is in fact a transformation of a theory. This process transforms not only the linguistic style but also the culture of the target language, and, moreover, brings a new way of theoretical thinking, which is often not foreseen by the original creator of the theory.[12]

Given that loss and transformation due to translation occurs, it is impossible to reproduce the true form of the original. Thus: "This original can never be recovered because it never existed as anything articulated or able to be articulated in any language. Translations of theory are therefore mistranslations of mistranslations, not mistranslations of some authoritative and perspicuous original".[13] Here, Miller applies the sharp tool of deconstruction to dissolve the true form of the theory, and starting from reading the theory in the original language, he emphasizes the untranslatability of the theory: any practice of paraphrasing (in the original language) and translating into another language can only result in mistranslation, similar to what Bloom calls "misreading". These are not bad things, because during the process of misreading and mistranslation, an unexpected outcome, "New Start", emerges. As a result, the original theory which may have lost its vitality has the opportunity to play a new role in another linguistic and cultural context. This is where the gains of translation outweigh the losses, and why translation is necessary. This is true for the translation of theoretical works, but even more so for the translation of literary works that have huge aesthetic space and tension. Of course, these examples can also be seen in the history of cultural translation at all times, at home and abroad.[14]

If Benjamin, in his discussion of literary translation, only emphasized the afterlife of the translation, Miller, following this line of thought, applied it to the translation of theory and developed the "afterlife" of deconstructive translation theory on a theoretical level by emphasizing that the translation of theory can lead to "New Starts". It is beyond doubt that this not only promotes the cultural turn of translation studies but also provides great insight for comparative literature scholars who investigate the reception, misreading and transformation of a theory (through the medium of translation) in another cultural context from the perspectives of reception-influence. This applies especially to our study of "sinicization" of various Western theories, including Marxism. The issue will be discussed later in this book.

4.2 The tension between foreignization and domestication

In the past decade or so, an increasing number of articles have discussed foreignization and domestication from the perspectives of literary and cultural translation, in the circles of translation and theoretical studies at home and abroad. Indeed, the issue of foreignization and domestication itself is a dichotomy in literary translation and cultural translation. This dichotomy is even more prominent when we translate foreign literary and cultural concepts into national languages: when the language and culture of a nation are in a strong position, the translated works must meet the conventions of the national language, in terms of language use and even specific forms such as the style of expression, otherwise readers will not accept the translation, or consider it a failure; conversely, when a national language and culture is in a weak position or they need help from the translated foreign culture, the argument of foreignization in translation will prevail, because foreign influence can accelerate the change of the national language and culture. The latter occurred before and after the May Fourth Movement in China when foreign literary works and academic thoughts were translated and introduced on a large scale. The pioneers of the May Fourth Movement had two main objectives: to promote the formation of Chinese cultural and political modernity, and to revolutionize the language of modern Chinese literature. It can be said that basically both have been achieved, although up till now many controversies remain. One of the responses to this is the phenomenon of "aphasia" in Chinese literary criticism, which has been widely talked about in domestic literary theoretical circles in recent years. The topic of faithfulness and fluency of individual translated texts is only discussed in translation criticism circles and does not involve issues such as the innovation and identity of language and culture. This is more or less the situation in China, where translation scholars involved in discussions about foreignization and domestication usually focus on the writings by Venuti who has given the clearest and strongest interpretation of this pair of concepts. Although this pair was not created by Venuti,[15] he wrote a book about it: *The Translator's Invisibility: A History of Translation*. The book systematically explains the translation strategies of foreignization and domestication, and describes the literary translation history of the Anglophone world since the seventeenth century through the tension and interaction between these two translation methods or strategies.

62 Deconstruction and cultural criticism

Besides this monograph that resembles a history of translation, Venuti also wrote many other important works and translated a large number of literary and theoretical works. He translates primarily Italian literature into English, which is related to the cultural background of his ancestors and his professional field. Venuti was born and raised in southern Philadelphia, USA. In the 1970s, he majored in English literature at Temple University and received his PhD in English and Comparative Literature from Columbia University in 1980. Upon graduation, Venuti returned to his alma mater, Temple University, and was appointed assistant professor and has since risen through the ranks to become a full professor of English there. As a translator and theorist, Venuti's major works on literary and cultural translation cover a wide range of topics, including *Rethinking Translation: Discourse, Subjectivity, Ideology* (1992), *The Translator's Invisibility: A History of Translation* (1995), *The Scandals of Translation: Towards an Ethics of Difference* (1998), and *Translation Changes Everything: Theory and Practice* (2013). He also edited *The Translation Studies Reader*, 2nd ed. (2004). In addition, he has published dozens of papers in more than ten well-known academic journals and review magazines, including *Critical Inquiry, Comparative Literature Studies, The New York Times Book Review*, which have had widespread influence. In American academic circles where Anglo-centrism dominates, translation has for a long time been marginalized in the academic system, but Venuti's breakthrough has greatly promoted translation studies in the field of the humanities and he is considered one of America's most prominent translation theorists after Lefevere. *The Translator's Invisibility: A History of Translation* is generally considered his most representative work on translation issues.

The title of the book suggests that it is a comprehensive investigation of the history of literary translation in the West. Indeed it is so, especially as one in the English-speaking world since the seventeenth century from a stance of postcolonial cultural criticism. From diverse and changing translation views, Venuti abstracted two roughly parallel and intertwined translation trends: the fluent-domesticating practice that appeals to the reading habits of the target language readers and the foreignizing practice that appeals to the transformation of the target language. The former represents a strong imperialist cultural strategy of ethnocentrism, while the latter is a "decentralized" deconstructive postcolonial view of translation. Venuti obviously approves and supports the concept of foreignization in translation. He was inspired by Derrida's deconstructive theory, acknowledging the differences between different languages and cultures and the paradox that translation is both impossible and inevitable. He calls for an end to the translator's invisibility by emphasizing a kind of foreignizing strategy, thus promoting the subjectivity and creative construction of the translator. This is one of the main purposes of his book. At the same time, Venuti also tried to criticize English cultural hegemony in a postcolonial way, to "fundamentally highlight the existence of differences and strong measures to adopt them".[16]

The Translator's Invisibility is divided into seven chapters. Venuti has reviewed the history and tensions of the development of foreignization and domestication in the history of literary translation in the West, mainly in the English-speaking world, based on the translation situations in different languages and cultures. In Chapter 1, Venuti makes clear at the outset that in the long history of Western literary translation, the position of translators has always been suppressed. Compared with authors, translators have always been in an "unseen", invisible position. The needs of the readers have, to a large extent, replaced the translators' personal aesthetic pursuits. Over time, translators have often consciously or unconsciously reached a consensus that translation must be unconditionally faithful to the original to reach a kind of "transparent" state. The ideal of making the translation "transparent" does not require the translator to bend to the meaning of the original, but forces the translator to make every effort to ensure fluency of the translation without any trace of translation, and even the translation style of the translator. Comments in various newspapers and magazines are evidence of the widespread and lasting influence of this strategy of fluency in literary translation in the Anglophone world. Venuti did the opposite—from the start he revealed the passive and disadvantaged position of the translator, laying the groundwork for vigorously promoting the rights and status of the translator later. In Chapter 2, Venuti traces the beginning and evolution of domesticating translation in the culture of the Anglophone world, arguing that it originated from seventeenth-century England with Sir John Denham and John Dryden as its representatives. Back then translators in general applied the domesticating strategy to meet the needs of most readers and the market, and they made every effort to enable the translation to read smoothly and fluently, so that it was almost the same as the original without showing any trace of the translator. Since then, the criterion of domestication equaling fluency has actually become an important indicator or benchmark of the success of a literary translation. This in fact stifled the creativity of the translator, but on the other hand, it paved the way for the rise of the opposite direction—foreignization. In the third chapter, Venuti explores the rise of the tendency toward foreignization in literary translation. This approach originated in a lecture given by Schleiermacher in 1813. He formally proposed foreignization and domestication as the two basic strategies of translation which run through the translation history in the West before and after Schleiermacher's lecture. Later, translation researchers generally considered Schleiermacher's lecture to be an important sign of the rise of foreignizing translation. Yet back then foreignization remained insignificant because of the long-standing tradition of domestication. It was only recognized by a small number of people in a relatively narrow and closed circle, but, after all, the dominant position of domestication was disrupted, and different voices in the translation world emerged, and some foreign words and exotic expressions infiltrated the standard English language. The fourth chapter is a case study about Italian literature that Venuti is familiar with, and he affirms Italian writer and translator Iginio Ugo Tarchetti's foreignizing way of rewriting and translating which brought a new spirit to the Italian literary world. Venuti points out that such rewritten translations actually played a role that national literature could not play, and that they contributed to promoting the reform of national literature and culture. In Chapter 5, Venuti focuses on the translation practice of the American imagist poet Ezra Pound. He emphasizes that the long-term impact of domestication standards such as "transparency" and fluency is the reason why the foreignizing translation strategy that modernist literature advocates is not accepted by the majority of translators and readers. Domesticating translation is still more popular among readers to a certain extent. At best, modernist translation experiments were only recognized within the elite circle of a few, or discussed by a few academic translation researchers. In Chapter 6, Venuti proposes a resistant translation strategy, based on his translation of the Italian poet Milo De Angelis, to reproduce the characteristics of the original poems. At the same time, he also emphasizes the equal status that both the translator and the original author should enjoy. In the last chapter, Venuti suggests that the translator should adopt a resistant translation strategy, which is not only of benefit to retaining the exotic style and rhythm of the original work but can also highlight the translator's status, so that he gradually rises from his "invisible" second-rate status to a "visible" prominent position. From Venuti's point of view, outstanding translators should be creative writers, and they should therefore be treated and respected in the same way as authors, in particular when literary translation reflects the translator's creativity. However, in the current environment which is unfavorable towards translation, people are not optimistic about the situation of literary translation. Therefore, colleagues in the translation field should take action and try to promote the co-existence of different translation theories and practices.

From the rich contents and detailed historical descriptions throughout Venuti's book, we can extract two revolutionary ideas: (1) the tension between foreignization and domestication, and (2) the promotion of the translator's subjectivity and the deconstructive resistance against colonial discourse. Thus, even though the concepts of foreignization and domestication were not created by Venuti, it is thanks to his theoretical exposition and creative efforts that they have become the theoretical topic widely discussed by translation researchers in the postcolonial context today. These two ideas will be further discussed below.

As mentioned above, all scholars in the translation world know that the terms foreignization and domestication were introduced by the German theologian and linguistic philosopher Friedrich Schleiermacher (1768–1834). In the lecture that he gave at Berlin's Royal Academy of Science on 24 June 1813 entitled "On the different methods of translating" (Über die verschiedenen Methoden des Übersetzens), he formally presented these two very different yet complementary approaches to translation:

> Now as for the translator proper who truly wishes to bring together these two quite separate persons, his writer and his reader, and to help the reader, though without forcing him to leave the bounds of his own native tongue behind him, to acquire as correct and complete an understanding of and take as much pleasure in the writer as possible—what sorts of paths might he set off upon to this end? In my opinion, there are only two possibilities. Either the translator leaves the author in peace as much as possible and moves the reader toward him; or he leaves the reader in peace as much as possible and moves the writer toward him. These two paths are so very different from one another that one or the other must certainly be followed as strictly as

possible, any attempt to combine them being certain to produce a highly unreliable result and to carry with it the danger that writer and reader might miss each other completely.[17]

Here, Schleiermacher chose the two most representative approaches to translation from many diverse and complex translation methods, and he made it clear that he favored foreignizing translation. For Venuti, therefore, the rise of foreignization in the English-speaking world originated in this lecture with a wide and lasting impact. As a supporter and advocate of foreignization, Venuti condemned the domesticating strategy of strong cultures. At the same time, he tried to emphasize a foreignizing strategy of postcolonial resistance to the violence and suppression of domestication against weaker languages and cultures. Some people in China think that the foreignizing strategy is the same as literal translation, which obviously is not true at all. Literal translation is basically a conversion at the linguistic level, whereas foreignizing translation involves profound cultural transfer, cultural criticism, and deconstruction. Based on existing studies, Venuti's theory on the foreignization strategy is obviously not equal to literal translation in traditional translation methods. It has a richer and more complex cultural connotation which is specifically manifested in seven aspects: (1) the "foreignness" of foreignization is manifested in the selection of "foreign" texts; (2) it is manifested in the "difference of languages" and the "difference of cultures", and the latter is more distinctive; (3) it is manifested in the "foreign style" of the translation; (4) foreignization has a problem of degree; (5) foreignization as a cultural strategy has the function of cultural intervention; (6) foreignization as a minority attempt or minority translation strategy possesses a strong sense of "elitism"; (7) foreignizing translation tries to enhance the cultural status of translators and translated texts.[18] Of course, we can sum up more features but these seven aspects are sufficient to illustrate the profound cultural implications of the foreignizing approach. It can be seen that Venuti's stress on foreignization has profound cultural critical implications and it is an important phase in the cultural turn of translation studies as a whole. However, in the long practice of translation, how was this foreignization strategy implemented? And how did it emerge in the long history of Western translation and become a translation method and cultural critical strategy with progressive universal significance? We can answer all these questions by carefully reading Venuti's book.

In the first chapter of the book, Venuti mentions a thought-provoking phenomenon: "The dominance of fluency in English-language translation becomes apparent in a sampling of reviews from newspapers and periodicals". From this, we can deduce: "The more fluent the translation, the more invisible the translator, and, presumably, the more visible the writer or meaning of the foreign text".[19] How did this norm come about? What is its purpose? It is well known that when a nation is in urgent need of the nourishment of foreign literature, to advance its own national literature, it will often show a mentality of worshipping the original. The translator must first acknowledge the classic and iconic nature of the original and then strive to bend himself to the original, be faithful to it, and even imitate it as much as possible in the translation. On the other hand, facing the book market and readers in general in China, translators have to yield to another god, and have to wipe away any traces of the translator that may have appeared in his translation, so that the translation looks "transparent". Venuti then notes that this illusion of "transparency" is at work:

> The dominance of transparency in English-language translation reflects comparable trends in other cultural forms, including other forms of writing. The enormous economic and political power acquired by scientific research during the twentieth century, the postwar innovations in advanced communications technologies to expand the advertising and entertainment industries and support the economic cycle of commodity production and exchange—these developments have affected every medium, both print and electronic, by valorizing a purely instrumental use of language and other means of representation and thus emphasizing immediate intelligibility and the appearance of factuality.[20]

This is a profound revelation of the immense political and economic interests that lie behind the appearance of such smooth translations. In cultural exchange and dissemination, the translator is at best a tool. He is often in a passive state of being "employed", so he can never enjoy the same status and respect as the original author. Furthermore, the copyright of technical and commercial translations is often a one-off purchase which forces the translator to give up their attribution rights. However, what Venuti shows in this book is quite the opposite: the emergence of this phenomenon in the post-war, post-industrial, and post-modern consumer society is no accident; it has a long-term historical continuity. Therefore, in order to deconstruct the transparency of translations and the invisibility of translators, we must trace the historical and cultural roots. After careful investigation and research, Venuti discovered that the strong position and centrality of English culture is the foundation on which it has been able to maintain its cultural hegemony and impose violence on other languages and cultures.

Yet, violence on languages and cultures is not one-sided. Strong languages and cultures can suppress translation, and translation can resist the invasion of strong languages and cultures by using an anti-suppression strategy. Therefore, what often happens is a kind of postcolonial "interaction" and "mutual infiltration" which manifests itself especially in the practice of literary and cultural translation:

> The violent effects of translation are felt at home as well as abroad. On the one hand, translation wields enormous power in the construction of national identities for foreign cultures, and hence it potentially figures in ethnic discrimination, geopolitical confrontations, colonialism, terrorism, war. On the other hand, translation enlists the foreign text in the maintenance or revision of literary canons in the target-language culture, inscribing poetry and fiction, for example, with the various poetic and narrative discourses that compete for cultural dominance in the target language.[21]

The large-scale introduction of foreign literary works in Chinese translation during the May Fourth Movement helped to a certain extent to construct a modern Chinese literary canon: it is different from both the Chinese literary tradition and modern Western literature, so it can engage in dialogue with both simultaneously.[22] If we investigate translated literature in the history of modern Chinese literature from the perspective of the domestication-foreignization strategy, it is certain that the rise of this new phenomenon is the result of a combination of foreignization and domestication with the latter prevailing in the end. Until today, there is still debate among academics about the success or failure of this practice. However, objectively speaking, the pace of modernization of Chinese language and culture is unstoppable. The continuous rise of the status of novels in the history of modern Chinese literature was probably directly affected by the impact of translated literature. It is well known that China was once known as the "Kingdom of Poetry". Even during the May Fourth Movement, when it was the trend to translate foreign novels and plays for performance on a large scale, the position of Chinese poetry remained stable. In recent times, however, while the interest in literature is generally declining, novels still top all genres, and drama (in particular modern drama and Peking opera) is in the second place thanks to their performing nature and attracting some aficionados, but poetry is totally out of favor. Except for established poets, emerging young poets often have to fork out a considerable amount of money to publish poetry collections at their own expense. Upon publication, they can at most only gain popularity among a very narrow circle of readers or indulge in self-appreciation. Instead, a variety of sub-literary works, such as documentary literature and biographies, have flooded the book market and gradually eroded the literary market. In recent years, newly emerging Internet literature has posed severe challenges to print publications. The translation of theories has also formed a unique landscape: the theoretical works of Friedrich Nietzsche, Martin Heidegger, Jean-Paul Sartre, Sigmund Freud, and Jacques Derrida are not only compulsory reading for theorists, but even once became "consumer goods" for readers with a little theoretical knowledge. When studying the penetration and generative influence of modern Western literary theories on the discourse of contemporary Chinese literary criticism, some scholars propose to distinguish two different concepts: Western literary theories and Chinese translations of Western literary theories. These two are not the same, and the main difference is the medium of translation.[23] Contemporary Chinese literary criticism is full of Western discourse precisely because of the mediation and revolutionary transformation of translation. As a result of this, by extension, some people hold that contemporary Chinese literary criticism is suffering from "aphasia", as every critical concept and theoretical model used by contemporary scholars are from the West.[24] This also has its repercussions in circles of translation studies, as will be discussed in detail.

In order to reverse the dominance of domestication in the history of translation, Venuti deconstructed the illusory central sense of domestication-fluency, and then he took his own translation practice as the starting point to propose a postcolonial resistant foreignizing translation strategy. However, as he sincerely admits in his book, even for him as a well-known translator, it was difficult to use a foreignizing strategy. After he finished his translation of the poems by the Italian poet Milo de Angelis, the manuscript was rejected by two relatively famous publishing houses (including a university press) for the reason that the reader was unable to accept this "resistant" foreignizing-style of translation. Eventually, after many twists and turns, the manuscript was accepted by a small publisher that advocated avant-garde experimentation. Therefore, Venuti learned from the experience that:

> If the resistant strategy effectively produces an estranging translation, then the foreign text also enjoys a momentary liberation from the target-language culture, perhaps before it is reterritorialized with the reader's articulation of a voice—recognizable, transparent—or of some reading amenable to the dominant aesthetic in English. The liberating moment would occur when the reader of the resistant translation experiences, in the target language, the cultural differences which separate that language and the foreign text.[25]

Although Venuti was aware that constructing a new translation model could not be done in one day, he found it worthwhile to put in a certain amount of effort. Therefore, in the last chapter of the book "Call to Action", after enumerating a large number of practitioners of foreignizing translation with a strong sense of elitism who had suffered setbacks and still acted tenaciously, he put forward his agenda of action:

> Yet alternative theories and practices of translation are worth recovering because they offer contemporary English-language translators exemplary modes of cultural resistance, however qualified they must be to serve a new and highly unfavorable scene. The domesticating translation that currently dominates Anglo-American literary culture, both elite and popular, can be challenged only by developing a practice that is not just more self-conscious, but more self-critical. Knowledge of the source-language culture, however expert, is insufficient to produce a translation that is both readable and resistant to a reductive domestication; translators must also possess a commanding knowledge of the diverse cultural discourse in the target language, past and present. And they must be able to write them. The selection of a foreign text for translation and the invention of a discursive strategy to translate it should be grounded on a critical assessment of the target-language culture, its hierarchies and exclusions, its relations to cultural others worldwide.[26]

Of course, for Venuti this is only an ardent wish and he himself does not know how this wish can be realized, but in any case, after his theoretical and practical deconstruction and impact, domesticating-fluent translation at least should not become the only standard for translation and in the process of the decolonization of national culture, a kind of foreignizing translation is slowly moving from the periphery to the center, and will eventually become a positive and critical cultural strategy.

Now let us turn to the attitude of Chinese translation theorists toward the foreignization-domestication strategy. It is no coincidence that Chinese translation studies circles are enthusiastic about the foreignization-domestication issue which is closely related to the translation practice of twentieth-century Chinese literature and culture, and the various theoretical viewpoints surrounding this practice. It is my belief that even today, the large-scale introduction of Western literature and cultural academic thoughts in the May Fourth Movement and the previous period from the late Qing Dynasty to the early Republic of China is historically significant. Even though those May Fourth pioneers ignored translating the traditional culture and excellent classical literature of China while translating foreign literature and cultural academic thoughts extensively, it is understandable because back then the Western and Japanese academic circles were far less interested in China than they are now. Even if there had been good translations, they would have been rejected or marginalized by the European, American, and Japanese markets where domesticizing translations prevailed. Yet now that China's economy is developing rapidly, the status of China as a political and cultural power should be established accordingly. Judging from a growing Western interest in China, we should and can afford to introduce Chinese literary works and cultural theories to foreign readers through translation, at least contributing to the formation of a truly multicultural pattern to break the monopoly of Western-centrism in cultural ecology. In this way, the interest of the Chinese translation community in Venuti's theory of foreignization-domestication is of strong practical significance. His preliminary achievements in the practice of foreignization can be used as a reference and precedent when we implement the strategy of making Chinese culture, philosophy and social sciences go global.

It should be acknowledged that despite the radical and resistant concept of foreignization presented in his book, Venuti, as a literary translator, still pays attention to the necessary formal skills, though he places more emphasis on the translation's function of cultural transmission and reconstruction of translation, and he believes that:

> Translation is a process that involves looking for similarities between languages and cultures—particularly similar messages and formal techniques—but it does this only because it is constantly confronting dissimilarities. It can never and should never aim to remove these dissimilarities entirely. A translated text should be the site where a different culture emerges, where a reader gets a glimpse of a cultural other, and resistancy, a translation strategy based on an aesthetic of discontinuity, can best preserve that difference, that otherness, by reminding the reader of the gains and losses in the translation process and the unbridgeable gaps between cultures.[27]

There is no doubt that, in creating a new setup for international cultural ecology, where diverse cultures can co-exist, Venuti's cultural translation strategy is very similar to the decolonizing efforts of postcolonial theorists Gayatri Spivak and Homi Bhabha, but in terms of translation practice and research, Venuti goes much further. His efforts are both tragic and heroic as well as admirable, given that he struggled many years on the forefront singlehandedly as a translator and theorist. His tortuous experience in translating from Italian into English may be useful for us today when we translate Chinese literary works into English and other major world languages. While we conduct such experiments, we may have to initially look for native speakers to cooperate with in order to achieve the purpose of effectively disseminating Chinese literary thoughts and cultural theories. We may even have to go so far as to follow the tradition of domestication and make the translator invisible. However, once we occupy a certain share of the market, and once readers of the target language understand the inherent Chinese mindset and cultural conventions, they will gradually become used to our foreignizing translations. Then gradually by reading translations of Chinese literary works, they will grasp the true essence of Chinese literature and culture. This may be a long process, but in the course of time, the historical merits and the significance of Venuti's efforts will become increasingly clear. Thus, when Chinese scholars in the humanities and social sciences vigorously implement the strategy of "going global" in philosophy and social sciences, referring to and learning from Venuti's theory and practice will undoubtedly prevent us from making detours and will help us to introduce our own academic research to the world as soon as possible. This will help disrupt the de facto hegemony of Western-centrism in the world's cultural landscape. It is gratifying to know that an increasing number of academic works by Chinese scholars have been translated and introduced to the world by way of joint Sino-foreign collaborations, ever since the National Philosophy and Social Sciences Planning Office launched the Chinese Academic Translation Project.

4.3 The visibility of translation and the awakening of the translator's subjective consciousness

When discussing the important contribution of Venuti's translation theory to the cultural turn of contemporary translation studies, it is obviously insufficient to argue only at the seemingly technical level of foreignization and domestication, because behind these two terms lies a profound postcolonial cultural criticism. As shown by the title of his book, Venuti profoundly criticized and deconstructed the long-standing tradition of suppressing translation and translators in the history of Western literary translation, and at the same time called for the awakening of the translator's own subjective consciousness. The latter of course depends on many subjective and objective factors, among which the theorist's appeal also plays an important role. In this regard, Venuti has always been at the forefront of the battle. As he frankly admits:

> The project of the present book is to combat the translator's invisibility with a history of—and in opposition to—contemporary English-language translation. Insofar as it is a cultural history with a professed political agenda, it follows the genealogical method developed by Nietzsche and Foucault and abandons the two principles that govern much conventional historiography: teleology and objectivity.[28]

This suggests that his book is of great political significance in highlighting the subjective creativity of the translator. The starting point of his deconstruction and the perspective of his discussion is cultural translation and the role of the translator in the translation and its development and evolution. Obviously, Nietzsche's challenge to the supremacy of God and Foucault's dismantling of the author's authority give profound insights to Venuti. However, Foucault only deconstructs the author's authority and uniqueness in general but does not deal with the authority of the original author in the translated text. Venuti did not follow Foucault's method to completely deconstruct the author's authority. He only wanted to highlight the role of the translator when acknowledging the author's right to the translation, thus returning to the Benjamin-like style of proposition: an excellent (translated) literary work is the result of the joint efforts of the author and the translator, rather than a product created independently by the author. However, this fact actually has not been widely recognized by readers and scholars and even many translators are not concerned about it because they have become used to their long-standing status of invisibility. Since the invisibility of the translator has become a well-known phenomenon, it is unnecessary for Venuti, who has also for a long time been involved in translation practice, to avoid this unjust phenomenon. Instead, he aims to break the so-called objective attitude of history writing and intervenes in this struggle with a distinct stance in politics and an attitude of cultural criticism. From the way he wrote *The Translator's Invisibility: A History of Translation*, we can see that Venuti did not describe historical translation events and introduce major translators and their translation methods in an "objective" chronological order, like how previous historians did. Rather, he elucidates his viewpoint right from the beginning—the objectivity of history is also an illusion, and it is not a true record of historical events, but a "textualized" history narrated by later generations using the power of language. One can say that in this respect Venuti was influenced by the historiography of New Historicism. At the same time, just like the new historicism in contemporary English literary criticism, he strongly deconstructed the prejudices against translators (recipient-interpreters) in translation history.

As mentioned before, there are many reasons for the phenomenon of the translator's invisibility. Besides the huge economic and political benefits hidden behind translation and the standard of domestication-fluency popular in translation circles, there is another important factor: the translator's own rights. That is, should translators enjoy the same rights as the author or should they play only a minor role in the translation process? This is the key when it comes to viewing the role of the translator. From the traditional point of view of domesticizing translation, only the author is the laborer with originality, and the role of the translator is only secondary. The task of the translator is to faithfully reproduce the original intention of the author. He must yield to the original work, must not interpret or develop it in any other way, and at most can just make some linguistic adjustments, so only one person can hold the right of the work, and that is the original author. The translator, like a cheap laborer, gets remuneration paid in a lump sum, unlike the author who can always enjoy the income of the royalties. Even worse, many translators are willing to remain anonymous and gain temporary benefits for this invisibility.

Venuti believes this is the crux of the matter, so he believes it necessary for scholars in translation studies to fight for the rights and interests of translators, and further points out:

> The translator's invisibility is also partly determined by the individualistic conception of authorship that continues to prevail in Anglo-American culture. According to this conception, the author freely expresses his thoughts and feelings in writing, which is thus viewed as an original and transparent self-representation, unmediated by transindividual determinants (linguistic, cultural, social) that might complicate authorial originality. This view of authorship carries two disadvantageous implications for the translator. On the one hand, translation is defined as a second-order representation: only the foreign text can be original, an authentic copy, true to the author's personality or intention, whereas the translation is derivative, fake, potentially a false copy. On the other hand, translation is required to efface its second-order status with transparent discourse, producing the illusion of authorial presence, whereby the translated text can be taken as the original.[29]

The humiliation suffered by the translator is obvious, and his position is thus very embarrassing: while he is not respected like an author, he may even be criticized for the translation lacking fluency and readability. A few translators who translate famous writers' influential works may be considered fame seekers, like "dwarfs standing on the shoulders of giants" and so on. The reasons are probably no more than these two: firstly, there must be an original work before someone can translate it; and the content of the original and the demand of the market determine whether it is worth translating into another language, so the content of the original comes first and the translator is merely a hired worker. Of course, there is some truth to it, but in essence, it ignores the enormous effect of the translator on the original: when a foreign literary work is translated by a translator who is well-known in the world of target language, the result will be that not only will the work have a huge market value, it will also make the original author more popular in the target language than in the source language. Here are just two examples. The first is the anonymous epic *Beowulf* in the history of English literature. This classic masterpiece was for a long time unpopular in the contemporary English-speaking world since it was difficult to read and the translations into modern English were too prose-like, so university lecturers of English literature stopped teaching this work altogether and started from Chaucer instead. However, at the turn of the century, a dramatic change took place: the modern English poetry translation of *Beowulf* by famous Irish poet and Nobel laureate Seamus Heaney appeared suddenly on the bestseller list, reviving the literary classic from "the state of death". Although Heaney's translation is only an "intralingual conversion" from Old English into Modern English, it is equally difficult as translating from a foreign language. Therefore, rather than *Beowulf* boosting Heaney's reputation, it was Heaney's retranslation that brought this dying classic to life in the afterlife. Ironically, readers still don't know who wrote the classic epic but they do know that the translation that they are reading is by the famous poet Seamus Heaney. There is no lack of similar examples in China. The famous Chinese writer and translator Fu Lei translated the novels of Honoré de Balzac in the early years of his career, which remained popular among readers for a long time, and earned Balzac higher status as a classic writer in China than that in the history books of French literature published abroad. As a result, Fu Lei's name is as well-known as Balzac's name among general Chinese readers, and both are widely respected in China. Although scholars who strictly abide by the linguistic conventions of translation would accuse Fu of too much creativity and embellishment in his translations, as he often replaced Balzac's tedious and heavy narrative with his own fluent and even elegant style, at least later retranslations of the same works by Balzac were never as successful as Fu's. Later versions were either inferior to Fu's in terms of print run, or rarely cited by readers or researchers. Even though there were some famous names among those translators, their names are inevitably overshadowed by the aura of Fu as a translation master. These two examples not only confirm the translator's role in the process of canonizing a translated work in the target language but also prove the win-win situation for both the original author and the translator. The translations are the products of tacit cooperation between the author and translator, so they are not equal to the original but have the same value as the original. Of course, Venuti may not agree with Fu's translation because Fu is a typical translator of domesticating strategy. The linguistic violence he inflicts on Balzac's original text in fact constructs a new Balzac in the Chinese context. However, this example eloquently demonstrates that the translator's huge impact on the original author and work cannot be ignored. Admittedly, the fame of the original author can raise the translator's status and boost their fame, but a well-known translator in turn can help the original work achieve a lasting "afterlife" in different cultural contexts. In this sense, therefore, the role of the translator cannot be ignored. Nevertheless, what is the status of translators in the contemporary Anglophone world? Venuti further reveals:

> The translator's shadowy existence in Anglo-American culture is further registered, and maintained, in the ambiguous and unfavorable legal status of translation, both in copyright law and in actual contractual arrangements. [...] The translator is thus subordinated to the author, who decisively controls the publication of the translation during the term of the copyright for the "original" text, currently the author's lifetime plus fifty years.[30]

Of course, such provisions favoring the protection of authors' rights and interests are not enjoyed by translators, so in Venuti's view, translators hardly receive extensive recognition by society for their creative work.

Indeed, if we don't deny that the success of a literary translation is the product of a tacit collaboration between the author and translator, then we will certainly see that this type of copyright law is beneficial to the original author without considering the translator's legitimate and proper rights. While the translator works hard to produce high-quality translations that also have great market value, the author and legal heirs are waiting for royalties. Moreover,

> [t]he translator's authorship is never given full legal recognition because of the priority given to the foreign writer in controlling the translation—even to the point of compromising the translator's rights as a British or American citizen. [...] Copyright law does not define a space for the translator's authorship that is equal to, or in any way restricts, the foreign author's rights. And yet it acknowledges that there is a material basis to warrant some such restriction.[31]

This shows that the situation of the translator is extremely unfavorable when confronted with the author and the copyright law of their own country, so they have no choice but to work hard to earn an income. While famous writers can leave their names in literary history, translators can only do the work for others in silence and ultimately maintain the fame of the original work at the cost of exhausting all their energy. For a successful translator and translation theorist like Venuti it is impossible to be indifferent to such a situation. Therefore, he calls on translators to act if they want to fight for their legitimate rights and status. In the last chapter of his book, he makes an appeal to all translators:

> Translators must also force a revision of the codes—cultural, economic, legal—that marginalize and exploit them. They can work to revise the individualistic concept of authorship that has banished translation to the fringes of Anglo-American culture, not only be developing innovative translation practices in which their work becomes visible to readers, but also by presenting sophisticated rationales for this practice in prefaces, essays, lectures, interviews. Such self-presentations will indicate that the language of the translation originates with the translator in a decisive way, but also that the translator is not its sole origin: a translator's originality lies in choosing a particular foreign text and a particular combination of dialects and discourses from the history of British and American literature in response to an existing cultural situation. Recognizing the translator as an author questions the individualism of current concepts of authorship by suggesting that no writing can be mere self-expression because it is derived from a cultural tradition at a specific historical moment.[32]

Of course, in his capacity as a translator and researcher, Venuti's call for the rights and status of translators is quite justifiable and undoubtedly has important practical significance. Nonetheless, to draw such a simple conclusion would obscure the more ambitious goal he is trying to achieve: arousing the translator's subjective consciousness and constructing the translator's status as a creator. I believe that this is another contribution of Venuti's monograph.

It is well known that the invisibility of translators generally manifests itself in the following three ways. The first is economic exploitation. Indeed, it is a common belief, both in China and in the West, that the author of a book is the original worker and deserves respect from society, while the translator who translates a foreign text into a native language cannot have the same status as the author because the (ambiguous) translator's creative labor is based on a ready-made original, therefore his status is not equal to that of the author. Of course, in general situations this makes sense but there are special exceptions. Some people who are already famous ask others to ghostwrite their life feelings for them in the form of an autobiography and publish it under their own name. Of course, this is sometimes done with the market in mind, but one wonders whether they should enjoy the privilege of the author. Of course, this is easy for authors, but for translators, they have to spend double the energy: first, they must have some knowledge of the life and experiences of the author, and second, they must have some knowledge of the background and circumstances in which the author wrote the book. Furthermore, the translator must also gain an understanding of the author's state of mind and way of expression in order to express the contents with a similar style in the translation. Moreover, the translator sometimes has to provide clear translations and interpretations of the vague places in the original. To be sure, the quality of the translation often directly affects the success of the original work in another language and culture, and sometimes the translator has to advertise or even promote the work in order to receive great market benefits. However, what is the result? The original author still collects the royalties while the translator only receives a one-off remuneration, which obviously does not match the hard work of the translator.

The second is the lack of recognition of the translator's name. If this suppression of attribution is somewhat better in the West, it is a really serious issue in China. Some scholars who are not rigorous in their scholarship often deliberately overlook the existence of translators when quoting translations of Western theories, for instance, as "Quoted from Hegel's *Aesthetics*, Chinese edition", with the page number. Sometimes when the translator is well-known the situation is slightly better. For example, when quoting Hegel's *Aesthetics*, most scholars will mention "Zhu Guangqian's translation",[33] but if the translator is not very famous, some of them simply ignore the existence of the translator altogether. In the last three decades or so, since China joined the Berne Convention for the Protection of Literary and Artistic Works,[34] and strengthened the contract with the author and the translator, translators have had the opportunity to fight for the right to have their names on the cover of the translated work next to the author's name. However, when translating a Chinese text into foreign languages, the situation is often far from ideal. The English edition of *Social Sciences in China* stipulates that the name of the translator appears at the end of the article. In translations of some national government documents or speeches of leaders the name of the translator rarely appears. The situation has not yet changed so the fight for translators' rights will remain a long-term task.

Finally, the translator has low social and academic status. Since translation is not considered creative work, it has led to the formation of a new hierarchical order within the field of literary creation and academic research. If we look at the academic careers of the translation theorists discussed in this book, they all started out as translators. For example, Derrida translated *The Origin of Geometry* by Edmund Husserl, and Spivak translated Derrida's *Of Grammatology*. However, neither was satisfied merely playing the role of translator, so they wrote a translator's foreword to express their own understanding and interpretation and finally, they played the dual role of translator and author. As soon as they were successful, they stopped doing translations and took the path of original theorists. It is likely that nowadays, researchers of Benjamin will seldom mention his translations of Baudelair's collection of poems *Tableaux Parisiens* [*Paris's Sights*] and Proust's *À la recherche du temps perdu* [*Remembrance of Things Past*] but they cannot fail to mention "The Task of the Translator" because that essay heralded the rise of deconstructive translation theory and method. In all fairness, the status of literary translators in China is not low in the field of contemporary literary creative circles. The Chinese Writers Association has admitted many members whose main work is translation, some of them even serve as committee chairs or bureau members, and some well-known translators make use of their "cultural capital" in translation to publish some essays and articles about their translation experiences from time to time. This shows that translators are not completely invisible in China, and some of them can use translation to develop their academic careers, thereby increasing their income as well as their popularity and influence. However, all this comes at the cost of this situation: the current book market is full of shoddy translations, while the work of Chinese scholars is marginalized which disrupts the balance of cultural ecology. This may be the reason why some people blame translation for being the culprit of cultural colonization. Of course, on the other hand, it must be admitted that translated works have not got the attention of Chinese academic circles that they so deserve. Some scholars with considerable academic attainments and theoretical accomplishments are not promoted in their professional ranks because they spend so much time and energy translating foreign academic works into Chinese and less on writing their own monographs. In contrast, there are some opportunists who take advantage of their foreign language skills to compile and rewrite the ideas of foreign scholars which they then publish as their own monographs. As a result, they make rapid advances in their career, which is not uncommon in academic circles in China today.

The issue of promoting translators' subjective consciousness cannot be discussed unless we take into account the above-mentioned factors. In the case of literary translation, we believe that the translator is in the first place the reader and recipient of a work, and the lack of attention directed to the translator is closely related to the long-standing lack of attention directed to literary reception. In the past, the mode of literary historiography was nothing more than writing the history of ideas, complemented with the biographies of authors and analyses of works, with little mention of the reception of the works after publication. In the late 1960s, literary history emerged as a kind of "challenge" to literary theory in reception aesthetics, especially reflected in the provocative essay "Literary History as a Challenge to Literary Theory" [Literaturgeschichte als Provokation, 1967] by Hans Robert Jauss (1922–1997). The English translation was published in volume 2 of the journal *New Literature History* in 1970. From the perspectives of reader's reception, this article draws attention to a field that has long been neglected by literary historians: reader's reception of literary works. According to the theorists of reception aesthetics, a literary history can only be credible and complete if it takes into account the important role played by readers' reception in constituting the history of literature.

It is beyond doubt that the two theorists of reception aesthetics Jauss and Wolfgang Iser challenged the traditional literary historiography that ignores the role of the reader from different angles. Their challenge has laid the foundation for us to construct a new literary history from a new angle. Just as Jauss questioned the practice of linking the literary evolution with social history,

> [f]rom this perspective, [...] must it not then also be possible to place the "literary series" and the "non-literary series" into a relation that comprehends the relationship between literature and history without forcing literature, at the expense of its character as art, into a function of mere copying or commentary?[35]

Obviously, reception aesthetics by theorists such as Jauss was not motivated by anti-historical purposes but rather an attempt to divorce the history of literature from its close association with social politics and ideology, while adding cultural and formalist elements in order to emphasize the literary and aesthetic functions of literary works. Although their efforts have become history, they are still important inspirations for us today to re-examine established literary classics and propose active strategies for their reconstruction. Besides, since translators are the first dynamic recipients of a literary work, they also play the role of interpreter and creative writer who produces it in another language, and they may have a huge effect on the canonizing process of the translated work in the target language. Therefore, the creative subjective role of the translator should not be overlooked.

In *Contemporary Translation Theories*, Edwin Gentzler discusses Venuti meaningfully in a chapter outside of deconstructive translation, possibly because he wanted to demonstrate that Venuti's translation theory is based on multiple sources, among which deconstruction is important, followed by Foucault's historical theory, German reception aesthetics and postcolonial theory and cultural studies in the Anglophone world. Worth citing is the paragraph, where he acknowledges Venuti's contributions:

> I am not alone in rethinking translation along such lines. Perhaps the most influential translation studies scholar of the last decade in North America has been Lawrence Venuti [...]. Venuti's contributions to translation studies are multiple. First, and perhaps most importantly, he criticizes the humanistic underpinnings of much literary translation in the United States and shows how it reinforces prevailing domestic beliefs and ideologies. Secondly, he provides a new set of terms and methods for analyzing translations. And finally, he offers a set of alternative strategies he would like translators to try.[36]

Admittedly, Gentzler's comments are obviously representative, at least it shows that in today's American translation theory circles, Venuti has intervened in translation and translation studies from the perspectives of deconstruction and postcolonial cultural criticism, advancing the cultural turn in translation and its studies, and promoting the indispensable role of translation in the process of cultural transmission and cultural change. In addition, Venuti himself has constantly kept abreast of the times. In recent years, in the face of the rising world literature fever in the circles of comparative literature and literary theory, he has again devoted himself to it with great passion and discussed the relationship between world literature and translation. In his article "World Literature and Translation Studies", he starts by pointing out:

> World literature cannot be conceptualized apart from translation. In most historical periods as well as in most geographical areas, only a small minority of readers can comprehend more than one or two languages, so that considered from the reader's point of view, world literature consists not so much of original compositions as of translations [...][37]

It is not all words and no action: Venuti never forgets to promote the translator's subjectivity, and always emphasizes the important role of translation in the construction of the world's literary canon. In this article, for example, he even cites several sinologists' writings in English when referring to Chinese writer Lu Xun's role in the use of "literary translation as a means of altering China's subordinate position in global political relations, they drew on minor literatures".[38] Thus, in this regard, even scholars specializing in translation theory are also aware of their language limitations, and they often have to rely on translation if they want to engage in the study of comparative literature and world literature across cultural traditions.

Notes

1 For more on De Man's views on translation issues, see De Man, P. 1986. Conclusions: Walter Benjamin's "The task of the translator". In *The Resistance to Theory*. Minneapolis: University of Minnesota Press, 73–105.
2 In fact, Venuti was not included among the names of deconstructive translation theorists in Gentzler's *Contemporary Translation Theories*. Instead, Venuti's role in promoting the cultural turn of translation is emphasized. Chinese scholar Guo Jianzhong was the first to introduce Venuti's translation theory in the context of China. See his papers: Guo, J. 1998. Cultural aspects in translation: Domestication and foreignization. *Waiguoyu* [Journal of Foreign Languages], (2): 12–19; Guo, J. 2000. Venuti and his deconstructive translation strategies. *Zhongguo Fanyi* [Chinese Translators Journal], (1): 49–52. Indeed, from Venuti's understanding, interpretation and follow-up on Derrida's thoughts on translation, his deconstructive tendency is rather obvious. On the other hand, as a translator (translating from a secondary language into a primary language), he has deconstructive views that are closer to Spivak's strategies of postcolonial criticism.
3 Translators' note: Miller gained his BA from Oberlin College and his MA from Harvard University.
4 Translators' note: Miller joined Yale University in 1972.
5 For details of the dialogue between Miller and Zhang Jiang, see the letters I was invited to edit for *Comparative Literature Studies* in the United States: Zhang, J. & Miller, J. H. 2016. Exchange of letters about literary theory between Zhang Jiang and J. Hillis Miller. *Comparative Literature Studies*, 53(3): 567–610.
6 Miller, J. H. 1993. Foreword. *New Starts: Performative Topographies in Literature and Criticism*. Taipei: Academia Sinica, vii. For an interpretation of Miller's view on translation, see Ning, Y. 1999. Miller on the translation of literary theory. *Waiyu Yu Waiyu Jiaoxue* [Foreign Languages and Their Teaching], (5): 37–39.

7 Ibid., p. 3.
8 Ibid., p. 6.
9 Ibid., p. 8.
10 Ibid., p. 13.
11 Ibid., pp. 25–26.
12 Late in his career, Miller turned his attention to the role of cultural translation and the status of literature in the era of globalization. See Miller, J. H. 2007. A defense of literature and literary study in a time of globalization and the new tele-technologies. *Neohelicon*, *34*(2): 13–22.
13 Miller, J. H. 1993. Foreword. *New Starts: Performative Topographies in Literature and Criticism*. Taipei: Academia Sinica, 26.
14 For "New Starts" in the translation of theory into another language and culture, see Sheng Anfeng's long article on the translation and transformation of postcolonialism in China: Sheng, A. 2008. The travel and variation of theory: Postcolonial theory in China. In N. Wang (ed.), *Wenxue Lilun Qianyan* [Frontiers of Literary Theory]. Vol. 5. Beijing: Peking University Press, 121–164.
15 In this regard, Wang Dongfeng is of the opinion that in the Chinese context, the translation practice and foreignization strategy of Lu Xun came out much earlier than Venuti's. See Wang's latest article: Wang, D. 2008. A comparison of Venuti's and Lu Xun's views on foreignization in translation. *Zhongguo Fanyi* [Chinese Translators Journal], (2): 5–10.
16 See Feng, Y. 2006. On Lawrence Venuti's deconstructive translation strategy. *Wenyi Yanjiu* [Literature and Art Studies], (3): 41.
17 Schulte, R. & Biguenet, J. (eds.). 1992. *Theories of Translation: An Anthology of Essays from Dryden to Derrida*. Chicago, IL & London: The University of Chicago Press, 41–42.
18 See Jiang, X. & Zhang, J. 2007. Reinterpreting Venuti's theory of alienated translation—debating with Professor Guo Jianzhong. *Zhongguo Fanyi* [Chinese Translators Journal], (3): 40–41.
19 Venuti, L. 1995. *The Translator's Invisibility: A History of Translation*. London & New York: Routledge, 2.
20 Ibid., p. 5.
21 Ibid., p. 19.
22 For the role of translation in the construction of modern Chinese literary classics, please refer to my article: Wang, N. 2002. Modernity, translated literature and the reconstruction of modern Chinese literary classics. *Wenyi Yanjiu* [Literature and Art Studies], (6): 32–40.
23 See Dai, X. 2008. Thirty years of literary theory in the new age: A review and reflection. In N. Wang (ed.), *Wenxue Lilun Qianyan* [Frontiers of Literary Theory]. Vol. 5. Beijing: Peking University Press, 87–120.
24 For a discussion of "aphasia" in contemporary Chinese literary theory, see the following two articles: Cao, S. & Li, S. 1996. The basic ways and means to reconstruct the discourse of Chinese literary theory. *Wenyi Yanjiu* [Literature and Art Studies], (2): 12–21; Cao, S. & Li, S. 1997. Revisiting the reconstruction of the discourse of Chinese literary theory. *Wenxue Pinglun* [Literary Review], (4): 43–52.
25 Venuti, L. 1995. *The Translator's Invisibility: A History of Translation*. London & New York: Routledge, 306.
26 Ibid., p. 309.
27 Ibid., p. 306.
28 Ibid., p. 39.
29 Ibid., pp. 6–7.
30 Ibid., pp. 8–9.
31 Ibid., p. 9.
32 Ibid., p. 311.

33 Translators' note: Zhu Guangqian (1897–1986), who was educated in Hong Kong, the United Kingdom and France, made important contributions to the study of aesthetics in China, by translating major Western works on aesthetics and publishing his own works on the subject.
34 Translators' note: This happened in 1992.
35 Jauss, H. R. 1982. *Toward an Aesthetic of Reception*. B. Timothy (trans.). Minneapolis: University of Minnesota Press, 18.
36 Gentzler, E. 2001. *Contemporary Translation Theories* (2nd ed.). Clevedon: Multilingual Matters, 36.
37 Venuti, L. 2012. World literature and translation studies. In T. D'haen, et al. (eds.), *The Routledge Companion to World Literature*. London & New York: Routledge, 180.
38 Ibid., p. 181.

5 The theory and practice of postcolonial translation

As a strongly revolutionary and deconstructive cultural critical theory in its broad sense, postcolonialism has been one of the most influential, interdisciplinary, intercultural, and intercivilizational cultural theoretical trends since the 1980s. It has been most comprehensively and deeply interpreted and practiced by critics such as Edward Said (1935–2003), Gayatra Chakravorty Spivak (1942–), and Homi Bhabha (1949–). There is no doubt that postcolonialism's deconstruction and critique of imperialist cultural hegemony is predominantly reflected in literary and cultural criticism but also in literary translation and research. It can be said that in a sense, the formation of postcolonial translation theory was a direct result of the promotion of various poststructural theories centered on deconstruction within the field of translation studies. The most influential among those were the theories of Derrida and Foucault. This chapter will mainly discuss the contributions of Spivak and Bhabha, who are the most representative postcolonial theorists, to the theory and practice of cultural translation. It will also discuss some of Said's theoretical concepts that are relevant to postcolonial cultural translation.

5.1 The critique of Orientalism and the traveling of theory

Undoubtedly, compared with the other two postcolonial theorists mentioned above, Said is considered the most prominent representative and leader of the postcolonial theoretical trend. As a result, his popularity has remained the highest and his writings have been the most frequently discussed and quoted in the field. This is undoubtedly related to his productivity and early rise in American academia. Said was born in Jerusalem, on November 1, 1935 to a property-owning Christian family. His father ran a well-established stationery business in the Middle East, while his mother's interest was in literature and the arts. These greatly influenced the development of his musical talents. In 1951, Said moved to the United States with his family, and began to receive education there (he began to receive education before moving to the US). He gained his BA degree from Princeton University in 1957, MA degree from Harvard University in 1960, and PhD from Harvard in 1964. Said started teaching British and American literature and comparative literature at Columbia University in 1963. In 1992, he was awarded the title of University Professor of English and Comparative Literature at Columbia University, while he was also elected fellow of the American Academy of Arts and Sciences. On 24 September 2003, he died in New York of cancer which he had battled for many years.

If Spivak's postcolonial theory has obvious feminist and deconstructive tones and Bhabha's theory has strong characteristics of "Third World" cultural criticism and "minority" studies, then there is no doubt that Said's early theories have strong ideological and cultural-political criticism, directed at Western imperialist cultural hegemonism and power politics. The cornerstone of his critical theory is "Orientalism". His provocative work *Orientalism*, which was first published in 1978, is generally regarded as the seminal work of postcolonial theory. While constructing Orientalism in this book, Said stresses that:

> Therefore, Orientalism is not a mere political subject matter or field that is reflected passively by culture, scholarship, or institutions; nor is it a large and diffuse collection of texts about the Orient; nor is it representative and expressive of some nefarious "Western" imperialist plot to hold down the "Oriental" world. […] Indeed, my real argument is that Orientalism is—and does not simply represent—a considerable dimension of modern political-intellectual culture, and as such has less to do with the Orient than it does with "our" world.[1]

Obviously, the Orientalism that Said refers to here is not a concept that people from the East have developed; instead, it is an indeterminate concept with multiple meanings, an illusion fabricated by Western media with a series of reproduction means over a long period of time. If this term is translated into Chinese, the Chinese translation is either "dongfang zhuyi" [Orientalism] or "dongfang xue" [Oriental studies]. Moreover, Said's original intention of the book was to criticize the Oriental studies in the West since the eighteenth century. However, once Orientalism is expressed as a discipline in Chinese, it may cover up its distinctive ideological meaning.[2] Therefore, most researchers in the Chinese context tend to translate it into "Orientalism" to highlight its distinctive ideological significance, but even so, without further explanation, there is still a risk of theoretical misunderstanding. In this regard, Said tried to clarify that "Orientalism" has at least two meanings: the first refers to a way of thinking based on the ontological and epistemological differences between the (imaginary, poetic) "Orient" and the "Occident". The East and the West are geographically located in opposite hemispheres of the earth, and in other aspects, they are also in a state of long-term opposition due to the huge unbridgeable differences in politics, economy, language, and culture. The second meaning of Orientalism refers to the way in which the West, in a strong position, has long dominated and reconstructed the East, in a weak position, and oppressed its power of discourse. The relation between the East and the West is thus often viewed as one of influencing and being influenced, restricting and being restricted, and giving and receiving. In this unequal relationship, the so-called "Orientalism" has become an "Oriental myth" created by Western people out of their ignorance, prejudice and curiosity about the vast East or Third World. In other words,

"Orientalism" itself had nothing to do with the East in the geographical sense but was merely a concept that was "constructed" artificially. However, Said also points out that Orientalism lies at the overlap between three areas: (1) the 4,000-year-long history of the cultural relations between Europe and Asia; (2) the discipline that trained experts in Asian languages and cultures since the nineteenth century; (3) the "otherness" of the "East" that has been developed by generations of Western scholars.[3] As a result of this long-lasting prejudice against the East, the people in the East are on the one hand labeled "lazy" and "stupid" by Western people, but on the other hand, the East itself is not without some beckoning "mystery". Ultimately Orientalism is in essence a political doctrine created by Western colonialists who tried to gain control over the East and has always served as an ideological pillar of Western colonialism as a deep-rooted epistemological system of the East. Obviously, through this "reproduction-style" cultural translation, Said constructed an object for his critique and deconstruction, which inspired, as it were, all subsequent postcolonial translation theories and practices.

Said's construction and criticism of Orientalism have indeed opened up a new theoretical perspective in interdisciplinary cultural scholarship, directing the tentacle of research to an area that has all along been neglected and deliberately marginalized by mainstream Western academic circles: The East or the Third World. It is geographically separated from the West, occupying two parts of the globe, but "the East" not only denotes its geographical location but also has profound political and cultural connotations. Thus, Said's attempt also has a strong effect of "decentralization" and "deconstruction". In fact, it is the precursor to the phenomenon of "demarginalization" that emerged in the West after the decline of postmodernism.

However, as many scholars in the East and the West have noticed, there are limitations to Said's criticism and construction of the "Orient" and "Orientalism". These limitations are manifested at geographical, cultural, and literary dimensions, and provide a theoretical basis for Third World scholars and critics to question and rethink. It is true that the publication of *Orientalism* not only established Said's academic reputation and status, but it also marked the start of the construction of his postcolonial theoretical system. Later, although on other occasions he added and corrected the intension (term in semantics) and extension of "Orientalism", the theoretical core basically had no other breakthrough.

In light of the controversy that followed after the publication of *Orientalism*, especially from the camp of Oriental scholars, Said responded in various venues. His most powerful and striking response was his article "Orientalism Reconsidered" published in 1985, in the fall issue of *Race and Class*. The article was later reprinted in 2000 in the edited volume *Reflections on Exile and Other Essays*. In this article, Said first briefly reiterates his three-fold definition of Orientalism:

> As a department of thought and expertise, Orientalism of course involves several overlapping aspects: first, the changing historical and cultural relationship between Europe and Asia, a relationship with a 4,000-year-old history; second, the scientific discipline in the West according to which, beginning in

the early nineteenth century, one specialized in the study of various Oriental cultures and traditions; and third, the ideological suppositions, images, and fantasies about a region of the world called the Orient.[4]

He then added, "This is, however, neither to say that the division between Orient and Occident is unchanging nor is it to say that it is simply fictional".[5] As a result of these complex factors, the concept of Orientalism has been proposed and created with various subjective and objective factors and inevitably it arouses criticism and controversy. In response, Said does not sidestep this but further refines the definition and description of Orientalism by probing its essence through various superficial phenomena.

> For the reconsideration of Orientalism has been intimately connected with many other activities of the sort I referred to earlier, and which it now becomes imperative to articulate in more detail. Thus, we can now see that Orientalism is a praxis of the same sort as male gender dominance, or patriarchy, in metropolitan societies: the Orient was routinely described as feminine, its riches as fertile, its main symbols the sensual woman, the harem, and the despotic—but curiously attractive—ruler. Moreover, Orientals, like housewives, were confined to silence and to unlimited enriching production. Much of this material is manifestly connected to the configurations of sexual, racial, and political asymmetry underlying mainstream modern western culture, as illuminated respectively by feminists, by black studies critics, and by anti-imperialist activists.[6]

We can see from Said's own construction of and reflections on Orientalism that after years of debate about the concept of Orientalism and Oriental studies in academic circles, he has to a certain extent incorporated some of the remarks made by critics and made some corrections to his own past constructs. Although Said does not specifically discuss translation issues, he is engaged in an important concept of cultural translation: cultural reproduction, or cultural translation in the broad sense, namely, the purpose for which people from the West translate and reproduce the East as "Other", different from itself. From his analysis and criticism, we can see that the "demonized" image of the East and its people in the eyes of the West is deeply ingrained, which results from not only a distortion deliberately used by Western media as a means of expression, but also a practice of "self-Orientalization" by authors and intellectuals with an Oriental cultural background living in the West. One of the important factors is translation, or cultural reproduction through translation.[7] As such, the East always plays the role of "Other" in the eyes of the West.

Said's engagement with cultural translation is also reflected in his important concept of "traveling theory". In the early 1980s, his edited volume *The World, the Text and the Critic* (1983) included one of his most famous and widely cited articles "Traveling Theory", which was originally published in *Raritan Quarterly* in 1982. In this article, Said used the translation and dissemination of the theory of reification proposed by the Hungarian Marxist theorist Georg Lukács in different eras and different regions which result in different understandings and interpretations to illustrate this point: theory can sometimes "travel" to another era or another scene, and in the course of traveling it often loses some of its original power and rebellious nature. The emergence of this situation is mostly subject to the modification, tampering, and even domestication of that theory when it is received by people at that time and place, so deformation of a theory is entirely possible. Here, the mediation of translation cannot be overlooked, which not only Said but also the deconstructionist Miller illustrated. According to Said, the travel of a theory or concept, generally speaking, has four stages and takes four forms:

> First, there is a point of origin, or what seems like one, a set of initial circumstances in which the idea came to birth or entered discourse. Second, there is a distance transversed, a passage through the pressure of various contexts as the idea moves from an earlier point to another time and place where it will come into a new prominence. Third, there is a set of conditions—call them conditions of acceptance or, as an inevitable part of acceptance, resistances—which then confronts the transplanted theory or idea, making possible its introduction or toleration, however alien it might appear to be. Fourth, the now full (or partly) accommodated (or incorporated) idea is to some extent transformed by its new uses, its new position in a new time and place.[8]

This is in fact intended to show that it is not only difficult to remain faithful in the translation and dissemination of theories, nor is there need to be so faithful. Sometimes, the mutation of a theory when it takes root in the cultural soil of another nation may even have an expediting effect on the establishment of the new culture of the nation. This has already been explained in the previous chapter where we discussed Miller's translation theory. Here we might as well extend it to the context of Chinese culture for further discussion.

It is beyond doubt that Said attempted to give some universal significance to his concept of "traveling theory". Indeed, if it is applied to modern Chinese literature, we may well conclude that the formation of new culture and new literature and even the modern Chinese language since the May Fourth Movement to a large extent results from Western culture, including theories, which traveled to China with the mediation of translation. This issue will be discussed later in this book. It is therefore appropriate to use this concept to explain the spread and reception of Western theories, including postmodernism and postcolonialism, in the Third World and Eastern countries, as well as the ensuing misunderstandings and misconstructions. As far as the concept of "postcolonialism" itself is concerned, it also has a dual meaning. In terms of time, it is a new period following the disintegration of colonialism, during which colonialism changed its face and penetrated and invaded the Third World culturally in the form of neocolonialism. Therefore, "postcolonialism" implies both "transcending colonialism" and "neocolonialism". When we translate this word into Chinese, we must explain its complicated dual meaning, otherwise it will cause unnecessary misunderstanding. This shows that the argument about "traveling theory" is highly influential. Although Said is aware of this, he always felt the need to further reconsider it and elaborate on it. His article "Traveling Theory Reconsidered", originally written in 1994, is included in the edited volume *Reflections on Exile and Other Essays* published in 2000. There he stresses how Adorno was inspired by Lukács' theory and then he points out its connection with the critical theory of postcolonialism. Here the intermediary is Frantz Fanon, a pioneer of contemporary postcolonial criticism. This is beyond doubt an example of how Lukács' theory traveled to another place and mutated through the medium of translation. After tracing the link between Fanon's postcolonial criticism and Lukács' theory, Said concludes:

> There is concurrence here between Fanon and this more (and perhaps only momentarily) radical Lukács on the one hand, and between Lukács and Adorno on the other. The work of theory, criticism, demystification, deconsecration, and decentralization they imply is never finished. The point of theory therefore is to travel, always to move beyond its confinements, to emigrate, to remain in a sense in exile.[9]

To a certain extent, this repeats the deconstructive principle of translation and interpretation: the connotation of theory is infinite, and therefore the translation and interpretation of meaning is also endless. Wherever theory travels, it will inevitably interact with the cultural reception soil and their surroundings at that time and place, and this will produce new meanings. It can be said that the resonance and repercussions of Said's postcolonial criticism, which are centered on Orientalist cultural critique, in the Third World, especially in China, prove the validity of his "traveling theory".[10] At the same time it has also influenced contemporary postcolonial translation and translation studies, as we can see from the discussion of the following two postcolonial cultural translation theorists.

5.2 Deconstructive translation and interpretation

In contemporary trends of postcolonial theories and feminist movements in the West, Spivak's name has increasingly drawn attention. After Said passed away in 2003, Spivak became the most outstanding representative of postcolonial theory and criticism. She is not only an excellent translator of literature and theory but is also very much concerned about translation studies and has published translations and critical texts, so she is one of the most important theorists and practitioners of postcolonial translation. Her two major contributions to postcolonial translation theory and practice are: the "Translator's Preface", which is over 80 pages in length, to her English translation of Derrida's *Of Grammatology* and the article "The Politics of Translation". The latter in particular has become a classic in the field of postcolonial translation theory. Furthermore, she has published some articles in journals discussing cultural translation in a more general sense. She has also written the foreword and postscript to her translation of the short story collection *Imaginary Maps* by the Bengali female author and activist Mahasweta Devi from India, contributing to the cultural and political turn of translation.[11]

Gayatri Spivak was born in 1942 to an intellectual family in Calcutta, India. Her father was a doctor and although her mother was very young when she married and had children, she continued her studies and obtained a master's degree in Bengali literature from the University of Calcutta in 1937. Spivak retains a deep affection for her homeland; in order to keep her unique identity as a Third World intellectual, she still holds an Indian passport. In 1959, Spivak graduated from the University of Calcutta with a BA degree in English literature. Like many of her peers living in the former colonies of the British empire, she aspired to continue her education at prestigious universities in the UK or the US. That is how, after graduating from college, she went to Cornell University, where she gained an MA degree in English in 1962 and a PhD in comparative literature in 1967. Her supervisor was the well-known Yale University Professor Paul De Man. He was the authority on research into Romantic literature and the most prominent representative and leading figure in deconstructive criticism in the US. After graduation, Spivak did not return to India, but taught at several universities, including the University of Iowa, Emory University, the University of Texas at Austin, the University of California and the University of Pittsburgh. Since 1991, she has been teaching at Columbia University where she has been Avalon Foundation Professor in the Humanities and served as the Director of the Center for Comparative Literature and Society. Since 2008, she has held the position of University Professor at Columbia University, as the successor of Said. Spivak has written extensively and translated numerous literary and theoretical works, among which the most representative are: *In Other Worlds: Essays in Cultural Politics* (1987), *Outside in the Teaching Machine* (1993), *A Critique of Postcolonial Reason: Towards a History of the Vanishing Present* (1999), *Death of a Discipline* (2003) and the English translation of Derrida's *Of Grammatology*. She has also published many articles and literary translations.

There is no doubt that among the "three musketeers" of postcolonialism, Spivak is considered a theorist that has the closest connection with translation and translation studies. Some of her works on translation have also been recognized by traditional translation scholars, although many feel that she has overemphasized the political aspects of translation and focused less on the academic nature and linguistic reproduction of the discipline of translation itself. This is in fact one of the characteristics of postcolonialism, and this also shows that for Spivak, who has multidisciplinary knowledge and accomplishments, translation is only a small aspect of her academic research. Her objective is not to get involved in the discipline of translation studies but rather to deconstruct and criticize the culture and language of colonialism through translation. Her academic career started with the translation of Derrida's *Of Grammatology*. She is not only the major English translator and interpreter of Derrida's work but also the one who has the most accurate and profound understanding of Derrida's theory among the postcolonial theorists, which is essentially reflected in her "Translator's Preface". In Spivak's view, the fact that Derrida emerged in Western philosophy is by no means a coincidence but has a profound theoretical origin. The origin of this theory can at least be traced back to Kant. Hence, that is where her interpretation of Derrida's theory starts. By comparing the ideas of Kant, Nietzsche, and Heidegger, Spivak concludes that since Kant, philosophy has realized that it has to take responsibility for its own discourse:

> And if the assumption of responsibility for one's discourse leads to the conclusion that all conclusions are genuinely provisional and therefore inconclusive, that all origins are similarly unoriginal, that responsibility itself must cohabit with frivolity, this need not be cause for gloom.[12]

In a sense, this confirms Derrida's criticism and dismantling of Western metaphysics and also explains and defends the legitimacy of his deconstruction.

An important point of deconstructive theory is its powerful critique and erasure of the position of "logocentrism" that has long dominated Western philosophy and the history of language. An important basis for this dismantling strategy is to question the hypothetical centrality and metaphysical wholeness of everything. In the postcolonial debate, this kind of centrality clearly refers to the cultural hegemony of imperialism which of course includes the hegemony of language. In translation practice, one of the concerns is the question of who should be at the center of translation. Scholars in traditional linguistic translation studies believe that translation is the practice of changing from one language into another, so the original should be the center and the translator has no choice but to be faithful to the original. Yet, Benjamin believed that if a work is not being translated then it is in a state of death, and only when it is translated, especially by an excellent translator, is it possible that an original work radiates into a new life or an afterlife. Sometimes an outstanding translation can even help an original become a classic in the target language, and conversely, a poor translation of a classic may lose its quality in the target language. Therefore, the mediating role of translation is very important, and deconstructive translation follows this line of thought. The same goes for Spivak as the main English translator of Derrida's work. Since in Derrida's view, no conclusion is absolutely reliable or of ultimate value, the reading and interpretation of a text cannot be final, and the final conclusion can never be reached. This is the open principle prescribed for deconstructive reading and interpretation, and this principle has been applied by Derrida in translation studies. In deconstructionism, the ultimate interpretation of meaning is absent and not present; thus, what is presented to the reader can only be an "absent presence", which is exactly what continuously delays the meaning. Spivak was very much aware of this, and after carefully reading Derrida's work, she points out:

> Derrida seems to show no nostalgia for a lost presence. He sees in the traditional concept of the sign a heterogeneity [...]. It is indeed an ineluctable nostalgia for presence that makes of this heterogeneity a unity by declaring that a sign brings forth the presence of the signified.[13]

The uncertainty of the signifier and heterogeneity of the signified, as well as the sliding between the two result in the impossibility of obtaining the ultimate meaning. This is the attitude of deconstructive critics toward the reading and interpretation of texts. It can be said that the principle of postcolonial translation is deconstruction and decentralization. Its strong political ideology and cultural critique against colonialism and imperialism are even more distinct.

It is well known that one of the key features of deconstructive translation theory is its appeal to difference, which Spivak also has a marked preference for and has interpreted in her own way. In her view:

> Armed with this simple yet powerful insight—powerful enough to "deconstruct the transcendental signified"—that the sign, phonic as well as graphic, is a structure of difference, Derrida suggests that what opens the possibility of thought is not merely the question of being, but also the never-annulled difference from "the completely other."[14]

In this way, differences will always exist, and their traces cannot be erased. Therefore, structural unity claimed by the structuralists is clearly out of date. In the practice of translation, the meaning of linguistic signs is uncertain, and thus the faithfulness of expression in the target language is also highly questionable.

Although Spivak does not specifically discuss translation issues in the traditional sense in her "Translator's Preface", in her careful and explanatory review she has nevertheless outlined the main points of such a profound and obscure work as *Of Grammatology*:

> *Of Grammatology* is the provisional origin of this Preface. But we have not kept track of the book's outline. We have considered instead the importance of erasure in Derrida; provided some ingredients for the computation of the intertextuality between Derrida, and Nietzsche, Heidegger, Freud, Husserl; given some indications of Derrida's view of Structuralism, especially of the metapsychological practice of Jacques Lacan; commented on the place of "writing" in Derrida's thought, hinted at the chain of its substitutions, given the recipe for deconstruction.[15]

This is a reminder that it is necessary to involve the works of other philosophical writers, when reading *Of Grammatology*, because of its intertextual nature. Therefore, in the course of translating the book, the translator in fact played the role of a "dual reader", a dynamic recipient of the source text and a translator-interpreter in the target language.

In the long "Translator's Preface", Spivak also explains and extends Derrida's important theoretical concepts from a unique perspective of cultural and theoretical interpretation: différance, difference, dissemination, logocentrism, phonocentralism, structure, traces, tracks, etc. The preface also refers to Derrida's other works including *Writing and Difference, Speech and Phenomena, Dissemination, Margins of Philosophy* and *Glas*, as well as his forerunner, Heidegger's *Being and Time* and Derrida's early translation of Edmund Husserl's "The Origin of Geometry". It can be said that the "Translator's Preface" has opened a new possibility for the translation of academic works in the humanities—interpretation. It is a kind of metaphysical interpretation of culture and theory not limited to a specific text, paragraph, or structure of the original work, but leading the reader into an abstruse theoretical work from a macroscopic perspective. Therefore, it is best to read Spivak's "Translator's Preface" before reading her English translation of *Of Grammatology*. In terms of depth and impact, Derrida's original French work and Spivak's English translation plus the "Translator's Preface" are equal in value. The worldwide popularization of Derrida's theory of deconstruction has largely been mediated by American circles of translation and scholarship. In this regard, Spivak's contributions should not be overlooked. As mentioned before, when French readers today come across an issue that is incomprehensible in *De la grammatologie*, they will always find the answer by consulting Spivak's English translation. It is probably a height that is difficult to reach for general translators of theories.

Of course, it is difficult for any translation to avoid misinterpretation, which Spivak is well aware of. While she points at Derrida's misreading of Husserl, she involuntarily wonders if she herself has misread Derrida. It is unfortunately unavoidable, because according to the deconstructive translation principle, the original work is both translatable and untranslatable. In the case of Derrida's work, the untranslatable elements far exceed the translatable ones. However, for Derrida's works to have an impact on the world, they must be translated into English, and Spivak can be said to be the best translator that could be selected from among the English academic circles at the time. It is clear from the efforts she put in the "Translator's Preface" that she had read almost all the theories of Western philosophy mentioned by Derrida in his book, as well as Derrida's own works that were published before the mid-1970s. Therefore, over the course of the translation, a resonance arose between the translator and the original author on many issues and they cooperated tacitly. Furthermore, Spivak admits frankly that Derrida's English was better than her French, so Derrida knew best whether Spivak had misinterpreted any of his ideas. Nevertheless, Derrida also understood that for the dissemination and popularization of his theory in the English-speaking world, a kind of misread version and a creative interpretation was needed. Perhaps it is exactly this kind of conscious misreading and "over"-interpretation that helped Derrida get into the Anglophone humanities directly, especially American literary criticism, and produce a huge and far-reaching impact. Just like Spivak, Derrida started his writing career with translation as the springboard, but he was extraordinary and amazed the world with his lengthy translator's preface to Husserl's original work which almost obscured the brilliance of it. Therefore, he must have his own views on the gains and losses of translation. For Derrida's view of translation, Spivak concludes the preface with the following summary:

> [...] Derrida's theory admitted—as it denied—a preface by questioning the absolute repeatability of the text. It is now time to acknowledge that his theory would likewise admit—as it denies—translation, by questioning the absolute privilege of the original. Any act of reading is besieged and delivered by the precariousness of intertextuality. And translation is, after all, one version of intertextuality. If there are no unique words, if, as soon as a privileged

concept-word emerges, it must be given over to the chain of substitution that is translation be suspect? If the proper name or sovereign status of the author is as much a barrier as a right of way, why should the translator's position be secondary?[16]

Spivak clearly returned again to Benjamin's standpoint: the translator and the original author are equally important, and the former is absolutely not secondary. It is precisely on this point, that Spivak accomplished both cultural translation and linguistic translation of Derrida's book. This demonstrates her own theoretical qualification, which laid the foundation for her to discuss the issue of theoretical translation.

5.3 The cultural and political strategies of translation

If Spivak had not ventured beyond the translation and interpretation of the works of master theorists such as Derrida, she would not have been so widely influential as she is today. Indeed, as many of her colleagues in academia have said, Spivak's academic career started with her translation of Derrida's work as a springboard, for she never translated another work by Derrida, nor did she continue to focus on explaining and criticizing his theories. Later in her academic career, she was influenced by deconstruction and Marxism simultaneously, and as a Third World postcolonial female scholar, she participated in the international feminist debates and criticism, and has been recognized by her peers for her commitment in all three fields. Therefore, in her own works the co-existence and interaction of these three elements are fully visible, which of course appears in texts where she discusses translation. Spivak's specific views on translation are mainly concentrated in her articles such as "The Politics of Translation", and the translator's prefaces and postscripts. "The Politics of Translation" was originally written in 1992 for a collection of essays on feminist controversy, and was later included in her own edited volume *Outside in the Teaching Machine*. One of the points emphasized in this essay is that any translation is not only linguistic conversion, but imbued with cultural critical meaning in terms of politics, ideology, and so on. This is especially true of the translation of works by women writers from the Third World into languages of imperialist hegemony. Admittedly, as a scholar of comparative literature studies involved in translation studies, Spivak attaches great importance to mastering various languages of the East and the West, and she takes the study of every language extremely seriously, not only to learn how to read fluently but also to achieve basic communication skills. However, her learning of foreign languages is not only for translation but even more so in order to be able to do research into theoretical issues with universal significance. In 2002, Spivak who was already well known by then, resolutely started to take a Chinese course in the Department of East Asian Languages and Cultures, Columbia University, as a regular student and insisted on taking the exams. In her view, lacking Chinese language knowledge would be a great shortcoming for someone involved in the comparative study of Eastern and Western literature and culture. She has mastered several

Western languages including English, French, and German, and is proficient in many Eastern languages, including Bengali and Hindi. With knowledge of Chinese on top of that, she is fully qualified to engage in the comparative study of Eastern and Western literature. However, she believes that comparing Eastern and Western literature only is not enough, and we should also include comparisons of literatures from the South and the North, i.e., literatures written in minor languages which "are doomed to extinction". In her view, working on comparative literature studies is in fact also practicing translation and cultural translation at a higher level. Spivak has always believed that:

> In my view, language may be one of many elements that allow us to make sense of things, of ourselves. I am thinking, of course, of gestures, pauses, but also of chance, of the subindividual force-fields of being which click into place in different situations, swerve from the straight or true line of language-in-thought. Making sense of ourselves is what produces identity.[17]

However, language is only a form of translation for her. The crux of the matter lies in who uses different languages to express meaning on what occasion. In this regard, Spivak does not deny the unique perspective of female writers and attempts to discern the differences between male and female writing.

In the same vein, female translators engaged in the practice of translation have an identity that is different from male translators. From the very start, Spivak was aware that her own position was doubly marginalized: an intellectual from the former British Raj or colonial India, and a woman from the Third World. As a result, this type of translation practice is not only a practice of linguistic resistance and decolonization but also bears distinctive gender and racial characteristics. She argues that:

> The task of the feminist translator is to consider language as a clue to the workings of gendered agency. The writer is written by her language, of course. But the writing of the writer writes agency in a way that might be different from that of the British woman/ citizen within the history of British feminism, focused on the task of freeing herself from Britain's imperial past, its often racist present, as well as its "made in Britain" history of male domination.[18]

In this way, the task of the translator is not merely to give life to the original work in the afterlife as Benjamin said, but translators should also undertake the dual historical task of removing gender oppression and the cultural hegemony of colonialism. Obviously, this cannot be accomplished at the linguistic level alone, but at least the purpose of decolonization can be realized partially through translation as a discursive practice. Her own translation practice can be considered a typical example.

As a result, Spivak also set the task for postcolonial female translators from her own marginalized dual gender/racial perspective:

The task of the translator is to facilitate this love between the original and its shadow, a love that permits fraying, holds the agency of the translator and the demands of her imagined or actual audience at bay. The politics of translation from a non-European woman's text too often suppresses this possibility because the translator cannot engage with, or cares insufficiently for, the rhetoricity of the original.[19]

Therefore, this kind of translation just scratches the surface and is totally ineffective. Only with deep sympathy and love for the works written by postcolonial female authors can translators accurately reproduce the style of language and rhetorical features of the original. Admittedly, only postcolonial intellectuals with a Third World background like Spivak can meet this kind of requirement for translators because they already have an awareness of postcolonial resistance and decolonization, when translating Third World texts into hegemonic discourse; whereas for white translators without a Third World background, it is difficult to feel sympathy for and cooperate tacitly with the original authors and their works.

Of course, only stressing the political side of translation would obviously take it to extremes. In this regard, Spivak believes that the politics of translation and the ethics of translation are closely related

The jagged relationship between rhetoric and logic, condition and effect of knowing, is a relationship by which a world is made for the agent can act in an ethical way, a political way, a day-to-day way; so that the agent can be alive, in a human way, in the world. Unless one can at least construct a model of this for the other language, there is no real translation.[20]

It is true that different translators have different attitudes toward the original. Besides deep love for postcolonial literature, Spivak also believes that in the process of translation and representation, the translator should also faithfully interpret the original with an "ethical attitude". The translator should not randomly add content that is not in the original. Only then can the translator construct a world in the target language that is similar to that of the original and faithfully reproduce the local customs and expressions of the original postcolonial literature. This is obviously difficult to accomplish for translators from the First World who look down on Third World literature.

While both Benjamin and Derrida were engaged in translating from one imperial language into another, thereby not going beyond the Western cultural context, Spivak mostly translates from minor languages of the Third World into the hegemonic languages of the First World, except for *Of Grammatology*. Therefore, in this respect:

First, then, the translator must surrender to the text. She must solicit the text to show the limits of its language, because that rhetorical aspect will point at the silence of the absolute fraying of language that the text wards off, in its special manner. Some think this is just an ethereal way of talking about literature or philosophy. But no amount of tough talk can get around the fact that translation is the most intimate act of reading. Unless the translator has earned the right to become the intimate reader, she cannot surrender to the text, cannot respond to the special call of the text.[21]

Only if the translator gets inside the special context of the original work, or the special view of the author, sharing the author's grief and joy, can the translator become an intimate reader who gains a thorough understanding of the original. In this regard, colonial translators, who look down on the original work and criticize the language for nonstandardness and impurities, are incapable of this.

This shows that there are unique advantages to having Third World texts translated by translators with a Third World background. However, there are not many people who can do this after all. As a female intellectual and postcolonial critic from the Third World, Spivak has always maintained close ties with the academic community of her homeland India, and she has engaged in her unique way with the activities of the "Subaltern Studies". Almost every year she travels to India to give lectures or attend academic conferences, and she openly declares that she is a postcolonial critic and a Subaltern Studies scholar. She notes that:

> In my view, the translator from a Third World language should be sufficiently in touch with what is going on in literary production in that language to be capable of distinguishing between good and bad writing by women, resistant and conformist writing by women.[22]

It can be said that because of the efforts of Spivak and others, postcolonial scholars from India have been able to make their voices heard in Western and even international academic circles and Spivak's strategy of cultural and political translation has basically achieved the desired effect.

In today's translation community and translation studies circles, some scholars involved in translation studies often withdraw from translation practice, or think it is not worth doing at all, considering it a superficial skill of linguistic conversion, but Spivak has a different view. She was engaged in translation practice on two fronts almost simultaneously. In the early years, she translated Derrida's work (written in a First World imperial language) into another more popular First World imperial language. This is perhaps considered by many as her springboard into academia, but she did not stop there. She quickly drew on theoretical resources from deconstruction and used them for resistant translations of colonial discourse. This is especially evident when she translated the works by the Bengali female writer Mahasweta Devi from India, written in a minor language of the Third World, into the imperial language of the First World. Therefore, she has first-hand experience and knowledge of both the theory and practice of translation. In discussing how she handles the relation between the two, she points out that:

> The understanding of the task of the translator and the practice of the craft are related but different. Let me summarize how I work. At first I translate at

speed. If I stop to think about what is happening to the English, if I assume an audience, if I take the intending subject as more than a springboard, I cannot jump in, I cannot surrender.[23]

In other words, her translation of Devi's work goes through a process of first loving it and sympathizing with it, then resonating with it, and thereafter considering the reception of the target readers on the basis of her deep understanding of it. In this respect, she is still somewhat different from Benjamin's promotion of the role of the translator. Perhaps this is what she calls the politics of postcolonial translation.

However, the translated text must face the readers of the target language. In case the target readers do not approve of the translation, it will not only fail to endow the original with a new life or an afterlife, it will even cause the well-written original to lose its inherent brilliance. Spivak has a profound understanding of this, so in her view, the translator should also consider the reception of the reader. In the introduction to her English translation of Devi's *Imaginary Maps*, she frankly states

> I am aware that the English of my translation belongs more to the rootless, American-based academic prose than to the more subcontinental idiom of my youth. This is an interesting question, unique to India: should Indian texts be translated into the English of the subcontinent?[24]

Obviously, this seems impossible to Spivak, because according to her postcolonial cultural and political strategy, the reason why she chose to translate Devi's novels from Bengali into English is to help them enter the mainstream Anglophone world smoothly, thereby dispelling the cultural hegemony of colonialism. So, this is also a practical strategy that she was forced to apply. As she worked on translations from two different foreign languages into English, i.e., translating Derrida's French works into English for an American audience and translating Devi's Bengali works into English primarily for the English-speaking world but also for India's own English-speaking audience, some readers accused her of failure to grasp the essence of Derrida's French, as well as failure to grasp Devi's Indian spirit. In fact, Spivak has her own political and cultural strategies for this. Indeed, she was also criticized by some scholars for her familiarity and reliance on Western theories in her work, to which she responded in a very calm way:

> I am not interested in defending the post-colonial intellectual's dependence on Western models: my work lies in making clear my disciplinary predicament. My position is generally a reactive one. I am viewed by the Marxists as too codic, by feminists as too male-identified, by indigenous theorists as too committed to Western theory. I am uneasily pleased about this. One's vigilance is sharpened by the way one is perceived, but it does not involve defending oneself.[25]

Admittedly, in addition to her profound learning and knowledge, Spivak's rise to distinct prominence in the acclaimed academic circles of American literary theory and comparative literature was not unrelated to her dual identity as a postcolonial intellectual and a Third World female scholar. In a multicultural society like the United States, academia does not advocate convergence but pursues differences. Those who completely follow the discourse of Western white men are doomed to lose their identity and be despised by Western mainstream scholars, while those who go their own way, distancing themselves from mainstream discourse, can at best only conduct narcissist monologues in a narrow circle but cannot have a wide-ranging impact. Therefore, Spivak's success is due to a large extent to her postcolonial cultural translation strategy. In other words, she is not only active in the teaching machine and the academic system, but was also constantly advancing from universities with a marginal status to ivy league colleges till gradually she gained a high position in the world-renowned Columbia University. On the other hand, she was "outside" the teaching machine and academic system, and with a unique sense of social responsibility and mission characteristic of public intellectuals, she enthusiastically followed and actively participated in the "Subaltern Studies" of Third World intellectuals and contributes to their "demarginalization" and "decolonization" efforts. This may be characteristic of nearly all postcolonial translators and researchers, and in this regard, Spivak's tremendous influence must be acknowledged.

"Translation as Culture" is an article by Spivak written for inclusion in the volume *Translating Cultures* edited by three Spanish scholars in 1999, and it was later reprinted in the journal *Parallax*, vol. 6, issue no. 1, in 2000. In this article, Spivak starts from the Viennese psycho-analyst Melanie Klein's view of translation, pointing out at the outset: "In every possible sense, translation is necessary but impossible".[26] This is actually a repetition of the principle of Derrida's Tower of Babel, in that translation is dualistic and a paradox. But she goes on to elaborate:

> To plot this weave, the reader—in my estimation, Klein was more a reader than an analyst in the strict Freudian sense—, translating the incessant translating shuttle into that which is read, must have the most intimate knowledge of the rules of representation and permissible narratives which make up the substance of a culture, and must also become responsible and accountable to the writing/translating presupposed original.[27]

This quite clearly shows a few of the most important aspects of translation: to grasp the tension between the translatability and untranslatability of the original, to fully consider the readers' reception in the process of converting the original into the target language, and finally, in retrospect, to consider whether we have fulfilled our dual responsibility towards the original and the translation. It should be said that this view does not deviate far from the conventional view of translation, and therefore they are comparatively easily accepted by translation studies scholars.

When it comes to the relation between the translator and the original, Spivak notes that:

> In the sense that I am deriving from Klein, *translation* does indeed lose its mooring in a literal meaning. Translation in this general sense is not under

the control of the subject who is translating. Indeed the human subject is something that will have happened as this shuttling translation, from inside to outside, from violence to conscience: the production of the ethical subject. This originary translation thus wrenches the sense of the English word *translation* outside of its making.[28]

Since there is a source text against which the translation can be checked, translators, as the subjects or masters of translation, often cannot control their own translation, but must follow the rules of the tension between translatability and untranslatability of the contents of the original and surrender to it in an ethical way; on the other hand, they have no choice but to express the meaning and style in the target language based on their own understanding and style of representation. In this way, translation as a type of culture translated into another, sometimes has to deviate from the original meaning of translation in the conventional sense, bringing along the translator's even greater subjectivity and creative construction. This is perhaps what makes postcolonial cultural translation different from literal translation in the general sense.

With regard to Spivak's translation theory and practice, Western translation scholars have different views, but in general, they agree and give her high praise. However, they also point out the bias and limitation in her cultural and political translation view. This can be seen in a summarized evaluation given by Edwin Gentzler as follows:

> In terms of theory, thus, Spivak accomplishes a kind of double-writing in her translation, critiquing Western metaphysical, humanist thinking and at the same time creating openings to imagine real cultural differences at work. She also unveils the highly polyvalent and multicultural conditions that characterize the "original" culture. And she is well aware of the impact her translations have upon the source culture; subsequent to Spivak's translations, Devi has moved from being a marginal writer to a well-known national as well as international figure. Both Spivak's translation work as well as her theoretical writing are meant to intervene and transform. Her translations of Devi thus supplement her work on Derrida, whose works she perhaps finds insufficient to address specific political situations such as those of the Indian tribal. And her writings about Derrida supplement her translation work, raising questions about representation, meaning, and translatability of "original" cultures and texts. Both are aimed at providing an opening for new ways of conceiving and responding.[29]

It should be said that Gentzler's comments are relatively factual, and meanwhile, it confirms that translation studies scholars recognize and value Spivak's translation theory and practice. It shows that the theory and practice of postcolonial translation cannot be ignored in the cultural turn of contemporary translation studies. It has not only a powerful impact but also a strong vitality and a broad influence. In this regard, Spivak's contribution is pivotal, and at the same time, her own unique ethnicity, gender, and cultural identity are not unrelated to it.

5.4 Mimicry, hybridity, the third space, and the strategy of cultural translation

When contemporary scholars involved in postcolonial translation discuss postcolonial translation theory, they often refer to the concept of cultural translation by Homi Bhabha. Although this concept was not first proposed by Bhabha, it is his interpretation and new reconstruction that give it a distinct postcolonial and deconstructive meaning. Bhabha had been relatively unknown due to his being young and having few publications to his name, but he became extremely active over the past decade or more. His works on postcolonial theory and criticism have seen a high citation rate in contemporary European and American literary theory and cultural critical circles, circles of cultural studies, and even circles of cultural translation, which earn him admiration from his peers. Although to date he has only published one monograph, which is a compilation of topical studies that were published elsewhere before, what is so admirable is that the citation rate is so high that not many can match it. Indeed, in the past 20 years, nearly every important paper or edited volume that Bhabha has published led to a rush of thousands of readers and critics to read, cite and discuss. This is no small feat for a postcolonial critic at the forefront of contemporary academia.

As one of the most influential and critical postcolonial theorists in the academic world of English literature and culture, Homi Bhabha's theoretical achievements are mainly reflected in the following aspects: (1) he creatively combined Marxism, psychoanalysis and (Foucault's) poststructuralist theories into one, applied it quite effectively to his own critical practice of culture and art, and developed a challenging and deconstructive style of postcolonial cultural studies and cultural criticism based on this; (2) his theoretical concepts of hybridity and third space had an impact on the study of national and cultural identities in today's global postcolonial context, and he proposed detailed strategies for Third World critics to enter the academic mainstream and make their voices heard; (3) his concept of mimicry and close reading of colonial-themed works have had a huge enlightening effect on the efforts of Third World critics who oppose Western cultural hegemony, and have somewhat contributed to the reconstruction of literary classics; (4) the theory of cultural translation that he developed also had a strong impact on translation studies which had for a long time been dominated by textual translation mainly based on linguistic conversion, dispelled the language-centered logocentrism at the cultural level, and played an important role in promoting the cultural turn in translation studies.

Homi F. Bhabha (1949–) was born in Mumbai, India, to a merchant family, and educated in schools in India. It is said that he has Persian ancestors and this "hybrid" ethnic identity gave him personal experience to study both national and cultural identities, as well as minority literature and culture, so he has a great say in these issues. Later on, Bhabha went to the UK to pursue his studies with the famous Marxist theorist Terry Eagleton and obtained his PhD from the renowned University of Oxford. Upon graduation, he taught at the University of Sussex for more than ten years, during which he frequently received invitations to lecture at well-known universities in the United States. In 1994, Bhabha was appointed Chester D. Tripp Professor in Humanities at the University of Chicago, while he also lectured as Visiting Professor at the University College, London. Since late 2000, Bhabha has served as the Anne F. Rothenberg Professor of English and American Literature and Language at Harvard University, while at the same time serving as the director of the History and Literature Center which was exclusively set up for him. He is now the director of the Humanities Center and deputy provost in charge of humanities. It can be said that Bhabha, like his peers in postcolonial criticism, has achieved his long-time aspiration of demarginalization and entrance into the academic mainstream.

It is true that Bhabha has not published as many works as the two other currently very active and productive postcolonial critics Said and Spivak. So far, Bhabha has only published one monograph *The Location of Culture* (1994), in addition to a few articles, and prior to this, he also published an edited collection of articles *Nation and Narration* (1990), but his huge academic reputation and influence are largely based on these two books. Although *Nation and Narration* is an edited volume, it is enough to attest to his unique editorial vision. It was the first time that he intervened in and criticized those writings of "Essentialism" that try to define and domesticate Third World ethnicity by assuming the traditional method of convergence and historical continuity, among which Foucault's influence is extremely obvious. In his view, these writings falsely define and guarantee their subordinate status, and are therefore unreliable. As he clearly points out in the introduction of *Nation and Narration*

> Nations, like narratives, lose their origins in the myths of time and only fully realize their horizons in the mind's eye. Such an image of the nation—or narration—might seem impossibly romantic and excessively metaphorical, but it is from those traditions of political thought and literary language that the nation emerges as a powerful historical idea in the west.[30]

This means that the nation itself is a kind of narrative and its uncertainty and "non-authenticity" are as unreliable as the narrative itself. If Said's postcolonial criticism originated in criticizing Orientalism, then it can be said that Bhabha's postcolonial criticism originated in debunking the myth of the nation. It is exactly dispelling the nation's authenticity that to some extent laid the foundation of Bhabha's theory of postcolonial criticism. Prior to this and ever since, Bhabha has all along held on to his cultural strategy of "hybridity", and in his writings, he developed a set of powerful terms of deconstructive "ambiguity" and "ambivalence". One can say that in a series of works after that, Bhabha developed this strategy of cultural criticism to varying degrees. It is this kind of "hybrid" strategy of criticism against essentialism and against cultural authenticity that has kept Bhabha dynamic and creative throughout his career as a critic.

Different from Spivak, Bhabha seldom engages in translation practice. Apart from frequent publications of art review articles in *Artforum*, he rarely ever discusses translation issues. In fact, if the three aspects of Jakobson's definition of translation are considered, Bhabha's written interpretation of art works is similar to intersemiotic translation and translation researchers can learn from the gains and losses. However, since his intersemiotic translation is basically still limited to the Western linguistic and cultural context, and has not yet reached the context that crosses Eastern and Western cultures, it is beyond the scope of this book. His only widely discussed article that focuses on cultural translation is "How Newness Enters the World: Postmodern Space, Postcolonial Times and the Trials of Cultural Translation", which is included in the book *The Location of Culture*.

In the first part of this article, Bhabha discusses Marxist theorist Fredric Jameson's work on postmodernism and the cultural logic of late capitalism from a macro-theoretical perspective. Starting from Jameson's class analysis and cultural reproduction in the era of transnational capitalism, he gradually extends the topic to include cultural translation in the broad sense. He believes that it is inevitable that something new will appear in such a postmodern space. But will these new things emerge suddenly or are they the product of transition from the old to the new era? This is something that Bhabha is most concerned about. In his view, new things can appear in the "interstices" of histories and ethnic cultures because of the development of history and the transition of time, as well as the expansion or even blurring of national boundaries. As a result, the experiment of cultural translation becomes possible. Here, cultural translation is similar to a transformation between cultures, and the task of the cultural translator is to relocate his or her national culture. Therefore, the mission of such a translation is obviously political and ideological. At the end of this section, Bhabha points out:

> The migrant culture of the 'in-between', the minority position, dramatizes the activity of culture's untranslatability; and in so doing, it moves the question of culture's appropriation beyond the assimilationist's dream, or the racist's nightmare, of a 'full transmissal of subject-matter'; and towards an encounter with the ambivalent process of splitting and hybridity that marks the identification with culture's difference.[31]

Bhabha's interpretation of globalization is obviously different from Eurocentric or Western-centric critics. In his view, on the one hand globalization has obscured the differences of national cultures, with the hegemonic culture using its own values to influence the weaker cultures, but on the other hand the weaker Third World cultures are unwilling to be outdone, carrying out silent and invisible protest all the time. This kind of resistance and revolt is mainly manifested in anti-infiltration in culture, so it is impossible to stop the trend of cultural diversity. There is no doubt that in the postmodern space and postcolonial era, cultural differences have become more prominent. Even the purest culture of white hegemonic culture and colonial discourse have been made "hybrid" and "ambiguous" by postcolonial critics. It is in the interstices created by this "hybridity" that some new things have appeared, and they formed a kind of "third space" that is neither here nor there and can be said to be the foundation on which cultural translation can experiment. In addition, his concept of "third space" has greatly influenced and inspired art criticism and interpretation.

However, on the other hand, Bhabha's postcolonial cultural translation, like deconstructive translation, is skeptical about the authenticity of the original work, and attempts using all means to attack from the margins, first to deprive its sacred aura through the strategies of hybridity and ambiguity, and then to construct something new through "secondary elaboration" in the sense of psychoanalysis. In Bhabha's view:

> If hybridity is heresy, then to blaspheme is to dream. To dream not of the past or present, nor the continuous present; it is not the nostalgic dream of tradition, nor the Utopian dream of modern progress; it is the dream of translation as "survival" as Derrida translates the "time" of Benjamin's concept of the after-life of translation, as *sur-vivre*, the act of living on borderlines.[32]

In actual translation practice, if this phenomenon is used to describe the relationship between the original and the translation, it implies that the translation is neither a passive reproduction of the original nor something new created entirely by the translator. It is in fact something new in between the two, something that resembles the original but keeps a certain distance from it. This reiterates Benjamin's concept of the "afterlife" of a translation from the perspective of postcolonial theory.

From the perspectives of deconstruction's multiple differences and the erasure of ethnic and national boundaries as a result of globalization, Bhabha proposed a theory of cultural "borderline": "To revise the problem of global space from the postcolonial perspective is to move the location of cultural difference away from the space of demographic *plurality* to the borderline negotiations of cultural translation".[33] There is no doubt that this "borderline" refers to the uncertain and ambiguous boundary between different cultures caused by mutual penetration in a complex state of cultural infiltration. Only at such a "close-to-border" point can it be possible to construct a "third space" and something new in the postcolonial sense. Borderline negotiations are a necessary means to create these new things, and its concrete manifestation is what Bhabha calls cultural translation. Obviously, here, the mission that Bhabha has bestowed on cultural translation is something that literal translation in the traditional sense cannot accomplish. So, in Bhabha's view, what is cultural translation? What are its characteristics of deconstruction and anti-colonial hegemony? As Bhabha explains:

> Translation is the performative nature of cultural communication. It is language *in actu* (enunciation, positionality) rather than language *in situ* (énoncé, or propositionality). And the sign of translation continually tells, or "tolls" the different times and spaces between cultural authority and its performative practices. The "time" of translation consists in that *movement* of meaning, the principle and practice of a communication that, in the words of de Man "puts the original in motion to decanonise it, giving it the movement of fragmentation, a wandering of errance, a kind of permanent exile".[34]

In Bhabha's view, in the performative process of cultural translation, the totality of the original work is disintegrated into fragments, and the task of the translator is to extract the components that most resemble the original and reassemble them, and finally construct something new. Although the new thing comes from the original, it is still different from the original. It is a "translation" recreated from the original but is different from the "translation" that in the traditional sense is very faithful to the original. It is a "third party" that is close to the original but also rebels against it. This shows that Bhabha's attitude towards the original is obviously different from Spivak's attitude to be subservient to the original and act as its "intimate reader", because the latter is mainly used to translate works from the Third World into the imperialist, hegemonic language, and therefore the translator must first have sympathy and or even affection for it, whereas Bhabha mainly refers to the "translation" and "transformation" of the hegemonic culture of imperialism.

Since Bhabha's article discusses how newness enters the world, he has to describe the specific characteristics of this newness from the perspective of cultural translation. For this reason, he proposes a concept of "foreignness" which is similar to the theory of "foreignization" in traditional translation theories:

> The "newness" of migrant or minority discourse has to be discovered *in medias res:* a newness that is not part of the "progressivist" division between past and present, or the archaic and modern; nor is it a "newness" that can be contained in the mimesis of "original and copy". In both these cases, the image of the new is iconic rather than enunciatory; in both instances, temporal difference is represented as epistemological or mimetic distance from an original source. The newness of cultural translation is akin to what Walter Benjamin describes as the "foreignness of languages"—the problem of representation native to representation itself. If Paul de Man focused on the "metonymy" of translation, I want to foreground the "foreignness" of cultural translation.[35]

What, then, is the "foreignness" of cultural translation? In Bhabha's view, it is neither the ancient modernity, nor the imitation of the original. Instead, it is the "third component" that is located in between the two and at the same time shares all the main characteristics of the two. It may appear different at first, but attentive readers will immediately be able to discern the shadow of the cultural matrix and its different characteristics. As such, "[c]ultural translation desacralizes the transparent assumptions of cultural supremacy, and in that very act, demands a contextual specificity, a historical differentiation *within* minority positions".[36] "The act of cultural translation works through 'the *continua* of transformation' to yield a sense of culture's belonging".[37] Obviously, from the traditional view of translation, Bhabha's cultural translation is a "foreignizing" translation which does not advocate convergence with the original, but rather ensures the deviation between the translation and the original, so that the translation has the same value as the original. Therefore, not surprisingly, the enormous impact of Bhabha's concepts of cultural translation and the third space on contemporary art creation is also beyond expectations.

It is clear that the meaning of cultural translation as advocated by Bhabha goes far beyond the mission that Benjamin assigned to translation in his "The Task of the Translator" and achieves a political and ideological meaning of cultural decolonization. Bhabha has always believed that nothing can stop the tide of globalization, but that is only one aspect of global trends. As he rightly pointed out in a speech in Beijing a few years ago:

> Du Bois's central insight lies in emphasizing the "contiguous" and the contingent nature of the making of minorities, where solidarity depends on surpassing autonomy or sovereignty in favor of an inter-cultural articulation of differences. This is a dynamic and dialectical concept of the minority as a process of affiliation, an ongoing translation of aims and interests through which minorities emerge to communicate their messages adjacently across communities. This enunciative concept of minoritization is much in advance of the anthropological concept of the minority that is in place in Article 27 of the International Covenant on Civil and Political Rights. In fact, this is another type of internationalization process.[38]

Therefore, in response to the increasing cultural homogeneity in the era of globalization, Bhabha proposes "minoritization" (in Chinese translation, this is also rendered, literally, as "vulnerable-group becoming") from another perspective, and he considers it another historical process similar to globalization. In fact, it is a way of emphasizing cultural differences and promoting the voice of minority groups. In this regard, traditional translation cannot undertake such a historical mission, and only cultural translation with the purpose of deconstruction and decolonization as advocated by Bhabha can accomplish it.

Cultural studies scholars have always attached great importance to postcolonial translation theory and practice, and examine them in the larger context of cultural studies. In the field of translation studies, however, scholars have different opinions and varying views. On the one hand, they welcome new ideas that postcolonial translation practice has brought to the literary translation world, but on the other hand, they have reservations about its overemphasizing translation's political nature and cultural critical spirit. Scholars who generally study translation from the perspective of linguistics seldom discuss or study the theory and practice of postcolonial translation, while scholars who study translation from the perspectives of comparative literature and cultural studies attach importance to deconstructive translation, but pass over postcolonial translation and often overlook its historical merits. Although Gentzler has a long chapter on deconstructive translation in his *Contemporary Translation Studies* (second edition, revised), there is no special section devoted to the discussion of postcolonial translation. He only uses a little over ten pages in the section "Deconstruction and Postcolonial Translation" to discuss Tejaswini Niranjana and Spivak, two postcolonial theorists heavily influenced by deconstructive theory.[39] While Gentzler gives some credit to Spivak for her achievements in translation theory and practice, he does not fully appraise the significance and value of postcolonial translation in general. In the foreword that he wrote for the collection of essays *Constructing Cultures: Essays on Literary Translation*, co-authored by Susan Bassnett and André Lefevere, he praised the two authors for their contribution to translation's cultural construction, and even wrote: "When I read work by Jacques Derrida, Homi Bhabha, or Edward Said, I am often struck by how naive their ideas about translation sound in comparison to the detailed analysis provided by translation scholars".[40] Although there is some truth in his brash judgment, on a deeper cultural level, it overlooks the huge and profound contribution of deconstruction and postcolonial theory to the cultural turn in contemporary translation studies. This is a limitation not only of Gentzler, but also of the knowledge and theory of most traditional translation researchers. This is also an important reason why traditional translation studies has been excluded from the mainstream of the humanities and social sciences for so long. Indeed, among the three aforementioned theorists, except for Said who only occasionally mentioned the role of cultural translation in discussing the phenomenon of the travel and dispersion of theories, Derrida and Bhabha both pay considerable attention to cultural translation and published a few works, albeit with profound philosophical insights. Derrida has a guiding significance for translation at a higher level of the metaphysical philosophy of language, while Bhabha guides translators in specific decolonization strategies, which should not be overlooked. Moreover, the actual impact that their theoretical viewpoints have on the humanities as a whole is unmatched by any professional scholar of translation studies. Not until we realize this can we have a full understanding of the historical merits and practical significance of postcolonial translation theory and practice.

Notes

1. Said, E. 1979. *Orientalism*. New York: Doubleday Books, 12.
2. Translators' note: If Orientalism is translated as "dongfang xue" [Oriental studies], it gives the impression of it being an academic discipline.
3. Said, E. 1979. *Orientalism*. New York: Doubleday Books, 1–28.
4. Said, E. 2000. *Reflections on Exile and Other Essays*. Cambridge, MA: Harvard University Press, 199.
5. Ibid.
6. Ibid., p. 212.
7. In terms of the formation of the image of the East and its people in the eyes of Western people, some works of Chinese diaspora writers in the West also played the role of "self-Orientalization" and even participated in the "demonization of the East" chorus of the Western media, and therefore, performed the function of "conspiring" with colonialism. For more details, see the relevant chapters in Lu Wei's monograph *Chinese American Literature: Towards Cultural Studies*. Beijing: Zhonghua Book Company, 2007.
8. Said, E. 1983. *The World, the Text, and the Critic*. Cambridge, MA: Harvard University Press, 226–227.
9. Said, E. 2000. *Reflections on Exile and Other Essays*. Cambridge, MA: Harvard University Press, 451.
10. For the translation and reception of postcolonial theory in China, see Sheng, A. 2008. The travels and variations of theory: Postcolonial theory in China. In N. Wang (ed.), *Wenxue Lilun Qianyan* [Frontiers of Literary Theory]. Vol. 5. Beijing: Peking University Press, 121–164.
11. In fact, the concept of "translation" that Spivak uses on different occasions has a far broader scope than the meaning of translation in the traditional sense, and carries the meaning of cultural transformation. For more on this, see the following two articles that

she wrote: Spivak, G. C. 2000. Translation as culture. *Parallax*, *6*(1): 13–24; Spivak, G. C. 2001. Questioned on translation: Adrift. *Public Culture*, *13*(1): 13–22.
12 Spivak, G. C. 1974. Translator's preface. In J. Derrida (ed.), *Of Grammatology*. Baltimore, MD: The Johns Hopkins University Press, xiii.
13 Ibid., p. xvi.
14 Ibid., p. xvii.
15 Ibid, pp. lxxviii–lxxix.
16 Ibid, p. lxxxvi.
17 Spivak, G. C. 1993. The politics of translation. In *Outside in the Teaching Machine*. London & New York: Routledge, 179.
18 Ibid., pp. 179–180.
19 Ibid., p. 181.
20 Ibid.
21 Ibid., p. 183.
22 Ibid., p. 188.
23 Ibid., p. 189.
24 Spivak, G. C. 1996. Translator's preface and afterword to Mahasweta Devi, *Imaginary Maps*. In D. Landry & G. MacLean (eds.), *The Spivak Reader*. New York & London: Routledge, 272.
25 Spivak, G. C. 1990. *The Post-Colonial Critic: Interviews, Strategies, Dialogues*. S. Harasym (ed.). New York & London: Routledge, 69–70.
26 Spivak, G. C. 2000. Translation as culture. *Parallax*, *6*(1): 13.
27 Ibid.
28 Ibid, p. 14. Translators' note: Italics maintained from original.
29 Gentzler, E. 2001. *Contemporary Translation Theories* (2nd ed.). Clevedon: Multilingual Matters, 186.
30 Bhabha, H. K. (ed.). 1990. *Nation and Narration*. London & New York: Routledge, 1.
31 Bhabha, H. K. 1994. *The Location of Culture*. London & New York: Routledge, 224.
32 Ibid., pp. 226–227.
33 Ibid., p. 223.
34 Ibid., p. 228.
35 Ibid., p. 227.
36 Ibid., p. 228.
37 Ibid., p. 235.
38 As regards to Bhabha's shift in academic thought over the last ten odd years, see his keynote speech "The Black Savant and the Dark Princess" which he delivered at Tsinghua University on 25 June 2002. The Chinese translation was published in *Wenxue Pinglun* [Literary Review], No. 5, 2002. Translators' note: The English version of the quote is from "Global Minoritarian Culture" by Homi K. Bhabha in *Shades of the Planet: American Literature as World Literature*, Princeton University Press, 2007, p. 191.
39 Cf. Gentzler, E. 1993. *Contemporary Translation Theories*. London & New York: Routledge, 176–186.
40 Gentzler, E. 1998. Foreword. In S. Bassnett & A. Lefevere, *Constructing Cultures: Essays on Literary Translation*. Clevedon & London: Multilingual Matters, xxi.

6 The intervention of comparative literature and cultural studies

As we have observed, translation has all along received attention and been promoted by scholars in three fields: contrastive linguistics, comparative literature, and cultural studies. For a long time, however, traditional translation studies have been dominated by a linguo-centric mindset. Scholars under the spell of this view held that translation is simply a conversion between two languages, and thus the only choice of the translator is to be faithful to the original and to express it fluently in the target language. With the intervention of comparative literature scholars, the factor of reception in translation began to be valued. Many translation researchers, in examining the actual relationship between two or more literatures, consciously focus on the reception and dissemination of one literary text in another cultural context through the mediation of translation, thus greatly increasing the elements of comparative literature and culture in translation studies. As this research progressed, they also found that the so-called influence of one national literature on another literature depends largely on the dynamic reception and creative interpretation by the readers of the other country. Therefore, under the influence of reception aesthetics, the new generation of comparative literature scholars were more concerned with the cultural variation resulting from this creative reception. The efforts of the scholars of cultural studies, especially postcolonial critical theorists, have led translation studies to pay more attention to such phenomena with elements of cultural studies: reconstruction, discourse, hegemony, manipulation, gender, race, colonization, identity, and so on, which greatly promoted the cultural turn of translation studies. This series of efforts has at least expanded the boundaries of translation studies, and the disciplinary status of translation studies has been raised correspondingly. Today's translation studies does show a pattern of pluralistic symbiosis, and the boundary between linguistics and culturology has been broken. Of course, this is inseparable from the writings and efforts of a large number of scholars from comparative literature and cultural studies, as well as the contributions of some open- and broad-minded scholars in the field of linguistics. We will summarize this new tendency and its future development in the last chapter. This chapter mainly discusses how scholars of comparative literature and cultural studies have intervened in translation studies and thus promoted its cultural turn.

6.1 Comparative literature and cultural studies: confrontation or dialogue?

Perhaps to the uninitiated, comparative literature and cultural studies should have a close relationship, because a large number of cultural studies scholars who are very active today were earlier literary scholars, and their broad interdisciplinary and intercultural perspectives and rich world literature knowledge make it easy for people to regard them as comparative literature scholars. However, this is not true. Comparative literature and cultural studies are obviously two different disciplines. With their respective developments, the territory of the former is increasingly encroached on by the latter, so some people exclaim that the prosperity of cultural research is sounding the death knell for the shrinking discipline of comparative literature. As two relatively independent disciplines and research methods, what is the relationship between comparative literature and cultural studies? Why are they both concerned with the role of translation and translation studies? I believe that there are at least the following different views and factors.

As for the development and current status of cultural studies in the West, we have provided an overview in the introduction of this book, and here we only discuss the current situation of cultural studies in China. Since the 1980s, various Western theoretical thoughts have swarmed into China, resulting in profound changes in contemporary Chinese literary criticism which has its own independent humanistic tradition. This has greatly contributed to the revival of comparative literature and literary theories in China. Since the 1990s, cultural studies has also entered China, which has a great impact on literary studies. Of course, the unilateral "traveling of theory" (Said's words) from West to East is not our ultimate goal. What we need is two-way travel and exchange of theories. From this perspective, we find that the comparative literature studies in this era of globalization is facing challenges from many aspects, especially from the cultural studies that points to the long-suppressed marginal cultures or even popular cultures. In view of the strong impact of economic globalization, consumer culture and literature is bound to be a hot topic that scholars of comparative literature and cultural studies must confront. According to Jonathan Culler's description, there is indeed a boundless pan-cultural tendency in the field of comparative literature: in addition to the comparative studies of literature across cultures and civilizations, it also involves discourses other than literature, such as philosophy, psychoanalysis, politics, and medicine. It is not surprising not only in Western academic circles but also in Chinese comparative literature circles for young scholars of comparative literature today to write doctoral theses on film, television, and popular culture. This has indeed made the disciplinary boundaries of comparative literature increasingly broad so that there is a tendency for culture to engulf literary studies in the traditional sense. Therefore, Culler says, "Treating literature as one discourse among others seems an effective and commendable strategy".[1] Apparently, Culler, a faithful interpreter of Derrida's deconstruction in American literary criticism, has felt the infringement on the discipline of comparative literature, and was thinking about the countermeasures to get rid of this crisis. However, other scholars believe that comparative literature and cultural studies can complement each other, so there is no need to form an antagonistic relationship with the latter.[2] Obviously, in the current context, the latter attitude should be more advocated, but the key problem is how to effectively ensure that comparative literature maintains its open and inclusive disciplinary characteristics, without completely disintegrating under the impact of many disciplines. The latest ten-year report of the American Comparative Literature Association, *Comparative Literature in the Age of Globalization*, edited more than a decade ago by Haun Saussy, a sinologist and comparative literature scholar, can be regarded as the latest response of American comparative literature to the consequences of globalization.[3] Of course, Chinese scholars have also responded actively with the current state of comparative literature research in China in a number of international contexts.[4]

Since comparative literature has been severely challenged and thus fallen into a new crisis, can we deny the value of its existence? Obviously not. There is no doubt that the emergence of the pan-cultural tendency in comparative literature is not accidental. It is closely related to the role of globalization in culture and literature. The trend of globalization in culture is directly linked to the reflection of postmodernism in culture and literature. In the postmodern era, elegant cultural products and works of art are regarded as consumer goods: the unrestrained reproduction of cultural products and the simulation, rewriting, proliferation and even mass production of literary classics have replaced the meticulous crafting of works of art in the modernist era. The flat characterization has replaced the in-depth portrayal of the characters' mental states in modernist art; and the fragmented or schizophrenic structure has substituted for the deep structure of modernist art, and so on. All these phenomena have undoubtedly aroused the concern of humanists and literary critics with a strong sense of social mission. In this respect, scholars of comparative literature have not evaded but intervened in the international theoretical debate on the issue of postmodernism with an active stance and published a large number of theoretical works. The rise of cultural studies provides another unique perspective for comparative literature. Through the analysis and interpretation of these phenomena, we may be able to put forward some positive strategies, so as to promote the coexistence and even complementarity of the two. In this way, the relationship between comparative literature and cultural studies is not necessarily an either/or dichotomy, but a harmonious relationship of coexistence and communion. The so-called return to the "authenticity" of comparative literature is impossible in this era. An effective strategy should be to put comparative literature research in a broad cross-cultural context: starting from the literary phenomenon, and then through the cultural perspective of literary text returning to the cultural interpretation of the literary phenomenon. This is perhaps a pragmatic and positive attitude. It is no coincidence that scholars in comparative literature and cultural studies are both concerned with translation and are interested in intervening in the cultural turn of translation studies. Therefore, they have come together at this point and jointly promote the development of it.

It should be admitted that the polysystem theory proposed by Itamar Even-Zohar, a scholar of comparative literature in Israel, has also played some role in promoting translation studies from the perspective of comparative literature. However, since this theory, when applied to translation studies, has not had a wide impact on the cultural turn in translation studies, and its formalistic overtones are still quite evident, this book does not intend to discuss it specifically. Both comparative literature and cultural researchers pay close attention to cultural identity. In discussing it in the context of the postcolonial world today, comparative literature scholars are faced with a new task: how to rewrite literary history from a new perspective? In this regard, our international counterparts have achieved a solid body of research results.[5] In my opinion, to rewrite literary history from the perspective of comparative literature, it is necessary to reach the point that the study of national literature cannot reach. If we cannot do this, it means that our research has not made progress, and it also shows that our writing of literary history has not gone beyond the established model. As scholars abroad have coincidentally recognized, Asian literature, including Chinese American literature, and the writing of ethnic minorities, such as black literature, have been integrated into the mainstream of contemporary American culture and literature. Their literary practice plays an important role in rewriting the history of American literature in this period. The study of these works is naturally a task incumbent on scholars of comparative literature and culture.

Moreover, almost all comparative literature and cultural studies scholars are interested in postmodernism and postmodernist issues. In his public speech delivered at the Chinese Academy of Social Sciences on July 31, 2002, Fredric Jameson made a new interpretation of the relationship between postmodernism and modernity. In his view, in the context of globalization, a new variant of postmodernism has also emerged, which forms a paradox with modernity. That is to say, if we want a thing to have the characteristics of modernity, it must first be postmodern or associated with postmodernism.[6] In the context of China, postmodernism is not only a foreign thing but also arises from the internal logic of the development of local culture and literature. In fact, it is a product of hybridization based on the fusion of foreign and local cultures, which is especially reflected in the modern Chinese literary tradition gradually formed under the influence of Western culture. There is no doubt that the formation of modern Chinese literary tradition benefits, to a large extent, from the mediation of translation, or inevitably results from a sort of cultural translation. Under the background of globalization, due to the increasingly frequent cultural exchanges and the increasingly evident hybridity of cultural and literary discourse, our comparative literature research has a new topic: the shift of the focus of Chinese and Western comparative literature in the context of "global localization".

In the face of the shift in the focus of Chinese and Western comparative literature, our strategy is that we might as well take the other extreme of globalization, that is, vigorously promoting Chinese and even Eastern culture to the world with the help of globalization. In order to achieve this great goal, we must undoubtedly rely on translation. In quite a long period of time, Chinese and Western comparative literature scholars in China spent a lot of time and energy exploring the external influence of Chinese literature, which is of course quite necessary, but we seem to forget another fact: if globalization is a process of travel, its route is two-way, with both a flow from the center to the periphery and a penetration from the periphery to the center. In the study of comparative literature, we should not only avoid a global strategy with imperialist hegemony but also overcome localism with narrow nationalism. As mentioned earlier, a "glocalization" strategy may prevent our discipline from falling into crisis again. It is true that it is necessary to maintain our national identity, but if localization is exaggerated to an inappropriate level, to the point of total rejection of any foreign influence, the result will be a vicious expansion of nationalistic sentiment, which will once again cast a shadow over our liberal cultural atmosphere. Therefore, we advocate facing the influence of globalization with an open mind: first, we should conform to this trend without sacrificing the spirit of our national culture, and then, with the trend of globalization, expand our cultural and academic exchange and dialogue with the international community, during which we will gradually influence our international counterparts. We are engaged in comparative literature studies, which should not be limited to comparing Chinese and Western literature but should also include comparing Chinese literature and that of Asian neighbors and other brotherly nationalities, and even comparing Chinese literature with African postcolonial literature, and, of course, comparing elite literature and popular literature in a cross-cultural context. In a word, this comparison should be cross-linguistic, cross-cultural, cross-civilizational and interdisciplinary, so that our literature studies is truly comprehensive and three-dimensional. Any comparative and intercultural study in this respect cannot do away with the mediation of translation, which is also an important reason why scholars of comparative literature and culture are actively involved in translation studies.

As mentioned above, scholars of comparative literature and culture pay close attention to the issue of cultural identity. The uncertainty of national cultural identity and the plurality of identity brought by globalization have prompted scholars of cultural studies and literary studies to focus their attention on the study of cultural identity. It goes without saying that the national identity of employees of multinational companies is uncertain. Similarly, in the intellectual and cultural academic circles, the expansion of knowledge and the travel of theory have also broken the boundaries between traditional disciplines, and the cultural identity of scholars from different countries and nationalities has become vague and uncertain. On the one hand, it is a challenge to traditional disciplines, but on the other hand, it has laid a foundation for the prosperity of cultural studies which crosses disciplinary boundaries. In addition, some scholars with a cultural background of the Third World take root and become famous in the Western mainstream academia, which also causes these intellectual elites to consciously "forget" or "blur" their inherent national and cultural identity. However, it is ironic that the background of their Third World national culture makes it possible for them to sing in an inharmonious voice in a multicultural society, and this inharmonious voice is exactly the resource for them to achieve innovation. In addition to the successful experience of postcolonial theorists such as Said, Spivak, and Bhabha, we can see the example of another non-Western literary theorist and thinker, Mikhail Bakhtin's "being discovered" and reinterpreted in the Western context. As early as the early 1980s, with the publication of the English translation of the Russian-Soviet thinker and literary theorist Bakhtin's main works, Bakhtin was considered world-class, because his theory involves linguistics, psychoanalysis, theology, social theory, historical poetics, human philosophy, and other fields. The study of Bakhtin was once a "prominent school" in Western academic circles, and his theory was also an important resource for structuralism, poststructuralism and postmodernism, cultural studies, and other theoretical trends. This fact is worthy of deep consideration by our Chinese scholars of comparative literature and culture.

In terms of the recent development in the Western cultural and theoretical circles, cultural studies can be basically divided into two orientations after a period of internal differentiation and integration: one is completely divorced from traditional literary studies, facing the whole popular culture, and more and more closely related to the contemporary media; and the other is to expand the boundary of traditional literary studies gradually, making it increasingly inclusive and cross-cultural. It certainly does cut into popular culture, but its attitude is to critically analyze and interpret it, and to a large extent to maintain its inherent position of elite cultural criticism. Earlier scholars of elite literature, such as the group of elite scholars around the journal *New Literary History*, were engaged in literary studies which, in fact, is expanded in terms of scope and amounts to the cultural studies of literature.[7] It can be seen that many theoretical topics of cultural studies come from literary studies, so some of its objects of inquiry can become the objects of literary studies in return, and have a positive and constructive effect on activating literary studies and expanding the scope of literary classics. There is also a good reason for comparative literature studies to break free from the purely empirical territory and to be compatible with and complementary to a kind of cultural criticism of literature.

So the question we now face is whether comparative literature studies and cultural studies should confront each other or coexist. Any scholar familiar with the history of Western literary studies in the twentieth century cannot deny that since the beginning of this century, literary studies in the broad sense has been impacted and challenged several times. The main impact came from the following two trends of thought: one is the impact of scientism, represented by Russian formalist criticism, which rose in the early twentieth century, and the result is literary studies becoming more and more scientific and formalized. Although hermeneutic theories of a humanistic nature still had considerable room for activity during this period, it was not until the later poststructuralist backlash that this predominance of formalism changed. The other is cultural studies, which started in the 1950s and rapidly entered the academic frontier in the late 1980s. Cultural studies has led to the breaking down of the original disciplinary boundaries, the blurring of the boundaries between elite and popular culture, and the move of Eastern and Third World cultures from the periphery to the center, and thus into the discourse of literary studies. Traditional literary studies gradually moved out of the ivory tower of elite scholars with its contemporary orientation and non-elite tendency gradually revealed, and its research results are increasingly marked with cultural and social analysis. The analysis of the formal structure that began with the New Criticism gradually gave way to a broader cultural analysis and theoretical interpretation. The "anthropological turn" that has emerged in the field of comparative literature and cultural studies in the past ten years or more is a new orientation and development trend similar to the "linguistic turn" in those years. It shows that a new critical method focusing on social and cultural analysis has occupied the leading position of contemporary criticism, and the traditional comparative literature studies has gradually developed from the study of the mutual influence of two or more kinds of literature, the internal aesthetic law and the parallel relationship to the comparative study of more than two kinds of culture and civilization across the disciplinary boundaries. Faced with the impact of this tide, the research territory of classical and comparative literature has undoubtedly become narrow, and its traditional methodology has also been challenged. Therefore, quite a number of traditional scholars doubt the future of pure literature and its study. The main representative of this attitude was Harold Bloom, one of the leading figures of the Yale School in those days. His hostility towards cultural studies and cultural criticism has long been found in his works. However, unlike those pessimists, Bloom bravely defended the increasingly narrow literary studies on all occasions. There are also scholars who are pessimistic about the future of comparative literature, such as Henry Remak, who once made an authoritative description of the definition of comparative literature based on the American School's position, and was extremely dissatisfied with his being marginalized for more than a decade. At the Sixth Triannual Congress of the Chinese Comparative Literature Association and International Conference held in Chengdu in August 1999, he made a speech entitled "Comparative Literature: Facing the Choice Again" in which he strongly attacked all kinds of new theoretical trends and was worried about the future of comparative literature.

However, some open-minded scholars of comparative literature are meeting the challenge of cultural studies. They hope that with the help of the impact from outside the literary circle, some reasonable factors and meaningful topics of cultural studies can be introduced into literary studies. This can not only expand the scope of literary studies but also provide some new topics or theoretical perspectives for future literary studies across Eastern and Western cultures. This group of scholars is represented by the literary theorist of the older generation, Ralph Cohen. Not only did he not object to the entry of cultural studies into literary studies, but he also paid close attention to the new developments in cultural studies and published several timely theoretically oriented articles (e.g., the special issue "Cultural Studies: China and the West" in Vol. 28 [1997], No. 1) as well as articles of disapproval and even criticism of cultural studies (e.g., a set of articles on the topic of "Revisionism Symposium" in Vol. 29 [1998], No. 1) in the authoritative journal *New Literary History*, for which he served as editor for 40 years. In this regard, we are willing to take this second attitude.

Cultural studies obviously has different disciplinary and theoretical sources, and there are some differences between British and American cultural studies. However, if we base ourselves on the cultural studies tradition of the Birmingham School, it is easy to grasp its origin with literary studies and the inseparability of the two.

Some well-recognized masters of literary studies, such as F. R. Leavis, Raymond Williams, and Terry Eagleton in Britain, Mikhail Bakhtin in Russia, Northrop Frye in Canada, Fredric Jameson, Edward Said, Gayatri Spivak, and Hillis Miller in the United States, have been considered the pioneers or important representatives of cultural studies (from the field of literary studies). Their works not only did not exclude literary studies, but also contributed to the expansion of the scope of literary studies, and thus had a significant impact on contemporary literary studies. Therefore, we can conclude that some theoretical methods of cultural studies can be introduced into literary studies and produce some new results. Since its first landing in the regions of Hong Kong and Taiwan in the early 1990s, cultural studies has become another popular topic in the whole of China after postmodernism and postcolonialism. It should be said that the introduction of cultural studies not only breaks the natural boundary between elite culture and popular culture but also paves the way for the dialogue between them. Its intercultural and interdisciplinary nature also breaks through the Western-centric mode of thinking and perspective. For the role and influence of cultural studies, Australian scholar Graeme Turner has made such a summary:

> Cultural studies does present a radical challenge to the orthodoxies within the humanities and social sciences. It has enabled the crossing of disciplinary borders and the reframing of our ways of knowing so that we might acknowledge the complexity and importance of the idea of culture. Cultural studies' commitment to understanding the construction of everyday life has the admirable objective of doing so in order to change our lives for the better. Not all academic pursuits have such a practical political objective.[8]

Such a comment is certainly comparatively objective. Today there are a growing number of treatises, translations, and papers on comparative literature and culture between China and the West, as well as similar international conferences held in China. A large number of scholars who have been active in literary theory, comparative literature and media studies are attracted by this appealing theoretical topic. On the one hand, they follow the latest progress in the field of Western cultural studies and introduce the latest research results to domestic academic peers. On the other hand, they are committed to applying this "translated" discourse of cultural studies in the Western context to the practice of Chinese cultural and literary criticism. As a result, it has significantly promoted the internationalization of cultural criticism of Chinese literature, popular culture studies and media studies.

In this way, it is not accidental for scholars of cultural studies to attach importance to translation and translation studies, and it is not groundless to call for a "translation turn" in contemporary cultural studies. In this period of global cultural transformation, how to grasp the future of translation studies, a "sub-discipline" which has long been suppressed in the margins of academic discourse is a problem that scholars of cultural studies need to face and seriously consider. In terms of the influence of various aspects on translation studies, it is appropriate to describe our time as an era of globalization. This feature is reflected not only in economy but also in culture. Since many translation researchers consider translation a cultural problem first, there is all the more reason to examine translation studies in the context of cultural studies in a broad sense, especially in the study of literary translation, which cannot be free from cultural factors. It is on this basis that we can make a more accurate understanding of the status quo and future of China's translation studies with intercultural and interdisciplinary characteristics.

There is no doubt that an important medium of cultural transmission is language, and the starting point of translation studies is naturally language. However, "language" without any ideological meaning should be extended to "discourse" with overtones of cultural hegemony and ideology because the connotation of translation in this era obviously involves the latter. In addition, the media character of contemporary cultural studies has become more and more obvious, and it has become almost inseparable from media phenomena, while its distance from elite literary studies in traditional culture is getting greater and greater. Since translation belongs to the category of media in the broad sense, it is undoubtedly appropriate to bring translation studies into the context of cultural studies.

Since cultural studies has an uncertain disciplinary boundary, it has different forms even in European and American countries. Even between the United Kingdom and the United States, two countries where English is spoken, cultural studies are in fact quite different, not to mention the differences between the academic circles of these two countries and the European continent. As far as the conservative characteristics of the European continent are concerned, although some theoretical founders of cultural studies were located on the European continent, it was only after their theories were translated and introduced to the United States that they received the most enthusiastic response. On the continent, their theories remained relatively silent for quite some time. Therefore, the popularity of cultural studies in the United States also depends to a large extent on the function of translation which is not limited to the function of paraphrasing at the linguistic level but has a broader function of cultural translation and theoretical interpretation.

Indeed, in the context of cultural studies, translation is moving from literal reporting to cultural interpretation and representation. Cultural globalization has not only broken the boundaries of culture, but also the boundaries of disciplines, which undoubtedly has a strong subversive effect on the old disciplines with strong traditional power, and provides a good opportunity for the rise of translation, a "subdiscipline" which has been on the periphery for a long time. In recent years, a large number of new theories and methods have been introduced into translation studies, including the perspectives and methods of cultural studies.

We say that translation studies is closely related to cultural studies, which can also be confirmed by the examples of literary theory and criticism. Generally speaking, most of the literary works that can be selected by translators should be classics, belonging to elite culture. Of course, there are also people who spend time repeating their work for profiteering, by "retranslating" literary masterpieces that have already been translated and are of excellent quality, or crudely translating some popular literature of poor quality. Despite this, the two factors— source text selection by the translator, and the actual process of translation and introduction—should be included in examining and studying translation. Therefore, translation studies actually plays a mediating role: it must first of all be through the efforts of translators that works belonging to different languages, different cultural backgrounds, and different literary levels get selected for translation, so the translator's ideological background and appreciation ability play a crucial role. This is especially reflected in the first translation of a work. At a time when the "Eurocentric" or "Western-centric" mode of thinking is bankrupt and culture itself is in some kind of crisis that is difficult to escape, some educated people in the West have begun to gradually recognize the value and profound connotation of Eastern culture. Therefore, it has become an inescapable obligation for translators to promote Eastern culture and enable it to have an equal and in-depth dialogue with Western culture. It can be said that cultural exchange and cultural dialogue cannot be achieved without cultural translation.

Because of the long-standing deficit in cultural and literary exchanges between China and foreign countries, it is necessary today to make an appropriate reversal and to focus more on introducing Chinese culture and literature abroad so that the world can learn more about China, so as to achieve the balance of mutual understanding and exchange. In order to engage in comparisons between different cultures or comparative studies of literary works based on different cultural backgrounds, especially cross-cultural comparisons between East and West, translation, as one of the indispensable intermediaries, has a role to play far beyond merely paraphrasing at the level of language and text. Cultural studies is a base for dialogue between the cultures of nations and regions, the various disciplines, and the various artistic disciplines. In particular, the discussion of postcolonial theory and the study of postcolonial literature have accelerated the process of "decolonization" in the East and the Third World countries, questioned and rewritten the traditional composition of the literary canon and its authority, and made Eastern culture gradually move from the periphery to the center, thus breaking the myth of a single Western center and bringing the world into an era of true pluralism and symbiosis, mutual exchange and dialogue rather than confrontation. Therefore, it will be more meaningful to translate and introduce Eastern culture to the world.

In terms of the distribution of disciplines, translation studies has long been dependent on contrastive linguistics or comparative literature studies. In some disciplines, translation studies is even not allowed to exist, and translation studies journals also face the screening of the market economy and find it difficult to survive. In the early 1980s, the resurgence of comparative literature in China made translation studies a branch within this discipline, namely, media studies. Now, by breaking down the natural boundaries between linguistics and literature, cultural studies has actually recognized the legitimacy of the existence of translation studies as a relatively independent discipline. Cultural studies can at least provide translation studies with theoretical weapons and observation perspectives so that we can stand apart from a single mode of thinking, and eventually make the conclusions we draw more universal in theoretical and disciplinary significance, rather than just solving a few specific problems about operational skills. Therefore, translation studies in the context of cultural studies will certainly help China's translation studies to converge with international translation studies as soon as possible, and also help translation studies occupy an important position in the humanities and social sciences with many sub-disciplines.

The significance of cultural studies to translation studies is also reflected in its criticism of power, especially linguistic and cultural hegemony which helps to eliminate a series of artificial binary oppositions and hierarchical boundaries, as well as the boundaries between popular culture and elite culture, so as to make intellectuals, who used to feel superior and pretend to be responsible for the mission of enlightenment, walk out of the ivory tower of knowledge and join the masses of people, and become part of society first before they can realize the ideal of "post-enlightenment". Cultural studies also helps to eliminate the natural barriers between Eastern and Western cultures, making cultural globalization a broad background for dialogue between different cultures. An important sign of cultural globalization is the infinite spread and expansion of information, all of which can be achieved through the Internet. At present, people contact and obtain information on the Internet mainly through English. Therefore, in a country where most people cannot use English effectively to communicate, the main means for people to obtain information is through translation, which leads to a "deficit" in translation. This is also the long-standing deficit in Chinese culture, especially in literary translation: the translation of foreign, especially Western culture and literature to China, either in terms of quality or quantity, is much better than the translation of Chinese culture and literature to foreign countries so that our understanding of the West is much better than Westerners' understanding of China. Therefore, "Occidentalism" is still a very mysterious (rather than derogatory) concept among a considerable number of Chinese people. In addition, from the perspective of the high requirements of cultural translation, the mastery of language skills alone cannot fully accomplish the important task of translating Chinese culture to the world, which will involve a series of complex cultural problems. Therefore, translation studies must transcend the limitations of language, and turn pure language-level reporting into the translation and interpretation of cultural connotations. Therefore, it is imperative to promote a kind of cultural translation and translation studies that crosses cultural traditions.

Many scholars are still pessimistic about the future of comparative literature. Indeed, since the world has entered the era of globalization, comparative literature, which belongs to the elite discipline, is bound to face more severe challenges: while the pressure of economic globalization is mainly reflected in the constraints of the laws of the market economy, the pressure of cultural globalization is clearly reflected in the rise of mass media and the shrinking of the elite cultural market. As far as this point is concerned, translation and its study will play an irreplaceable and historic role that no other sub-discipline of the humanities and social sciences can play: in an era of globalization and information expansion, people have more and more demand for translation, which undoubtedly has a large market, so the shrinking of the market will not have any side effect on translation; on the other hand, as an important medium of communication, it can also develop itself by taking advantage of the increased status of the media. In addition, the high requirements of information, computerization and digitization of language in the era of globalization also give rise to a higher requirement for our translators. Moreover, translation studies itself will gradually undergo a non-marginalization movement, eventually reaching the goal of becoming a relatively independent discipline characterized by the features of the humanities and social sciences, and at the same time by also being closely related to natural science.

The cultural translation theories and ideas discussed in this chapter were developed by two comparative literature scholars, who have been called the founders of the (cultural) "school of translation studies" by later researchers because their unique cultural perspective on translation goes far beyond the traditional language-based translation studies and takes on a more cultural dimension. Whether this label is appropriate or not, it has at least shown their objective influence. Therefore, it is not surprising that the starting point of their writings and the perspective of the issues discussed are comparative literature and cultural studies. They also focus less on translation in the traditional sense of language conversion and more on the translation and reception of literature from a cross-cultural perspective. Therefore, their efforts actually reflect the intervention of scholars of comparative literature and cultural studies in the cultural turn of translation studies.

6.2 Lefevere: translation and the manipulation of literature

It is generally held that the late Belgian-American comparative literature and translation studies scholar André Lefevere (1946–1996) was the leading representative of translation studies from a comparative literature perspective, so his untimely death was undoubtedly a major loss for the cultural turn in translation studies. Together with Susan Bassnett, he is called a representative of the "school of translation studies". Whether or not this "school of translation studies" exists, they have contributed greatly to the movement of the discipline from the periphery to the center, from scratch. Lefevere knew a lot of European languages and was keen on Chinese literature and culture. He used to teach at the Chinese University of Hong Kong and did translation in his spare time for many years. He was professor of comparative literature at the University of Texas at Austin before his death. Prior to his death, he supervised a Chinese scholar's doctoral dissertation devoted to translation thoughts in China, which also stimulated his interest in Chinese literature and culture. He published a lot, including *Translating Poetry: Seven Strategies and a Blueprint* (1975), *Literary Knowledge: A Polemical and Programmatic Essay on its Nature, Growth, Relevance and Transmission* (1977), *Translating Literature: The German Tradition: From Luther to Rosenzweig* (1977), *Translation/History/ Culture: A Source Book* (1992), *Translating Literature: Practice and Theory in a Comparative Literature Context* (1992), *Translation, Rewriting and the Manipulation of Literary Fame* (1992). He co-authored *Constructing Cultures: Essays on Literary Translation* (1998) with Susan Bassnett, and they also compiled a series of books on translation studies. In addition, Lefevere has published a large number of papers in academic journals, dealing extensively with such cutting-edge theoretical topics as the study of the reception and influence of comparative literature, the formation and reconstruction of literary classics, the manipulation and power relations of literary translation, and the cultural turn in translation studies. Among these works, the last three books mentioned above still have an important influence on the cultural turn of translation studies. The topics discussed in this section are mainly from these three books.

Translation, Rewriting and the Manipulation of Literary Fame discusses the writing (translation) practice of those who are not engaged in original writing but specialize in rewriting the works of others. The book argues that translation is a form of rewriting from the perspective of literary reception. Lefevere tried to show how rewriting—translation, anthologization, historiography, criticism, and editing—affects the process of literary works' reception and canonization. He pointed out that there are four main forms of rewriting, among which translation plays an important role and is also the focus of the author's discussion. Lefevere also revealed how the practice of rewriting manipulates the production and dissemination of literary works for various ideological and poetic purposes. It should be said that this monograph is a typical work of comparative literature studies. However, the author was not satisfied with the traditional reception-influence studies and parallel research methods of comparative literature but introduced some topics of cultural studies, such as hegemony and discourse. Lefevere placed literary production and reception in a broad cultural and historical frame of reference and revaluated the socio-historical context of literature from the perspective of Western Marxist theories of literary production. He also discussed such controversial ideas from the standpoint of literary studies: originality, inspiration, aesthetic excellence, and so on. As a scholar of comparative literature, the author has not only crossed the boundaries of languages but also the boundaries of countries and nations. In a broad European cultural context, the author examined the situation of these works of classical and modern literature in today's cultural context, as well as the dynamic and "manipulative" role of translation.

Lefevere first pointed out that all translation is actually rewriting the original, but the rewriters are not imitators without their own ideas. Rewriters are people who live in a specific cultural context and ideological environment, and have their own clear ideological purpose and aesthetic ideal, so to some extent

> Rewriting manipulates, and it is effective. All the more reason, then to study it. In fact, the study of rewriting might even be of some relevance beyond the charmed circle of the educational institution, a way to restore to a certain study of literature some of the more immediate social relevance the study of literature as a whole has lost.[9]

So what kind of process is rewriting? What is its purpose? Lefevere noted:

> The same basic process of rewriting is at work in translation, historiography, anthologization, criticism, and editing. It is obviously also at work in other forms of rewriting, such as adaptations for film and television... Since translation is the most obviously recognizable type of rewriting, and since it is

potentially the most influential because it is able to project the image of an author and/or a (series of) work(s) in another culture, lifting that author and/or those works beyond the boundaries of their culture of origin.[10]

This narrative vividly reproduces Foucault's description of the trinity of knowledge, power, and discourse: knowledge arises from power, and power is expressed through discourse so that discourse actually occupies a central position in the transmission and reproduction of knowledge. According to Foucault's theory, translation is also an "interlingual" discursive practice. Translators are often involved in two kinds of discourse: that of the source language and that of the target language. Therefore, successful translators are actually manipulating the reception and dissemination of the original works in the target language. Obviously, Lefevere's emphasis on rewriting is not only in line with Benjamin's view that translation gives an afterlife to the original, but also takes it to a new extreme.

On the other hand, since translation is a way of rewriting, then it is entirely possible for the translator to make arbitrary adaptations of the original to suit his or her needs for different purposes. It is precisely because the translator can rewrite the original at will that people's long-time prejudice against the translator can be summarized by the Italian adage: Traduttore, Traditore [literally, "Translator, Traitor", meaning the translator is a traitor]! However, for Lefevere, who has also been engaged in translation practice, this kind of betrayal is first of all inevitable. Therefore, he defended it:

> Translators, to lay the old adage to rest once and for all, have to be traitors, but most of the time they don't know it, and nearly all of the time they have no other choice, not as long as they remain within the boundaries of the culture that is theirs by birth or adoption—not, therefore, as long as they try to influence the evolution of that culture, which is an extremely logical thing for them to want to do.[11]

For translators, since they have been forced to take this path of "betrayal", they must do a better job of "betrayal", because indeed, as Lefevere realizes, a translator with a true sense of subjectivity is not willing to be subservient to the original work. S/he always wants to show their linguistic characteristics and expression style in various ways, so in translation practice, s/he has to play the role of a "rebel" who rewrites the original work, which is especially reflected in literary translation. All translators/rewriters with their own independent ideology and aesthetic/poetic ideals try to influence the cultural process of the target language with their own translations, so this form of rewriting has evolved into active "manipulation". Lefevere and some scholars with similar research methods are called the "manipulative school" of translation studies. In fact, they are not a school, but represent a tendency to study translation from the perspective of cultural studies.

According to Lefevere, another factor that influences the translator's rewriting is poetics: "The functional component of a poetics is obviously closely tied to ideological influences from outside the sphere of the poetics as such, and generated by ideological forces in the environment of the literary system".[12] For different poetic purposes, translators/rewriters can achieve different effects. Sometimes, the translator can introduce a new genre of literature to the target language through translation. As Lefevere noted, in the history of modern Chinese literature, Feng Zhi's translation of sonnets not only established the legitimacy of his own sonnet creation, but also introduced this ancient European literary genre into modern Chinese literature, and this is precisely what other forms of rewriters fail to do. Therefore, from the perspective of the composition and reconstruction of literary classics, the role of rewriting goes far beyond the shallow role of language conversion and achieves the goal of reconstructing the literary classics in the target language.

Undoubtedly, rewriting may manipulate the spread of a writer's literary fame in the culture of the target language. On this Lefevere held:

> Rewritten literature plays a vital part in this evolution. The struggle between rival poetics is often initiated by writers, but fought and won or lost by rewriters. Rewritings are also a perfect gauge to measure the extent to which a poetics has been interiorized... Rewritings, mainly translations, deeply affect the interpenetration of literary systems, not just by projecting the image of one writer or work in another literature or by failing to do so.[13]

From this point of view, rewriting does not only achieve the superficial purpose of manipulating the writer's reputation but also deeply affects the dissemination and reception of a writer and his works in another literature. It is true that every excellent literary work contains both translatability and untranslatability, and the translator's task is to find a balance in the tension between translatability and untranslatability, and bring its inherent translatability to its fullest potential. In this way, the translator not only conveys the basic information of the original but also reproduces the original author's ideology and poetics in the target language through his/her own style of expression.

Lefevere repeatedly emphasized in his book that "[t]wo factors basically determine the image of a work of literature as projected by a translation". These two factors are "the translator's ideology" and "the poetics dominant in the receiving literature at the time the translation is made". On the other hand, he pointed out that the two factors are not contradictory, and will go towards the same destiny in the end, because

> the ideology dictates the basic strategy the translator is going to use and therefore also dictates solutions to problems concerned with both the 'universe of discourse' expressed in the original (objects, concepts, customs belonging to the world that was familiar to the writer of the original) and the language the original itself is expressed in.[14]

Since the medium of translation is language, it is necessary to return to language. He proposed the concept of "discursive world" and thus eliminated the dichotomy between ideology and poetics. In this regard, he did not stray too far from the traditional emphasis on language in translation but expanded the role of linguistic expression considerably. He summarized the function of language in translation/rewriting as follows:

> Languages are different, and no amount of translator training is ever likely to reduce that difference. Translator training can, however, alert translators both to the relativity of translation poetics and to strategies that may be used not to "overcome" the differences between languages, which are an undeniable given, but to project "their" image of the original, which may be influenced by various considerations, not just of ideology and/or poetics but also of the intended audience of the translation. These strategies are by no means limited to the realm of linguistics alone. Rather, they operate on the level of ideology, poetics, Universe of Discourse, and linguistics.[15]

Thus, in Lefevere's view, through the mediation of translation, a literary work can be received in another cultural context, and the receiver is the so-called "intended audience". Here, Lefevere finished describing the four factors of translation studies and further ranked in the book to be discussed below those four factors as: (1) ideology, (2) poetics, (3) universe of discourse, and (4) language.[16]

As a scholar who taught comparative literature in college for a long time, Lefevere always put translation in a very prominent position and earnestly practiced what he advocated and spread this view among college students. He was invited by the Modern Language Association of America to write the translation textbook *Translating Literature: Practice and Theory in a Comparative Literature Context* for college faculties of the humanities (including the department of English, the department of comparative literature and the departments of literary studies of different countries). Some of the viewpoints in this textbook were scattered in his earlier works and papers. However, for Lefevere, whose mission is to establish the discipline of translation and to make it independent of the discipline of comparative literature, this is an excellent opportunity to enlighten young undergraduates and graduate students about translation. He therefore began his book with a chapter on "Translation Studies" and described the purpose of the book:

> This book tries to deal with translation in a way that goes beyond right or wrong. In this introduction, I try to explain why, and I also try to show that the approach I advocate can incorporate older approaches, complement them, and make them more fruitful for future research. I must first ask the reader to imagine the translation of literature as taking place not in a vacuum in which two languages meet but, rather, in the context of all the traditions of the two literatures. It also takes place when writers and their translators meet, an encounter in which at least one of the parties is a human being, made of flesh and blood and provided with an agenda of his or her own. Translators mediate between literary traditions, and they do so with some goal in mind, other than that of "making the original available" in a neutral, objective way. Translations are not produced under perfect laboratory conditions. Originals

are indeed made available, but on the translators' terms, even if these terms happen to produce the closest literal (faithful) translation.[17]

Here, he was very clear that the reconstructive function of translation is realized by human beings, who are never passive recipients. The extents to which translators with different ideologies and poetics have rewritten the original are obviously different, so the same original work is "rewritten" and received differently in different linguistic and cultural contexts. This is the reason why literary translation is different from general translation.

In the following chapters, he discussed some of the theorists who have emerged in the field of translation studies in the West in recent decades and their main theories, including Eugene Nida, John C. Catford, Peter Newmark, Mary Snell-Hornby, Gideon Toury, George Steiner, Itamar Even-Zohar, etc. Although these theorists or scholars have different definitions of translation and varied research perspectives, Lefevere, as the author of a textbook, felt the need to allow students to make their own judgments and choices among the many different translation theories. Finally, he unapologetically revealed his banner of "translation studies" and decisively stated his views on cultural translation:

> Paradoxically, perhaps the most productive insight generated by this school of translation studies is the conclusion that no perfect translation is possible. If that is so, acceptance or rejection of translation in a given culture may well have much more to do with power and manipulation than with knowledge and wisdom.[18]

It can be seen that in Lefevere's view, translators always have their own independent ideology and poetics. He did not conceal his views even in teaching but cultivated a group of such translators through the teaching of translation.

We say that Lefevere and Bassnett have greatly promoted the cultural turn of translation studies, which is also evident in their emphasis on the role of culture in the process of literary translation. Lefevere pointed out:

> This book subscribes to the thesis that translation is indeed acculturation. It rejects the finality of the old normative approach, while gratefully incorporating the legacy of some of its techniques, such as componential and functional analysis. Freed from the obligation to give rules for translating and criteria to judge translations by, it claims three areas for the study of literary translation: process, product and reception. It does not slight the study of nonliterary translation in any way: concentration on one aspect of a phenomenon does not imply any value judgment.[19]

It should be said that his open-ended translation research shares some similarities with Derrida's deconstructive translation theory: both of them are opposed to the fixation of translation standards, the former against making value judgments, and the latter having an ideal and most relevant standard of translation; the former studies translation in terms of process, product, and reception, while the latter highlights process. However, they are consistent in emphasizing the cultural factors in translation.

Of course, opposing value judgment does not preclude translation criticism. On the contrary, Lefevere attached great importance to the criticism of the translator and his translation from readers. He noted,

> Translators have to make decisions over and over again on the levels of ideology, poetics, and universe of discourse, and those decisions are always open to criticism from readers who subscribe to a different ideology; who are convinced of the superiority of the poetics dominant in their time and culture; and who are dissatisfied with the strategies translators have chosen to make universe-of-discourse elements intelligible or more easy to intuit.[20]

Since literary translation involves all aspects of literary production and reception studies, it is not surprising that it has a distinct ideological orientation and has given rise to critical controversies. Lefevere must be very clear about this.

As one of the advocators and pioneers of translation studies, Lefevere, like Bassnett, is very concerned about the positioning, current research status and future prospects of the discipline at all times. Although his main field of study is comparative literature, he always believes that in any form of comparative literature studies, scholars must be involved in translation, but in practice, they often regard translation as only a tool or means of research and do not give it due attention. As a result, translation studies has been marginalized for a long time. Lefevere tries to change this situation through teaching and research:

> I have tried to suggest a way of teaching literary translation that strikes a fair balance of the teaching of the product and the teaching of the process. I venture to think that this way of teaching literary translation could help move translation studies from the periphery of comparative literature and literary theory to a position closer to their center. In conclusion, I briefly explain why translation has been condemned to vegetate on the outskirts of literary theory and comparative literature and then suggest not only why this state of affairs should change but also how the kind of course proposed in this book could help change it.
>
> The study of translation has been eclipsed, and the status of the production of translations lowered, in the republic of letters by a combination of at least four factors: the Romantic idea of literature as "secular scripture" and the concomitant emphasis on originality, the Romantic equation of literature with language and the concomitant equation of language with nation, the nineteenth- and early-twentieth-century philologists' insistence on reading texts in the original only, and the enormous influence exerted by New Criticism with its almost exclusive emphasis on interpretation.[21]

Indeed, at least three of the four factors mentioned in the above citation play an important role in the formation of linguo-centrism in translation studies. Therefore, he believed that it is necessary to call for a cultural turn in translation to fundamentally change this situation. This actually served as a sort of precursor to Bassnett's later subversion of the hierarchical order of translation studies and comparative literature.

6.3 Comparative literature and translation studies: the overthrow of the hierarchical order

As a close collaborator of Lefevere, Bassnett's works have also greatly promoted the cultural turn of translation studies. Bassnett's talents are manifested in many ways. She began her academic career in Italy before moving to the United States and finally settling in the UK. She is now a professor of the Centre for Translation and Comparative Culture Studies at the University of Warwick, which she founded in 1980 and served as the first director for many years. She also served as Pro-Vice-Chancellor at the university and is currently Special Adviser in Translation Studies. She is still active in academia and media. Bassnett is a prolific scholar and has published nearly 20 works or edited books, including *Translation Studies* (1980), *Feminist Experiences: The Women's Movement in Four Cultures* (1986), *Sylvia Plath* (1987), and *Comparative Literature: A Critical Introduction* (1993). She edited or co-edited *Beyond Translation* (1989), *Knives and Angels: Latin American Women's Writing* (1990), *Literature and Translation* (1997), and *Post-Colonial Translation: Theory and Practice* (1999). As can be seen from the titles of these books, the breadth of the fields she has covered and the frontiers of the topics she has discussed are indeed rare among scholars of translation studies. In addition, she has compiled some monographs and anthologies with Lefevere and others. As a poet and translator, Bassnett has also published many poems and translations. It is generally believed that Bassnett's main contributions in the field of comparative literature and translation studies are embodied in two monographs—*Comparative Literature: A Critical Introduction* and *Translation Studies* (2002, third edition).

Comparative Literature: A Critical Introduction was published in 1993. At that time, the discipline of comparative literature was under the impact of various new theoretical trends, and its boundaries became more and more uncertain. In particular, the rise of cultural studies posed a powerful challenge to comparative literature. As we all know, as a discipline with a history of more than 100 years, comparative literature has experienced at least three major crises in the twentieth century: The first was a crisis in methodology and schools, which resulted in a new turn in comparative literature, long dominated by the French School of influential studies—the rapid rise of the American School and its move from the periphery to the center. The parallel and interdisciplinary studies promoted by the American School greatly expanded the boundaries of comparative literature studies, introducing elements of aesthetic analysis and interdisciplinary and cross-cultural studies. The second is the impact of new theoretical trends, especially the impact of postmodernism/poststructuralism and postcolonialism: in the face of the former impact, a large number of scholars of comparative literature actively participated in the international discussion of postmodern issues, while in the face of the latter impact, the established mode of "Eurocentrism" or "Western-centrism" of comparative literature was shaken, and scholars of comparative literature had to pay attention to Eastern and Third World literature. The ensuing impact of cultural studies further shook the elite status of comparative literature. Before the publication of her book, people had had great expectations for Bassnett, hoping that she could save the discipline of comparative literature from the crisis it was facing. However, after reading the book, people felt the strong impact of the author's deconstructive and constructive strategies: the deconstruction of traditional comparative literature and the construction of translation studies. Ten years later, comparative literature experienced a third crisis. This crisis came from the impact of the postcolonial theorist Spivak who published a book entitled *Death of a Discipline* in 2003 and officially declared the death of the traditional Eurocentric discipline of comparative literature and the birth of a new comparative literature.[22] It was imaginable that the publication of Bassnett's book created an uproar in comparative literature circles at the time. However, the author of the book did not take a nihilistic approach to the current state and development of the discipline of comparative literature but began with a historical tracing of its birth, its breakthrough to the European frontier, its presence in Britain, its multiple comparative identities after the Second World War, the impact of cultural studies, and the intervention of gender studies and thematic studies. Finally, considering the current situation of comparative literature, the author simply calls for a straightforward shift of interest from comparative literature to translation studies because, in her view, cultural translation in the broad sense actually covers comparative literature studies. Therefore, her book not only intervenes in translation studies from the perspective of comparative literature but also impacts the increasingly rigid comparative literature studies with the momentum of translation studies.

When we say that the discipline of comparative literature has undergone a series of crises, what does its inseparable relationship with translation studies mean in concrete terms? Bassnett pointed out several aspects, among which the impact of translation cannot be ignored:

> The spread of English and the decline of classical languages means also that comparative courses increasingly study texts in translation, which leads on to other methodological issues. If texts written in various different languages are read in translation, then one result of this can be reductive, in that they can all be made to appear to be part of the same literary system.[23]

Indeed, as many scholars of comparative literature have realized, the popularity of English has led to English translations of every classical European literary text. Most of them are domesticated translations, which have at least some "convergence" in terms of linguistic expression, and therefore read like an original work written in English. Since similarities outweigh differences, what is the significance of such a comparison?

Therefore, Bassnett simply announced, "Today, comparative literature in one sense is dead. The narrowness of the binary distinction, the unhelpfulness of the ahistorical approach, the complacent shortsightedness of the Literature-as-universal-civilizing-force approach have all contributed to its demise".[24] On the other hand, the paradox is that scholars of comparative literature are very active in this era of globalization. They are present at academic conferences in various fields and write books. Departments of comparative literature in universities are constantly holding various academic activities, and have a certain influence on the humanities as a whole. What is the explanation for this situation? Bassnett went on to point out:

> But it lives on under other guises: in the radical reassessment of Western cultural models at present being undertaken in many parts of the world, in the transcendence of disciplinary boundaries through new methodological insights supplied by gender studies or cultural studies, in the examination of the processes of intercultural transfer that are taking place within translation studies.[25]

All these phenomena show that the study of comparative literature has indeed fallen into a paradoxical crisis since the 1990s: as a discipline, its territory has become more and more narrow, and much of the original territory is either occupied by cultural studies or appropriated by critical theories; but on the other hand, comparative literature scholars' broad multidisciplinary knowledge and keen sense of cutting-edge theory, combined with their well-trained writing skills, make it easy for them to cross boundaries into new interdisciplinary fields and make new unique voices. This is in sharp contrast to the decline of the discipline itself. Of course, an inevitable result of this is that a significant number of scholars of comparative literature are not studying literature today, but rather are studying topics of other disciplines, such as media studies, gender studies, film and television studies, and ethnic minority studies, from a comparative perspective. On the other hand, these scholars have to be institutionally attached to the discipline of comparative literature, such as the late Lefevere and the still active Gentzler, who have been teaching and supervising graduate students within the program of comparative literature. Bassnett is also very clear about this phenomenon, so she has been looking for various opportunities to establish the disciplinary status of translation studies. Of course, the acceleration of globalization has also led to a fracturing of the world's language systems: the already strong languages, such as English, have become increasingly powerful and have taken on the role of the world's lingua franca, while previously weak languages have either died out or are increasingly shrinking. This leads to such a phenomenon:

> English writing should necessarily be seen as the dominant centre. Indeed, the impact of non-English writers whose native language is a variant of English is leading gradually to a shift in terminology: we now distinguish between "English Literature" and "Literature in English", a shift that has happened in the last two decades but which is crucially important for the future.[26]

The intervention of comparative literature and cultural studies 127

Under the impact of postcolonial theories, the study of international English literature has become a relatively independent discipline. Similarly, if we use it to describe the current situation of the development of Chinese, it is not difficult to find that due to the worldwide popularity of Chinese, it has itself undergone a fission. Chinese writing outside China's territory is developing rapidly, and Chinese is gradually changing from a national language into a more widely used regional language, and now becoming a major international language. There are more and more people writing in Chinese outside China's territory. Overseas Chinese literature has shown differences from Chinese literature. Therefore, the study of international Chinese literature will become a discipline, and the compilation of a history of Chinese literature will be a task for Chinese scholars of comparative literature in the future. Bassnett, limited by her Western-centric vision, could not have seen this at the time, but her call for a translation turn in comparative literature studies still seems forward-looking today.

As a practitioner and scholar of translation, Bassnett was naturally very concerned about the improvement of the status of translators, and like Venuti, she also made unremitting efforts for it. She pointed out in her book:

> The debates on translation that have raged on down the centuries have frequently concerned the visibility or lack of it of the translator. Is the translator a transparent channel, a kind of glass tube through which the Source Language text is miraculously transformed in its passage into the Target Language, or is the translator herself an element in that process of transformation? Similar questions have begun to be asked about map-makers, questions that challenge the supposed objectivity of a map and ask what the map might be for, what might it be seeking to represent.[27]

Different from Venuti, however, she did not cry out for the subjectivity of translators, but was more concerned about the development of translation studies as a discipline in recent decades. With the rise of the status of translation studies, it is natural that the status of translators will be improved correspondingly. Therefore, after discussing the relationship between comparative literature and translation studies in parallel, Bassnett pointed out boldly and frankly in the last chapter of the book "From comparative literature to translation studies" that in view of the decline of comparative literature,

> [i]n contrast, however, Translation Studies has been gaining ground, and since the end of the 1970s has come to be seen as a discipline in its own right, with professional associations, journals, publishers' catalogues and a proliferation of doctoral theses.[28]

Therefore, "[w]e should look upon translation studies as the principal discipline from now on, with comparative literature as a valued but subsidiary subject area".[29] It can be said that Bassnett's book at least theoretically deconstructs the discipline of comparative literature and constructs the discipline of translation studies. In view of the rapid development of translation studies all over the world today, her prediction is indeed forward-looking. On the other hand, it should be pointed out that in the era of globalization, comparative literature has not died out. Although the old Eurocentric comparative literature is shrinking day by day, the new discipline of comparative literature, which has expanded its boundaries and ushered in topics in cultural studies, still has great vitality and is flourishing in Eastern countries outside Europe and the United States. This phenomenon is probably beyond Bassnett's expectations but has proved true.

Translation Studies is one of the most important works that established Bassnett's position as a major scholar of translation studies. It has also been a popular textbook of translation studies during the past 20 years. In the three parts of this book, she first outlined the core issues of translation studies in recent decades, such as meaning, translatability and untranslatability, correspondence theory, and intercultural communication translation; the second part traces the evolution of translation theory from the perspective of historical development and the different understandings of translation concepts by scholars in different periods; the third part deals with the translations of specific literary genres and their problems, covering the translation of poetry, fiction and dramatic literature, and guides translators and researchers of European languages and literature to a certain degree. However, in consideration of the literature in different cultural contexts involved in the whole book, it should be an important work in studying translation from the perspective of comparative literature.

Of course, from the publication of the first edition of the book in 1980 to the third edition in 2002, great changes have taken place within the field of international translation studies. She has been involved in promoting the cultural turn of translation studies and has brought it into the mainstream of contemporary cultural scholarship. Therefore, in the preface of the third edition, she first made a clear distinction between linguistics and translation studies from the cultural perspective:

> The apparent division between cultural and linguistic approaches to translation that characterized much translation research until the 1980s is disappearing, partly because of shifts in linguistics that have seen that discipline take a more overtly cultural turn, partly because those who advocated an approach to translation rooted in cultural history have become less defensive about their position. In the early years when Translation Studies was establishing itself, its advocates positioned themselves against both linguists and literary scholars, arguing that linguists failed to take into account broader contextual dimensions and that literary scholars were obsessed with making pointless evaluative judgements. It was held to be important to move the study of translation out from under the umbrella of either comparative literature or applied linguistics, and fierce polemics arguing for the autonomy of Translation Studies were common. Today, such an evangelical position seems quaintly outdated, and Translation Studies is more comfortable with itself, better able to engage in borrowing from and lending techniques and methods to other disciplines.[30]

The intervention of comparative literature and cultural studies 129

In fact, Bassnett has already noticed that with the rise of cultural studies, the cultural turn of translation studies has changed the original meaning of translation. Scholars from different disciplines have made a new interpretation of the role of translation. In particular, the use of cultural translation strategies by postcolonial theorists has been distinctly political and ideologically critical. For example:

> Significantly, Homi Bhabha uses the term "translation" not to describe a transaction between texts and languages but in the etymological sense of being carried across from one place to another. He uses translation metaphorically to describe the condition of the contemporary world, a world in which millions migrate and change their location every day.[31]

There is no doubt that this large-scale immigration has led to more and more uncertainty about people's national and cultural identity. People from different cultural contexts need to coordinate and communicate, so the cultural characteristics and functions of translation become increasingly obvious. On the other hand, she also affirmed the achievements of the polysystem theory which is still characterized by formalism:

> Polysystems theory filled the gap that opened up in the 1970s between linguistics and literary studies and provided the base upon which the new interdisciplinary Translation Studies could build. Central to polysystems theory was an emphasis on the poetics of the target culture.[32]

Undoubtedly, from a historical point of view, the polysystem theory has also made some contributions to translation studies out of the prison of language, but such contributions were soon overshadowed by deconstruction and postcolonial translation theory with more impact of the cultural turn.

In the introduction, Bassnett reviewed the development of translation studies and pointed out that although translation studies covers a wide range of fields, it can still be clearly divided into four areas, or four categories: (1) history of translation, (2) translation in the TL (target language) culture, (3) translation and linguistics, and (4) translation and poetics.[33] In her opinion, the first two categories are the most discussed topics by translation scholars today, because they are especially closely related to culture.

Bassnett was very clear about the views of scholars outside the field on translation studies. As a still very young discipline, translation studies still lacks profound theoretical accumulation:

> The problem of evaluation in translation is intimately connected with the previously discussed problem of the low status of translation, which enables critics to make pronouncements about translated texts from a position of assumed superiority. The growth of Translation Studies as a discipline, however, should go some way towards raising the level of discussion about translations, and if there are criteria to be established for the evaluation of a

translation, those criteria will be established from within the discipline and not from without.³⁴

One of the biggest defects of the previous literary vs. linguistic translation debate is that both sides of the debate started from their own disciplines, without considering the uniqueness and independence of translation studies. She believes that this is one of the major reasons why the level of discussion on translation issues has remained low.

In her book, Bassnett spent considerable time reviewing the history of translation, but her entry point was the problem. She concluded:

> From this brief outline, it can clearly be seen that different concepts of translation prevail at different times, and that the function and role of the translator has radically altered. The explanation of such shifts is the province of cultural history, but the effect of changing concepts of translation on the process of translating itself will occupy researchers for a long time to come.³⁵

As a translator, Bassnett was also very concerned about the translation of specific literary genres, including poetry, drama, and fiction. However, she still identified some general patterns in them and theoretically explained them. She believed:

> The translator, then, first reads/translates in the SL and then, through a further process of decoding, translates the text into the TL language. In this he is not doing less than the reader of the SL text alone, he is actually doing more, for the SL text is being approached through more than one set of systems. It is therefore quite foolish to argue that the task of the translator is to translate but not to interpret, as if the two were separate exercises. The interlingual translation is bound to reflect the translator's own creative interpretation of the SL text. Moreover, the degree to which the translator reproduces the form, meter, rhythm, tone, register, etc. of the SL system, will be as much determined by the TL system as by the SL system and will also depend on the function of the translation.³⁶

It should be said that this is what she has learned from her own translation practice. Therefore, like Spivak, Bassnett was never satisfied with the superficial faithful representation of the original text. The function of the translator in her mind also includes the dynamic interpretation of the original text from her own unique perspective and vision of expectations, which may result in unfaithfulness in linguistic equivalence, but is more accurate in reproducing the cultural connotations of the original work, and even uncovers the potential meaning of the original. In this regard, like Lefevere, she believed that translation plays an important role in the canonization of the original in the TL.

After examining the English translation of some poems written in European languages, Bassnett also expounded the modernity of translation. She noted:

The intervention of comparative literature and cultural studies 131

> All the translations reflect the individual translators' readings, interpretations and selection of criteria determined by the concept of the *function* both of the translation and of the original text. So from the poems examined we can see that in some cases *modernization* of language and tone has received priority treatment, whilst in other cases conscious archaization has been a dominant determining feature.[37]

Whether from the translator's perspective or from the reader's perspective, translation cannot be separated from its own era, and therefore translators of each era should produce translations that are appropriate to it.

Although Bassnett has repeatedly emphasized the dynamic role of the translator, she still pointed out through the analysis of specific translated texts:

> It therefore becomes possible for a translator to see himself freed from the restrictions of those conventions governing translation that have prevailed at different moments in time and to treat the text responsibly as the starting point from which the metatext, or *translation-reading* (an interlingual reading) can begin…all kinds of different criteria come into play during the translation process and all necessarily involve shifts of expression, as the translator struggles to combine his own pragmatic reading with the dictates of the TL cultural system.[38]

In this way, the translator's task is not only to reproduce the original text linguistically but also to contribute to the construction of the culture of the TL. It should be said that this is one of the important missions of the so-called "cultural school" of translation studies, and in this regard, Bassnett's pioneering contribution cannot be ignored.

Finally, in the conclusion of her book, while she admitted that translation studies was still a young discipline, Bassnett further indicated:

> One great benefit to be derived from a more accessible terminology would be that we could move away from the old vague conflict between free and literal translation, with the attendant value judgements. We could also move away from the dubious distinction between author-directed and audience-directed translation.[39]

In this regard, Bassnett has obviously absorbed some translation principles of polysystem theory and deconstruction. Her purpose is to move the discipline's concerns increasingly in the direction of culture, without having to stick to unwarranted specific linguistic and textual arguments. It should be said that this is also the position maintained by most scholars of translation studies from comparative literature and cultural studies.

Today, in the context of globalization, the boundary of literature has greatly expanded. Many things that were not considered to be part of literature by the formalist literary theorists in the past have now entered the halls of literature with aplomb. One consequence of this is that not only has the face of comparative literature changed fundamentally, but cultural studies is also moving in a new direction. People may be concerned whether Bassnett still insists on the proper disciplinary status of translation studies. Will she still cry out for the legitimacy of translation studies as she did in those days? Surprisingly, in 2006, she published a shocking article "Reflection on Comparative Literature in the Twenty-First Century" in *Comparative Critical Studies* series, Volume 3, Numbers 1-2. In that article, she changed her radical position of favoring one over the other (comparison). Instead, she claimed more aggressively that her main motivation for writing the book *Comparative Literature: A Critical Introduction* back then was:

> as much about trying to raise the profile of translation studies as it was about declaring comparative literature to be defunct. Today, looking back at that proposition, it appears fundamentally flawed: translation studies has not developed very far at all over three decades and comparison remains at the heart of much translation studies scholarship. What I would say were I writing the book today is that neither comparative literature nor translation studies should be seen as a discipline: rather both are methods of approaching literature, ways of reading that are mutually beneficial. The crisis in comparative literature derived from excessive prescriptivism combined with distinctive culturally specific methodologies that could not be universally applicable or relevant.[40]

In this way, the topic of the crisis of comparative literature surfaces again, and it also implies an inherent crisis of translation studies. How will researchers respond theoretically to the new challenges posed by this phenomenon? Indeed, in an era when the golden age of cultural theory has passed, the function of theory has undoubtedly changed, pointing not only to literary texts composed of words, but also to visual texts composed of images and symbols. It is not surprising that comparative literature scholars have gone beyond the boundaries, and cultural studies scholars are gradually getting rid of the traditional method of "talking on paper". They are increasingly concerned with the visual culture that arises in our daily lives. In this regard, what will translation studies do? How does it get out of the closed "cage of language"? Should it also be concerned with the translation and interpretation of texts composed of various images and symbols surrounding us? We will discuss this in the next chapter.

Notes

1 For new crises faced by comparative literature, see Culler, J. 1995. Comparative literature, at last! In C. Berheimer (ed.), *Comparative Literature in the Age of Multiculturalism*. Baltimore, MD & London: The Johns Hopkins University Press, 117.
2 For the possible interaction and complementation between comparative literature and cultural studies, see Riffaterre, M. 1995. On the complementarity of comparative literature and cultural studies. In C. Berheimer (ed.), *Comparative Literature in the Age of Multiculturalism*. Baltimore, MD & London: The Johns Hopkins University Press, 66–73.

3 Cf. Saussy, H. (ed.). 2006. *Comparative Literature in an Age of Globalization*. Baltimore, MD & London: The Johns Hopkins University Press. In particular, the editor's long introductory article.
4 In this regard, please refer to the following English papers of the author: Confronting globalization: Cultural studies versus Comparative characteristics studies? *Neohelicon*, *28*(1) (2001): 55–66; Comparative literature and globalism: A Chinese cultural and literary strategy. *Comparative Literal Studies*, 41(4) (2004): 584–602; and Comparative Literature, in Robertson, R. & Scholte, J. A. (eds.) 2006. *Encyclopedia of Globalization*. New York & London: Routledge, 196–198.
5 One of the outstanding achievements in this respect is the multi-volume *The Comparative History of Literature in European Languages*, a large-scale international cooperation project sponsored by the International Association for Comparative Literature, which was published by John Benjamins Publishing Company of the Netherlands. At present, all the 24 volumes have been published.
6 See Fredric Jameson, "The retrogression of the present era", translated by Wang Fengzhen, in *Zhonghua Dushu Bao* [China Reading Weekly], August 14, 2002.
7 In particular, it should be pointed out that most of the articles published in *New Literary History* in the past 20 years encompass a broad cultural perspective, and some special issues, such as "Ecocriticism" (Vol. 30, 1999), "Ecological Culture" (Vol. 38, 2007), are actually the cultural study of literature. These all have a great influence on the interaction and complementarity between literary studies and cultural studies.
8 Turner, G. 1998. *Introduction to British Cultural Studies*. Tang, W. (trans.). Taipei: Asia Pacific Book Press, 298. Translators' note: In translating this passage from the Chinese we have consulted the third edition of the English original of the book published by Routledge in 2003, p. 230.
9 Lefevere, A. 1992. *Translation, Rewriting and the Manipulation of Literary Fame*. London & New York: Routledge, 9.
10 Ibid.
11 Ibid., p. 13.
12 Ibid., p. 27.
13 Ibid., p. 38.
14 Ibid., p. 41.
15 Ibid., p. 100.
16 Lefevere, A. 1992. *Translating Literature: Practice and Theory in a Comparative Literature Context*. New York: The Modern Language Association of America, 87.
17 Ibid., p. 6.
18 Ibid., p. 11.
19 Ibid., p. 12.
20 Ibid., p. 88.
21 Ibid., p. 134.
22 Cf. Spivak, G. C. 2003. *Death of a Discipline*. New York: Columbia University Press, Chapters 1 and 3.
23 Bassnett, S. 1993. *Comparative Literature: A Critical Introduction*. Oxford: Wiley-Blackwell, 45.
24 Ibid., p. 47.
25 Ibid.
26 Ibid., p. 67.
27 Ibid., p. 99.
28 Ibid., p. 138.
29 Ibid., p. 161.
30 Bassnett, S. 2002. *Translation Studies* (3rd ed.). London & New York: Routledge, 3.
31 Ibid., p. 6.
32 Ibid., p. 7.
33 Ibid., pp. 16–17.

34 Ibid., p. 20.
35 Ibid., pp. 79–80.
36 Ibid., p. 86. Translators' note: SL = source language, TL = target language.
37 Ibid., p. 106.
38 Ibid., p. 109.
39 Ibid., pp. 136–137.
40 Bassnett, S. 2008. Reflection on comparative literature in the twenty-first century. Huang, D. (trans.) *Zhongguo Bijiao Wenxue* [Comparative Literature in China], (4): 6. See also the discussion of this article by several Chinese scholars published in the first issue of the journal in 2009. Translators' note: we consulted Bassnett, S. 2006. Reflection on comparative literature in the twenty-first century. *Comparative Critical Studies*, *3*(1–2): 3–11.

7 Intersemiotic translation and the "visual turn" in cultural studies

Although scholars of translation studies still remember the three aspects of translation proposed by Jakobson from the perspective of linguistics over half a century ago, they tend to focus only on the conversion between different languages and consider it real translation when specifically discussing translated texts. Therefore, before we discuss intersemiotic translation, let us first review how Jakobson defined the three aspects of translation back then:

1 Intralingual translation or rewording is an interpretation of verbal signs by means of other signs of the same language.
2 Interlingual translation or translation proper is an interpretation of verbal signs by means of some other language.
3 Intersemiotic translation or transmutation is an interpretation of verbal signs by means of signs of nonverbal sign systems.[1]

Obviously, Jakobson referred to translation in the broad sense when he made this description, but he then revealed his bottom line: from the perspective of formalist linguistics, he believed that only the second form of textual translation is translation *per se* that is being discussed. However, the cases that emerge in the practice of literary translation raise new questions for the scholars of translation studies: the Irish poet Seamus Heaney's translation of the English literary classic *Beowulf* from Old English into contemporary English is by no means less difficult than the translation of a foreign classic into English; does this count as translation? Besides, does it count as translation that some Chinese scholars translated the classical work of literary criticism *Wenxin Diaolong* [The Literary Mind and the Carving of Dragons] into modern Chinese? If the answer is yes, then the boundaries of translation in the traditional linguistic sense have actually been widened.

In recent years, with the entry of globalization into China, the boundaries of culture have become wider and even more uncertain. Once held in high esteem by elite intellectuals, "elite culture" has been banished to the margins of contemporary life. Popular culture has penetrated more and more deeply into people's daily lives, not only influencing the intellectual and entertainment life of people, but also greatly affecting people's aesthetic taste and consumption habits, and made our era increasingly demonstrate the characteristics of consumer society. The language and words that once dominated people's aesthetic objects have been powerfully challenged, not to mention the elite literature made up of language and words. There is no doubt that this challenge comes from two sources: the rise of popular culture and consumer culture has fundamentally changed people's inherent elite cultural outlook and provided the possibility for most people to appreciate and "consume" high cultural products; and the rise of another medium of writing and criticism, the image, has fundamentally changed people's aesthetic interests and values. Today's postmodern consumer society enables people to aesthetically appreciate and even consume refined culture and its products—the work of art. Therefore, the emergence of iconographical writing with images as the main medium is a historical inevitability. It can meet the aesthetic needs of readers/viewers, and it also challenges our cultural scholars: since cultural studies investigates all the living cultural phenomena around us, should visual culture, which is composed of images and various symbols, also enter the vision of cultural studies scholars? Now that the phenomenon that people call "the age of picture reading" has come to the forefront, our scholars of culture and translation studies cannot help but confront these phenomena and perform rational analysis and research. Moreover, with the increasing popularity of images and their partial substitution for textual expressions to a certain extent, the practice and theory of translation need to give corresponding attention to images. The function of translation in this regard is manifested in two ways: one can translate and explain images in another cultural context with words, and at the same time, the words can also participate in the construction of a visual culture. This chapter intends to elaborate on these two aspects.

7.1   The aesthetic features of postmodern consumer culture

In the late 1990s, British Marxist theorist Eagleton gave a sober analysis of the phenomenon of "cultural proliferation" from the perspective of cultural criticism. In an article entitled "The contradictions of postmodernism" (1997), he expressed a different view on the postmodern fever and Western cultural fever in Third World countries. He sharply remarked:

> Why is everyone talking about culture? Because there are, of course, rather more important topics to talk about… everything is cultural… Culturalism inflates the importance of what is constructed, coded, conventional about human life…Historicism, likewise, tends to emphasize what is changeable, relative, and discontinuous about history, rather than what has remained massively, unmovably, and somewhat depressingly consistent about it. Culturalism belongs to a specific historical place and time—in our case, to an advanced capitalist West, but now increasingly, it would seem, about to be imported into China and other "emergent" societies.[2]

Eagleton's radical remarks obviously mean something. Before the publication of this article, in the keynote speech of the "International Conference on Cultural Studies: China and the West", he recalled that unlike his first visit to China in the early

1980s, Chinese society in the mid-to-late 1990s has become increasingly characterized by the features of a postmodern consumer society. It should be acknowledged that what Eagleton saw in Tiananmen Square in Beijing, China's capital, more than two decades ago was only a precursor to the rise of consumer culture, which has become a common phenomenon throughout the mainland of China's medium-size cities and beyond today. Here, Marxism and postmodernism encounter each other, and produce a certain degree of integration in the production and consumption of culture.[3] The starting point of Eagleton's discussion of postmodernism at that time was culture, but it was not the elite culture in the traditional sense of modernism, but the popular culture in the postmodern sense with more consumption characteristics, which naturally also includes visual culture. This mass or popular culture, which emerged from a consumer society, undoubtedly had a certain impact and deconstructive effect on the once dominant modernist elite culture and its product, literature. The rise of visual culture has also had a fatal impact on the production of elite literature, the main medium of which is the written word.

Not surprisingly, when talking about culture, people have begun to pay more and more attention to the consumptive characteristics of contemporary culture and the specific postmodern aesthetic characteristics that this consumer culture carries. The culture of postmodern society is obviously different from modern culture both in its essence and in its form of expression, so we must first make a distinction between different levels of culture. According to Eagleton, the word "culture" has always seemed both too broad and too narrow to be really useful: its aesthetic meaning includes Stravinsky's writings, but not necessarily science fiction; its anthropological meaning ranges from hairstyles and dining habits to the manufacture of drainpipes. In fact, the worry about the unlimited expansion of the concept of culture has long been reflected in his previous works. From a dialectical point of view, Eagleton always believes that there are at least two levels of culture that can be discussed. One is the "general culture" (Culture) that starts with a capital letter, and the other is the "specific culture" (cultures) of each nation that starts with a lowercase letter. The confrontation and struggle between these two cultures have led to an unrestrained expansion of the concept of culture, even to the point of being offensive. After analyzing different versions of the concept of culture, Eagleton concludes

> We see that the contemporary notion of culture has expanded so dramatically that we apparently share its fragile, troubled, material, physical, and objective human life, which has been unceremoniously swept aside by the folly of so-called culturalism. Indeed, culture is not something we live with, but in a sense, something we live for. [...] The culture of our time has become too conceited and brazen. While acknowledging its importance, we should decisively send it back to where it belongs.[4]

Since this postmodern consumer culture is everywhere and has directly affected our daily life and aesthetic concepts, we should analyze and study it.

Of course, this is the case when discussing different cultures. In discussing the issue of postmodernism, scholars have also found the forms of postmodernism at different levels. Postmodernism at the level of poststructuralism, that is, postmodernism with the deconstructive character of Derrida's and Foucault's theories, indicates a critique and deconstruction of the modernist conception of totality, a postmodernism at the metaphysical philosophical and intellectual level. The intellectual rebellion and radical artistic experiments of the avant-garde pushed the elite art view of modernism to the extreme, which actually inherited to some extent the experimental and avant-garde characteristics of high modernist art. Postmodernism, which is dominated by consumer culture and popular culture, embodies the impact and deconstruction of modernist elite culture. It should be pointed out that the visual culture and image art in the past ten years or more should also be included in the category of postmodern consumer culture, because it objectively satisfies people's visual aesthetic needs and meets the aesthetic needs that no other cultural form can provide. From this point of view, whether advancing, critiquing, or even dismantling modernism, the object of postmodernism's critique and transcendence has always been its predecessor and forerunner, modernism. One of the important reasons is that while modernism made culture accessible, appreciated, and even consumed by only a few, postmodernism made it accessible and consumed by the majority while greatly expanding the boundaries of culture. Therefore, the close relationship between postmodernism and consumer culture exists objectively. When discussing this relationship, we can't help thinking of or quoting "Postmodernism and consumer society" written by Jameson, a new Marxist theorist in the United States, in the early 1980s. In this article, he clearly stated that, in addition to examining the various characteristics of postmodernism, people

> can also come at the break from the other side, and describe it in terms of periods of recent social life. As I have suggested, non-Marxists and Marxists alike have come around to the general feeling that at some point following World War II a new kind of society began to emerge (variously described as postindustrial society, multinational capitalism, consumer society, media society and so forth). New types of consumption; planned obsolescence; an ever more rapid rhythm of fashion and styling changes; the penetration of advertising, television and the media generally to a hitherto unparalleled degree throughout society; the replacement of the old tension between city and country, center and province, by the suburb and by universal standardization; the growth of the great networks of superhighways and the arrival of automobile culture—these are some of the features which would seem to mark a radical break with that older prewar society in which high modernism was still an underground force.[5]

Jameson described the phenomenon, which is very different from modern society, as a phenomenon in postmodern society. If the Western postmodern theory introduced during Jameson's first visit to China in 1985 only resonated with a few elite intellectuals and avant-garde literary artists, the above passage could not be more accurate in describing the social and cultural situation in China at the beginning of the new century.[6] This is the foresight of Jameson's theory. This being the case, one might ask, what form will culture take after entering postmodern society? This is what many scholars in the East and the West who specialize in the study of postmodernism pay close attention to and try to answer. Let me take consumer culture as an example.

Let us review the characteristics of modernist culture and art: a sophisticated culture full of elite consciousness, a culture appreciated only by a few people, an aesthetic culture expressing the individuality of the self, and even the elite cultural concept of "art for art's sake", etc. Obviously, all these are what the postmodern artist wants to criticize and transcend. Therefore, it is not difficult to infer that the characteristics of postmodernism are anti-aesthetics, anti-interpretation, anti-culture, and anti-art. However, which level of culture is it against? This may be exactly what we easily ignore: it opposes the modernist aesthetics with its lofty characteristics and elitist consciousness, resists the modernist-centered interpretation and the mainstream culture held and dominated by a few elites, and transcends and criticizes the elegant literature and art of modernism. In a word, postmodernist culture and art are different from the elegant culture and art of modernism. It inherits some aesthetic principles of modernism in some aspects but criticizes and deconstructs them in more aspects. Therefore, a dialectical and analytical perspective is necessary to examine postmodernist culture and art, and this complex phenomenon must not be simplified.

In terms of Western Marxist studies of postmodernism, although Jameson took a critical attitude toward postmodernism from the height of cultural criticism, he still factually recognized many reasonable elements in postmodernist culture and gave full recognition to them. He believed that what postmodernism or postmodernity brought was not all negative. It breaks our inherent single-mindedness, makes us think about issues in a complicated way in such an era when the concept of time and space has been greatly reduced, and makes the pursuit of value standards also break through the limit of the simple either-or mode. If we examine postmodernism comprehensively from the aspects mentioned above, we can easily see:

> In the most interesting postmodernist works, however, one can detect a more positive conception of relationship, which restores its proper tension to the notion of difference itself. This new mode of relationship through difference may sometimes be an achieved new and original way of thinking and perceiving; more often it takes the form of an impossible imperative to achieve that new mutation in what can perhaps no longer be called consciousness.[7]

Therefore, in Jameson's view, the close relationship between postmodernism and consumer society is reflected in the characteristics of consumer culture. As a special reaction to the established form of modernist mainstream culture, postmodernism emerged with the obvious feature of dissolving the boundary between mass culture and elite culture, marking the end of the elite culture of modernism and the rise of postmodern consumer culture. It should be acknowledged that the issue of consumer culture, which is so hotly discussed in the field of cultural studies in the West today, is largely based on Jameson's critical construction of postmodernism.

In fact, Jean Baudrillard, another French post-Marxist thinker who contributed greatly to the postmodernist trend, was early on concerned with consumer culture and its impact on contemporary life. As early as 1970, he wrote a monograph *La Société de consummation* and stated at the beginning:

> Today, we are everywhere surrounded by the remarkable conspicuousness of consumption and affluence, established by the multiplication of objects, services, and material goods. This now constitutes a fundamental mutation in the ecology of the human species. Strictly speaking, men of wealth are no longer surrounded by other human beings, as they have been in the past, but by *objects*. Their daily exchange is no longer with their fellows, but rather, statistically as a function of some ascending curve, with the acquisition and manipulation of goods and messages:...[8]

Although Baudrillard's description above was based on European countries in the 1970s, it is still very appropriate to describe the situation of the consumer society in China today. As more and more Chinese translations of Baudrillard's work become available, his study of symbols and symbolic meanings of production and consumption will increasingly attract the attention of our cultural studies scholars and translation researchers. Undoubtedly, Baudrillard's generalization shows an obvious feature of postmodern consumer society: people have been increasingly shaped by the commodity economy, and the consumption of goods and the exchange of information dominate people's daily lives. Therefore, people living in the postmodern consumer society are not concerned with how to subsist, but with how to enjoy life more comfortably or "aesthetically". We say that an important feature of postmodern culture is its consumerism. Does it mean that postmodern culture has lost all its aesthetic features? No, it is just the opposite. In the postmodern society, especially in the era of globalization, people's material life has become greatly enriched, which makes them not only rely largely on the production of material culture but also advocate the enjoyment and consumption of these material cultures. If, in the modernist era, people's aesthetic concepts were mainly expressed in focusing on the production and practicality of cultural products, then in the postmodern society, their aesthetic values are more reflected in the packaging and consumption of cultural products. If, in the era of traditional industrial civilization, this kind of material and cultural consumption is only of the low-level "food and clothing type", then in the postmodern information society, there has occurred a huge increase in people's demand for material and cultural consumption. Postmodern society provides people with a variety of aesthetic choices: they don't need to spend a lot of time reading thick, long literary masterpieces, but just spend an hour or two in their "home theater" to enjoy the aesthetic pleasure provided by a masterpiece of world literature; at the same time, many students engaged in literary studies—the product of elite culture—have also changed their past practice of indulging in reading classic literary masterpieces in books and replaced it with watching and studying movies or television, which are more aesthetically stimulating. When they write their dissertations, instead of wandering quietly through the sea of books in the library and savoring the pleasure of books, as they used to do, they are immersed in images and enjoy the beauty of fast-paced music. All these show that in the postmodern society, people need to enjoy and consume these cultural products "aesthetically" rather than vulgarly. In China, even the elegant theories of Jameson and Baudrillard have become the literary products "consumed" by the new generation of young scholars. In order to consume these cultural products more "aesthetically", people need to grasp the aesthetic characteristics of consumer culture.

Contrary to the deep aesthetic value of modernist art, the consumer cultural products produced in the postmodern period have superficial and shallow aesthetic value. The concept of time and space of people living in postmodern society is quite different from that of people living in modern society: their life is fast-paced and ever-changing, which determines that their aesthetic interests should also change accordingly. Since the pace of life for people in modern consumer society is often very fast, it is impossible for them to carefully taste the elegant cultural products, but at the same time, it is impossible for them to spend money on the consumption of cultural fakes that cannot satisfy even their own vision. So what are the aesthetic characteristics of consumer culture? I will just make a brief summary here.

The first is performativity. Consumer cultural products are generally not finely crafted cultural masterpieces. Instead, they are often produced to attract people's visual attention in an instant and satisfy the aesthetic pleasure they provoke in a short period of time. In this way, they, especially some artistic sketches for stage performances, need to work on the performance process. Similarly, some consumer goods also need to show their "value" in the process of media advertising. Therefore, this kind of "performing" advertising, often joined by movie or television stars, can play a role in the promotion of such cultural products.

The second is ornamental value. If performativity is only reflected in the art sketches that can be used for stage performance, then the ornamental value of static art becomes an important link in attracting consumers in an instant. In order to attract people to spend money on consumption and enjoyment, these kinds of consumer cultural products are designed to attract people's attention with their appearance, make people's eyes delighted, and make consumers willingly spend money to consume and enjoy these products.

The third is packaging. Since consumer culture should first satisfy consumers' vision, what measures should be taken for those products with rough appearances? Naturally, it is through "packaging" that they become "beautiful" in appearance. Therefore, whether a consumer cultural product can go to the market smoothly depends to a great extent on how it is packaged. Although the content of most products is far from their external packaging, there is no shortage of a few true gems that can achieve consistency between the inside and the outside.

Finally, there is the timeliness of consumer culture. The culture of postmodern consumer society is a culture pursuing fashion. Since consumer culture only serves to meet people's visual aesthetic needs, or only the short-term aesthetic needs and enjoyment of consumers in postmodern society, such cultural products only reflect the fashion of the moment. When new fashion replaces old fashion, these products will only become "things of the past". This is the timeliness of consumer culture.

As mentioned above, all these aesthetic characteristics show that consumer cultural products in postmodern society appeal to people's eyes to a large extent, thus objectively laying the foundation for the rise of a new cultural form—visual culture. There is no doubt that visual culture is an imported product "translated" from the Western postmodern society. It is mainly a product of the post-industrial information society, but once it entered China, it quickly took on the characteristics of the local culture. So what changes has this visual culture brought to us? Next, we will focus on visual culture and the resulting "pictorial turn" in contemporary writing and criticism, in order to set the stage for our natural transition to a discussion of cross-cultural pictorial translation.

7.2 Visual culture and an "iconographical turn" in contemporary culture

Discussing the phenomenon of visual culture in a global context has become a hot topic in literary theory and cultural studies in recent years. This is bound to make people think of a new "pictorial turn" in contemporary cultural and artistic criticism. Since the images, which contain the meaning of the language, cannot be separated from the specter of the language, and to a large extent, they also assume the function of the original language and writing, we can call this phenomenon "an iconographical turn" which combines textual and pictorial language. Since entering the era of globalization in the new century, due to a new turn in contemporary literary creation—the gradual transition from traditional writing to the emerging image writing—there has also been a "pictorial or iconographical turn" in literary criticism. The original way of using words to convey meaning has been challenged by both popular culture and Internet writing, and thus the writing of words has also been strongly challenged by the writing of images. Facing the impact of this irresistible trend, traditional textual criticism should also shift its focus somewhat to image criticism. When we reflect on the road of literary and cultural criticism in the twentieth century, we can easily find that as early as the 1980s in Western criticism, when it was felt that postmodernism had become the end of the line, people competed to predict the landscape of literary theory criticism that would emerge after postmodernism. Some people predicted that in the postmodernism era, the main way of criticism would no longer be textual criticism, but more likely image criticism, because the popularity of images heralded the advent of an age of iconography, embodied in both literary creation and theoretical criticism.[9] Obviously, the main way of literary creation will gradually turn from literary writing to image expression, and with this turn comes a new critical mode: pictorial or iconographical criticism. Although many people are not aware of this, for us scholars engaged in literary theory criticism and translation studies, we should be aware of the significance of this turn and propose our responses. Therefore, in this sense, we find that due to the change of aesthetic taste in the postmodern consumer society, all kinds of elegant and popular cultural and artistic products can hardly escape the fate of being "consumed". Even the recognized works of elite theorists, such as Heidegger, Freud, Sartre, Derrida and Said, cannot get away from the fate of being "consumed" in the Chinese context, not to mention the illustrated works devoted to visual culture and art. A critical approach focused on pictorial texts will thus emerge with this new aesthetic principle in contemporary literary and art criticism, or in cultural criticism in general.

With the shrinking market of elite literature and the rise of popular culture in the era of globalization, people's visual aesthetic standards have also changed: from the traditional focus on reading textual texts to an increasing focus on reading and appreciating visual texts. The postmodern consumer society has changed people's aesthetic standards, and literary and artistic works have become high-end consumer goods to some extent. Different from the past, many literary masterpieces are also accompanied with exquisite illustrations and photos, which allow the reader to gain more direct sensory satisfaction. We can say that the emergence of this era of iconography today is in fact an inevitable product of post-industrial society reflected in postmodern literature and art. People may ask, since the aesthetic characteristics of modern consumer society have changed as a whole, what are the specific characteristics of the iconographical era arising from this context? If there is indeed such a "turn" in contemporary literary and artistic criticism, how does it differ from the previous textual creation and criticism? In this regard, let us begin by quoting W. J. T. Mitchell, a leading contemporary American picture theorist and cultural critic, who described the characteristics of the pictorial age in general:

> For anyone who is skeptical about the need for/to picture theory, I simply ask them to reflect on the commonplace notion that we live in a culture of images, a society of the spectacle, a world of semblances and simulacra. We are surrounded by pictures, we have an abundance of theories about them, but it doesn't seem to do us any good. Knowing what pictures are doing, understanding them, doesn't seem necessarily to give us power over them. [...] Images, like histories and technologies, are our creations, yet also commonly thought to be "out of our control"—or at least out of "someone's" control, the question of agency and power being central to the way images work.[10]

If this were coming from a painter or visual culture producer, it might be considered too radical, but it is precisely what Mitchell, longtime scholar and editor who has taught and researched literary theory and criticism, has concluded from the changes in his intellectual career. Mitchell has been the editor of *Critical Inquiry,* a well-known journal in the international circles of literary and cultural and theoretical criticism, for a long time, so he has experienced, to a great extent, the ups and downs of Western literary theory and cultural criticism in the past 30 years. He has not only actively advocated picture theory in the United States and Europe over the past 20 years, but also made a profound study of picture theory, and with great enthusiasm called for such a "pictorial turn" in contemporary literature and cultural criticism. In the last decade or so, as a result of his several visits to China to lecture and focus on contemporary Chinese art, and the recent release of the Chinese translation of his theoretical work *Picture Theory*, a "picture fever" seems to have entered contemporary Chinese cultural and artistic criticism. However, the translation studies community in China is relatively slow in responding to this. Even in the eyes of many translation studies scholars, the translation of pictures is not considered translation at all, and "linguo-centrism" still dominates the thinking and writing patterns of translation researchers. Therefore, it is no surprise that works on image criticism and its research are rarely written by scholars who specialize in translation studies, which is a pity. The reason for this should probably be traced back to the definition of the three forms of translation given by Jakobson back then.

Undoubtedly, when Mitchell first raised this issue in 1994, computers were nowhere near as widespread as they are today around the world, and in the world of literary creation and theoretical criticism, textual criticism had always been very strong, while in contrast, visual culture criticism or iconographical criticism were almost relegated to a "marginalized" situation. This is in sharp contrast with the ubiquity of pictures in today's society. In addition, people don't seem to realize that a new era of iconography will come with the digital development and the popularization of computers in the age of globalization. Mitchell's interdisciplinary and cross-artistic approach to both literary criticism and art criticism led him to foresee astutely the shift in critical attention that was bound to occur in the near future. As he pointed out at the international conference "Critical Inquiry: The End of Theory?" held in Beijing in June 2004 that when we opened *Time* at the turn of the century, we suddenly noticed that different images on the cover of the magazine in different periods convey different meanings. When a cloned sheep appears on the cover, it obviously implies that the myth of human invincibility is shattered and the era of "posthumanism" is coming. More and more people have realized that human beings can not only create all human miracles but also create things that can destroy themselves. However, the burning World Trade Center on the cover of the magazine after the 9/11 attacks is not surprising: the once noisy theory has no explanation for this tragic but vivid reality.[11] The weakness of the theory even made some of the theoreticians who originally fought for it lose confidence in it. There is no doubt that these profound pictures are much more advanced than the images created by ancient people. They are generated and supported by high technology in the global digital era, because these modern technologies have not only significantly updated the form of pictures, but also enabled their realistic assembly and even large scale "cloning" (reproduction). To express and interpret these pictures in words, we need the intermediary of translation, but such a difficult translation is no longer a task for the interlingual translator. It should be in front of the interlingual translator who has good artistic and textual training at the same time. In this way, the long-suppressed and even neglected intersemiotic translation has been able to emerge from the "surface" of contemporary visual culture studies.

In fact, scholars of semiotics have done a careful study of pictures, schemata and metaphors to distinguish three forms of iconographical symbols. In their opinion:

> Images are characterized by having simple qualities in common with their object. If a piece of a red carton is used as a sign exhibiting the color of the paint you want to buy, then it functions as a simple iconic sign, an image, of the desired color.[12]

Although they are not involved in iconographical criticism and intersemiotic translation, they have clearly revealed that pictures themselves also have a denotative function in terms of iconography and metaphor. To express the implied meaning, we need well-trained readers to translate and interpret it. However, in text-centric text, pictures are only regarded as additional images inserted into text, while in iconographical writing, pictures occupy a large part of the core of the text. Therefore, iconographical writing has many characteristics of postmodern culture. It indicates not only the decline of text writing and the rise of iconographical writing but also the rise of iconographical criticism dedicated to the examination and study of this genre of writing. Indeed, in a postmodern society, when people's lives are becoming more and more colorful and full of options, they can not only be satisfied with the traditional textual writing and criticism, because reading itself has become a kind of cultural consumption and aesthetic appreciation. According to Roland Barthes, reading should also become an aesthetic "pleasure". However, how to provide such aesthetic pleasure? Obviously, words are not enough to satisfy the eye. In the tedious daily life, it is easy for people to suffer from "aesthetic fatigue" due to reading various text-based documents all day long. Therefore, in order to meet the needs of the general public or consumers, a new form of writing and criticism has emerged, which mainly conveys information through images and pictures, and the information content is again highly condensed into the picture. This undoubtedly reflects the spirit and situation of the postmodern age: the reader is also the viewer, critic and interpreter, and his/her active acceptance and creative construction of the text/picture is beyond control. In addition, the popularity of the Internet makes these "netizens" more powerful. They can maximize their imagination and construct all kinds of beautiful pictures in a virtual cyberspace to meet their aesthetic pleasure and needs. Therefore, the pictorial turning in contemporary literary creation and theoretical criticism is an event that does not depend on people's will. Translation researchers have not yet had a clear understanding of this. However, as more and more pictures appear in the materials available for translators to translate, they cannot avoid the translation of pictures. If we take a closer look at the phenomenon of pictorial or intersemiotic translation in the modern history of China and the West, we can fully predict that this form of translation has not only sprouted in the past, but also has broad space for development in the future, and our research should keep up with it to provide accurate translation-interpretive guidance to our readers. We will discuss this in a later section.

7.3 Pictures crossing the border and the attempt to deconstruct

"Cross the border—close the gap" was a frequently discussed topic in early postmodernism.[13] This topic is often discussed in contemporary Chinese cultural studies, generally referring to crossing the boundary between elite culture and popular culture and filling the gap between high culture and popular culture. This concept is particularly applicable when it comes to the relationship between textual writing and iconographical writing. Since pictorial writing and its criticism also have this "border-crossing" feature, it is even more necessary to elaborate on its specific performance from the interdisciplinary and theoretical perspective. In the field of contemporary cultural criticism and comparative literature, a hot topic is "crossing borders", but more specifically, people put forward a question about the phenomenon of "crossing borders" in contemporary literature and culture: after the tide of postmodernism, where exactly is the boundary of literature? Or they ask further: where is the boundary of literary studies? Will the rise of cultural studies engulf literary studies? Perhaps some conservative literary scholars are very much worried about the "border-crossing" behavior of some young and middle-aged scholars with extensive knowledge and critical spirit. They are afraid that these new generations of literary scholars will overstep the boundaries of literary studies and move into other fields of study to play a large and unwarranted role, or to encroach on the territory of others. Others doubt the legitimacy of literary scholars' study on pictures, and even think that they are not doing their proper work. However, in the view of some open-minded literary researchers, this kind of "border-crossing" behavior not only reflects the characteristics of postmodern literary studies across the disciplinary boundaries, but also subverts the hierarchical order of literature and art, deconstructs the increasingly narrow disciplinary boundaries, and paves the way for interdisciplinary studies of literature and art in the broad cultural context. Moreover, this act itself is also characterized by interdisciplinary comparative literary studies.

As we all know, in the context of China, comparative literary studies has been free from the single distinction between the "French School" and the "American School" from the very beginning, and drawn from the practice of these two schools of thought what is conducive to the comparative study of Chinese and foreign literature. It has had all kinds of "border-crossing" characteristics from the very beginning, so it coincides with the definition of comparative literature given by Henry Remak:

> COMPARATIVE LITERATURE is the study of literature beyond the confines of one particular country, and the study of the relationships between literature on the one hand and other areas of knowledge and belief, such as the arts (e.g., painting, sculpture, architecture, music), philosophy, history, the social sciences (e.g., politics, economics, sociology), the sciences, religion, etc., on the other. In brief, it is the comparison of one literature with another or others, and the comparison of literature with other spheres of human expression.[14]

Generally speaking, there are at least some valid factors why this definition is used today. Even today, when comparative literature in the traditional Eurocentric sense is declared dead, according to Gayatri Spivak, who declared it dead, the new comparative literature should still "always cross borders".[15] This is the reason why comparative literature in China has never died despite the challenge of cultural studies in recent years. From the very beginning, comparative literary studies in China have taken great care to cross the boundaries not only of language but also of disciplines, arts, and cultural traditions. Since iconographical writing and its criticism were not introduced to China until after the discussion of postmodernism, we can regard it as a unique cultural and artistic phenomenon in contemporary postmodern society.

As an inevitable consequence of postmodern society and culture, the rise of iconographical writing is by no means accidental. It is also an inevitable outcome of postmodern consumer society. Like Internet writing, it emerged with the rapid development of information and electronic technology in post-industrial society, so its unique characteristics dictate that it can only emerge in today's postmodern consumer society, where people are more eager to read images than books. It's no surprise that when people finish a day's hard work, what they need most is relaxation, rather than reading books or professional journals assiduously in their spare time. Therefore, they need to consume a variety of cultural and artistic products in a relaxed and pleasant way in order to meet their visual needs. Since various pictorial texts are composed of colorful pictures, they can quickly stimulate people's eyes and satisfy their visual desire, so that they can easily and aesthetically appreciate the pictures and make various associations and imaginings by reading these pictures. It differs from traditional image art in that it progresses with the development of contemporary Internet technology: in a vast online world, tens of millions of Internet users are free to use their imagination and power to express themselves with words in the virtual cyberspace, write various vivid and interesting stories, combine and even collage pictures or images of various colors. In such a virtual cyberspace, classic literary and artistic works are often rewritten or even "spoofed" and lose their original essence. Beautiful pictures can be "made" through computer collage and combination, and even beautiful women and handsome men can be produced through cloning technology. Everything has become so false and fickle, and everything has become a fleeting disposable consumer product. Where has the refined aesthetic sensibility of the modernist period been banished to? This is what many postmodern intellectuals with an artistic conscience and elegant aesthetic taste think about.

There is no doubt that after all, all kinds of popular literary works, good or bad, exist together on the Internet. Some of the "cultural fast food" is thrown into the dustbin only after one-time consumption by consumers. This is also true of Internet art, as every Internet user can go online and function as an "artist" of his or her own. However, we cannot deny the fact that there are always a few truly outstanding works of art on the Internet, and they will gradually show their unique artistic charm and value, which may be drowned out by the current consumer tide, but will be discovered by future researchers. These works may eventually become classics. Moreover, Internet literature and art can also make a few truly outstanding works of art that have been "marginalized" in the contemporary market economy be appreciated by the majority of Internet users and thus return to the classics. In this sense, Internet writing also has the characteristics of "crossing the border" and "filling the gap" in the postmodern era. How does iconographical writing and its criticism that use pictures as the main means of expression "cross the border"? I think this is evident in the following areas.

First of all, all the main means of iconographical writing are images or pictures rather than texts. Here, the text still plays an important function, but it can no longer have the primary function of reproduction as it once had, thus reversing the hierarchy between text and picture and making these colorful pictures full of narrative potential and interpretive tension. It also leaves readers/interpreters/translators great room for association and imagination, in which they can construct and reconstruct freely. It also bridges the gap between readers and critics, so that every reader with certain artistic attainment can directly participate in literary appreciation and criticism. The finalization of the construction of meaning depends to a large extent on the active participation of the reader and the communication and interaction between him and the assumed reader. This undoubtedly reflects the characteristics of postmodern reading.

Secondly, the beautiful and elegant pictures in iconographical writing are largely the product of high technology and digitization in postmodern society, which seem to make the imitation of nature by art return to the primitive stage of mankind. These pictures are closer to nature on one hand, but on the other hand, they are obviously higher than nature after the aesthetic processing of artists. Thus, it transcends the boundary between nature and art, making the depiction and imitation of nature once again the sacred responsibility of the postmodern artist. Postmodern art is a nostalgic art like its predecessor modern art, so at this point, art once again returns to its original imitative character.

Moreover, the third feature of iconographical writing is that it shortens the distance between the author and the reader, or between the photographer and the viewer so that they can communicate and talk at the same level. In this way, the wider the reader's horizon of expectation, the richer content s/he can find in the pictorial text. It can be seen that iconographical writing is in no way a decline in the reader's reading function, but on the contrary, it greatly accentuates the reader's active understanding and creative construction and interpretation. To some extent, the reader of the iconographical text plays three different roles at the same time: reader, translator, and interpreter. The finalization of his/her construction of the meaning of the iconographical text mainly depends on the dual communication and dialogue between the reader and the author as well as between the reader and the text. It is this pluralistic communication and dialogue that makes the interpretation of the textual meaning pluralistic and rich. This in a way also breaks the modernist linguo-centrism and holistic concept.

It is true that Jacques Derrida's death announced the end of deconstruction, but the theory of deconstruction has fragmented into pieces, which in turn have permeated the entire contemporary humanities and social sciences and have had a profound impact on them. One of the important reasons is that his theoretical approach has become a part of the methodology within various fields of the humanities and social sciences. When we commemorate Derrida's historical contribution and summarize his legacy of critical theory, we especially emphasize that his theory deconstructs the long-established logocentric mode of thinking. If this is indeed one of his greatest contributions, then inspired by it, postcolonialism deconstructs the cultural hegemony of imperialism, New Historicism deconstructs the myth of "scientificity" and "objectivity" of history, ecocriticism deconstructs the myth of anthropocentrism, and the attempts made by the cultural translation school deconstructs the myth of literal "faithfulness", and so on. Therefore, where is the deconstructive power of iconographical writing and its criticism? In my opinion, it effectively deconstructs the linguo-centric thinking and writing style, and it liberates the creativity and critical imagination of artists and critics. This potential significance and value may not be recognized by many now, but that is what we will emphasize in this chapter.

Before we move to cross-cultural intersemiotic translation in the next section, I think it is necessary to first describe the expansion of translation frontiers in recent years: even though Jakobson did not regard intersemiotic translation as real (in the narrow sense) translation when he talked about the three aspects of translation, but in fact, his classification has left room for later translation researchers to discuss and develop. It also prefigures the legitimacy of cross-cultural intersemiotic translation studies. If we insist that only translation across language boundaries can be regarded as real translation, then the wave of cultural translation in recent years has actually cleared up this artificial boundary, and the transformation between two cultures realized through language is also regarded as translation in a broader sense. Then, why can't the intersemiotic translation across languages, cultures, and arts be regarded as a kind of translation? From the case study in the next section, we can see the historical origin and contemporary form of intersemiotic translation.

7.4 Intersemiotic translation and Fu Lei's cross-cultural intersemiotic translation

We say that a cross-linguistic and intercultural intersemiotic translation did not suddenly appear before us, so how has it manifested itself in history? Not to mention earlier eras, the differentiation, and analysis of poetry and painting in Gotthold E. Lessing's *Laocoon* in the Western Age of Enlightenment has got an element of intersemiotic translation. Unfortunately, Lessing has not been able to transcend the limitations of Western language and culture. In China, however, we can easily find such examples.

Coincidentally, 2008 marked the 100th anniversary of the birth of Fu Lei (1908–1966), a modern Chinese translator and art theorist. When people remember Fu's historical achievements in literary translation, they cannot help but find that his literary translation has actually transcended the mere transformation between words and reached the realm of intersemiotic translation where sound and pictorial symbols are transformed into words. Indeed, anyone familiar with the history of modern Chinese literature and literary translation cannot deny that Fu is a translator, artist, and writer with a unique position in the history of Chinese literature and cultural translation in the twentieth century. For many years, he has been studied in the domestic translation and cultural academic circles, but most of these studies are limited to his (verbal) translations of French literature, or only to an impressionistic analysis of his (verbal) translations, but not involving his profound artistic attainments and aesthetic pursuits. In fact, we have overlooked another important aspect of Fu's translation practice when evaluating the historical merits of his translations, namely, his translation and interpretation of works of art. It is his profound artistic attainments and unique aesthetic ideals that have made him achieve remarkable achievements in another field of translation: the cross-cultural translation and interpretation of pictures, which is reflected in his creative interpretation of famous European painters and their works in his *20 Lectures on World Masterpieces of Art*. It should be said that this is his most important contribution to cross-cultural intersemiotic translation, which also enables his translation practice to prefigure Jakobson's later theoretical description of the three aspects of translation. Although Jakobson might not know Fu's translation, Fu's practice was ahead of his theoretical description, at least in terms of time.

Admittedly, one might think that Fu's translation of works of art is quite different from his translation of French literature: the latter is essentially a display of his own re-creative style based on word-for-word and sentence-for-sentence rendering, which can be said to have reached a certain degree of re-creative "sense for sense translation", while the former is a kind of intersemiotic translation that reflects his profound cultural heritage and dynamic interpretative power. Therefore, it is not surprising that this kind of interpretative translation of works of art was not recognized by traditional translation researchers for a long time. However, in the face of the cultural turn of translation, such a narrow view of translation obviously does not meet the requirements and expectations of this age, and it is also one of the major reasons why translation studies has been imprisoned in the "cage of language" for a long time. In fact, more and more scholars of the humanities have begun to turn their attention to the historical role of translation and its new functions in this age of globalization. They realize that people today can hardly survive without translation. Of course, this kind of translation also includes one's own translation and assimilation of another culture's language and symbols as they enter one's brain. One of the tasks of today's cultural translation theorists and researchers is to thoroughly deconstruct the traditional view of translation confined to the linguistic level, and then introduce the factors of cultural translation and interpretation. Even in terms of the three aspects of translation described by Jakobson from the perspective of linguistic form—intralingual, interlingual, and intersemiotic translation—intersemiotic translation should at least be regarded as one aspect of (extended or generalized) cultural translation. In fact, many translators in history have made remarkable achievements in their own practice, and their successful experiences have left valuable research materials for our cross-cultural intersemiotic translation studies. Therefore, this aspect of Fu's translation practice naturally belongs to the category of cross-cultural intersemiotic translation. In order to confirm the legitimacy and validity of his translation practice, we first need to change the previous narrow definition and understanding of translation by starting from Jakobson's definition of translation.

We all know that translation research has long been dominated by the "linguocentric" mode of thinking, giving rise to translation studies being considered a branch of contrastive linguistics for a long time. Therefore, translation as it was understood in the past is basically a conversion between two languages, and it is essentially just a language conversion skill. Later, due to the intervention of comparative literature and cultural studies on translation, the scope of this word-for-word language-based type of translation has only gradually expanded to include translation and conversion between two cultures, but the mediator of meaning conversion is still language. Translation began to be examined and studied within the framework of both contrastive linguistics and comparative literature. Of course, in a modern era where textual texts occupy the main reading space of the general public, the translation of language and culture must be the main object of investigation by translation researchers. However, in this postmodern era of information and pictures, the media of information has undergone great changes, and the role of language has also been challenged by other media, especially by various pictures. In people's reading and viewing today, the omnipresence of pictures and the squeezing of textual space make people feel more and more as if we are in such an "age of reading pictures". What we often face is not a text composed mainly of words, but a text composed of both words and pictures, a "linguo-symbolic" or "iconographical" text. Sometimes pictures even occupy more space, while words only act as the incidental explanation of the pictures, which really brings great challenges to our contemporary readers. We should not only be able to read the part of the text that is illustrated, but also be able to read the rich information and meaning contained in the pictures. This requires that our reader-translators have a variety of talents: we should be able to express the meaning of pictures in the form of language (translation); and sometimes when faced with pictures from another language and culture, we also need to have the ability to carry out cross-cultural intersemiotic translation—while interpreting pictures, we also translate into the target language the historical and cultural background knowledge behind the pictures.

Wolfgang Iser, representative of contemporary reception aesthetics and theorist of literary anthropology, has always been concerned with cross-cultural translation and interpretation. When talking about the impact of the changing times on the concept of translation, he points out with great insight,

> We usually associate translation with converting one language into another, be it foreign, technical, vocational, or otherwise. Nowadays, however, not only languages have to be translated. In a rapidly shrinking world, many different cultures have come into close contact with one another, calling for a mutual understanding in terms not only of one's own culture but also of those encountered. The more alien the latter, the more inevitable is some form of translation, as the specific nature of the culture one is exposed to can be grasped only when projected onto what is familiar. In tackling such issues, interpretation can only become an operative tool if conceived as an act of translation.[16]

Although he does not mention intersemiotic translation, he puts forward the same views on the expansion of the territory of translation as we do. Indeed, according to Iser, interpretation is also a form of translatability, and it depends on what is translated. "Interpretation is therefore bound to be different", which is generally reflected in the following three situations:

1. when certain types of text, such as holy or literary ones, are transposed into other types, such as an exegesis of canonical texts or cognitive appraisals of literary texts;
2. when cultures or cultural levels are translated into terms that allow for an interchange between what is foreign and what is familiar, or when entropy is controlled, or when "reality" is to be conceived in terms of interacting systems;
3. when incommensurabilities such as God, the world, and humankind—which are neither textual nor scripted—are translated into language for the purpose of grasping and subsequently comprehending them.[17]

Obviously, we cannot do so if we follow the traditional translation in the narrow sense characterized by conversion between words. It is true that Iser does not mention art here, but from the different kinds of culture he mentions in general, this kind of interpretive translation should undoubtedly include art, because as a form of visual culture, art is also composed of specific pictures with cultural connotations. Therefore, the interpretation of art should also be regarded as an indispensable form of translation.

Looking back at the history of modern and contemporary cultural development in the West, it is not difficult to find that great translators and art theorists, such as Walter Benjamin, Roland Barthes, and Ernst Gombrich, have shown profound attainments in both text and picture, and they have reached an extremely high level in translating and interpreting them. A pictorial text without much explanation in words can be translated and interpreted into a large and rich linguistic text after they read it. However, the image translation they engaged in mainly faced readers in Western cultural contexts and did not reach the realm of image translation across different linguistic and cultural contexts. Of course, we know that contemporary art master Gombrich also had a keen interest in Chinese art during his lifetime, and even had the desire to learn and master Chinese, but his admirable wish was ultimately not realized. His unique interpretation of classical Chinese art through the media of English should undoubtedly be regarded as a cross-cultural intersemiotic translation. However, we know that for Gombrich, who could not read Chinese, the information he received about the historical and cultural background of Chinese art was largely mediated by translations, which, objectively speaking, was very limited. His interpretation of famous Chinese paintings from different dynasties is basically obtained by the historical documents translated into Western languages, previous studies, and his own artistic intuition. Therefore, he himself did not reach the status of cross-cultural intersemiotic translation, but only practiced intra-intersemiotic translation in Western cultural contexts. The intersemiotic translation discussed in this chapter is interlingual and intercultural semiotic translation. In other words, what can be called cross-cultural intersemiotic translation must have the following three basic conditions: first, it should be translation across different languages; second, it should be translation across different cultural traditions; finally, it should be interpretation (translation) across different disciplines and artistic categories. In this respect, Fu's image art translation is very unique. His cross-linguistic and intercultural intersemiotic translations transcend the Western-centric limitations of Benjamin and Gombrich and achieve the status of real intersemiotic translation across languages, disciplines, artistic categories and cultures, and can therefore be said to be intersemiotic in the true sense of the word. His successful translation practice not only provides the best cross-cultural example for the three aspects of Jakobson's translation, but also revises and supplements this relatively universal translation theory from the perspective of the practice of art translation in China. Next, we will discuss his translation practice through the interpretation of his *20 Lectures on World Masterpieces of Art*.

As we all know, written in the 1930s and taught as course material at the Shanghai Academy of Art, Fu Lei's *20 Lectures on World Masterpieces of Art* was intended for a Chinese audience, mostly Chinese students who did not know Western languages or who knew a little English but lacked background knowledge of Western history and culture. Some of them often just knew a little about the history of the development of Western art and began to boldly attack traditional Chinese art, and even put forward some radical anti-traditional art and "innovative" slogans, which Fu disagreed with. In the preface of the book, he pointed out bitterly:

Since the May Fourth Movement, the attitude of learning has become thinner and thinner with the world: speculation has become the norm, and there are those who use scholarship as a tool for gaining fame and fortune; in contrast, the former scholars who stuck to the form and were faithful to imitation were still willing to learn.[18]

Although Fu blamed the world going to the dogs on the negative consequences of the May Fourth New Culture Movement, he still attached great importance to the introduction of Western culture and art, and took up translation as a tool to try to enlighten the young students of the time (aesthetically). Of course, unlike Cai Yuanpei's aesthetic education based on text and theory, Fu chose art education.[19] In Fu's view, pictures give people a sense of art, which can cross the boundaries of language, so that even those who don't understand Western languages can appreciate these works intuitively, thus achieving aesthetic pleasure. However, most of the young students were still unfamiliar with the European art masterpieces at that time, and what was more unfavorable was that many textual materials to illustrate the historical background and implied meaning of the pictures were not readily available in Chinese translation, so Fu's aesthetic education must rely on his own selection and translation. It can be said that when teaching those European art masterpieces, Fu played a dual role as a translator: he not only interpreted the meaning of those art works with elegant modern Chinese literary language but also condensed and translated into concise Chinese the vast amount of historical and socio-cultural background information he had at his disposal to explain the meaning of those works. As he argued in the preface of the book:

> The production of art in a country is forced by the evolution of time, environment, and tradition, just as the growth of plants and animals in a country is forced by soil, climate, temperature, and rainfall. Raphael was born in Italy during the Renaissance, and Molière was born in France in the 17th century, just as orange and olive groves are found in the south. Tao Qian was not born in the West, and Dante was not born in China, as the situation is forbidden by the national nature of the environment. This is one of the things that cannot be ignored in the study of Western art.[20]

Obviously, inspired by Hippolyte Taine's philosophy of art, he realized that since there are so many cultural differences between the East and the West, it is necessary for people to know the Western culture before understanding the art that emerges from the specific Western cultural soil. Therefore, his lectures necessarily began with the religious and cultural-historical background of the West. Only those who are familiar with this historical and cultural background can effectively appreciate the art that emerges from this particular cultural soil. It can be seen that his image translation not only transcends the boundaries of disciplines and arts, but also transcends the boundaries of cultures and languages, so it should be regarded as the crystallization of intersemiotic translation in the broad sense of cultural translation. Although *20 Lectures on World Masterpieces of Art* was only a collection of lecture notes and it does not count as a work of art history for today's readers, Fu mentioned almost all the most important masters in European art in the limited number of lectures: Leonardo da Vinci, Michelangelo, Rembrandt, Peter Paul Rubens, Joshua Reynolds, etc. The detailed explanation of the first three artists is the most wonderful. Now let us take Da Vinci's *Mona Lisa* as an example to see how Fu went about cross-cultural translation and interpretation of the specific works.

As we all know, da Vinci's immortal masterpiece *Mona Lisa* has been favored by art lovers and professionals since it was created. Art theorists from different countries and eras have also tried to interpret, imitate and even parody this monumental European classic painting. However, just like the life span of a literary masterpiece composed of words, this constant interpretation makes the *Mona Lisa* obtain an afterlife in different cultural contexts and different times. From the Chinese translation of the painting used by Fu Lei, "Yaogongte", it is clear that he obtained the background information about the painting through the mediation of French. There is no doubt that Fu was an early artist and translator who interpreted this artistic masterpiece in a Chinese context. In the absence of background information in Chinese at that time, Fu's interpretation of this work is unique and well placed, given his ability to understand the language (in French) and to express it (in Chinese), as well as his ability to appreciate art. In *20 Lectures on World Masterpieces of Art*, he devoted two lectures to introduce da Vinci's life experience and his talents in various fields of art and science to Chinese readers in detail. At the same time, he gave a very precise explanation of the background of the birth of the

Mona Lisa and the profound meaning of the work itself. On the creation and artistic charm of this painting, he noted:

> This supernatural and mysterious charm can indeed describe the charm of Da Vinci's "Yaogongte" (i.e., "Mona Lisa"—cited). This face, once seen once, will never leave our memory. Moreover, "Yaogongte" has general admirers, just like the beautiful women of the world. The first one was, of course, Da Vinci himself, who painted with devout love, and for four years he surrounded the model with musicians, famous painters and comedians, so that her heart and soul would always be immersed in tender pleasure, and her beauty would reveal itself as an extraordinarily soul-stirring allure. Around 1500, Da Vinci took this rare treasure to France, where it was bought by King François I for 12,000 lire (French gold coins). It is clear that this painting was greatly appreciated at that time. Moreover, there is no other painting in the world that can be compared to this painting in terms of its many interpretations. The so-called interpretation is not criticism or analysis of the picture, but passionate exposition of poets and philosophers.[21]

The argument between the poets and the philosophers mentioned here obviously is about the rich aesthetic spirit and cultural meaning contained in this work of art. It is expressed in a still picture, but a dynamic is implied in this stillness, which gives rise to uncertain huge space for translation and interpretation. The translation and interpretation in each language can only approach its meaning from a certain side or angle, but it can never exhaust its profound meaning. Fu was very clear about this, so he believed that one of the incomparable aspects of this work lies precisely in its "multiplicity of interpretations". Today, after reading a lot about the history of art, when we reread his interpretation of art, we still find that many of his unique insights are unprecedented and inspiring even to contemporary appreciators and researchers. Therefore, it can be said that his (translational) interpretation still leaves room for us to undertake further (translational) interpretation. If the interpretation of the *Mona Lisa* by Western theorists from the same linguistic and cultural backgrounds has only reached the point of crossing the boundaries of disciplines and art categories, then there is no doubt that Fu's interpretation of the *Mona Lisa* in another language from a linguistic and cultural context different from that of the West carries the significance of translation that crosses Eastern and Western cultural contexts, and (pictorial) intersemiotic translation.

What is more important to emphasize here is that Fu himself was also very accomplished in music, which has been reflected in his translation of Roman Roland's masterpiece *John Christophe*. In the interpretation of the *Mona Lisa*, he also gave full play to his musical talent, explaining Mona Lisa's smile and eternal charm from the perspectives of scale, harmony, melody, and rhythm. He concluded:

> In music, for example, the commonplace "Carnival of Venice" can also be in harmony with your personal feelings.[22] When you are in pain, it is moaning and hooting; when you are in joy, it becomes a happy chant.

The enigmatic smile of "Yaogongte" is in fact the result of its ability to give us the most elusive, the most "trance-like", the most unpredictable realm. In this respect, Da Vinci's art can be said to be in harmony with the spirit of Eastern art. Chinese poetry and painting, for example, both have the elements of infini and indéfini, allowing the reader's mind and soul to be free to experience and appreciate the world.[23]

It should be said that the examples he gave here of Chinese poetry and Chinese painting are also unique: both have a distant mood, and both have an indefinite space for interpretation. Contemporary aesthetic researchers later saw the commonality between classical Chinese aesthetics and Western phenomenology and hermeneutics, but Fu's artistic intuition made him see this commonality early. However, it is a pity that in many places he only stopped at that point, but did not carry out in-depth theoretical elaboration. After all, he is not a theorist, but an art translator and critic. Therefore, to achieve in-depth theoretical elucidation, it is far from enough to rely on one's language skills, years of artistic experience, and artistic intuition. The translator must also have extensive knowledge of the culture in which the source language symbols (images) are located and be able to express them eloquently in the literary language of the target culture. As for the era of da Vinci, Fu also put it very briefly: in his age, painters were devoted to technique, and demanded perfection of light and darkness, perspective, and anatomy; he had studied these techniques, but he put the bull's-eye of art beyond all these techniques and wanted art to be the only expression of human passion; the knowledge of all techniques is but the most powerful tool. At last, he came back to make the finishing point: in this way, the clear-sightedness, virtue-loving, and gentle mood of the fifteenth century reached its peak with da Vinci.[24] In my opinion, even such a brief summary also shows that Fu had extensive knowledge and profound artistic attainments in cross-cultural intersemiotic translation, which is an important aspect that makes him superior to his contemporary translators and art theorists. At the same time, his successful practice of cross-cultural intersemiotic translation also prefigured Jakobson's theoretical elaboration on intersemiotic translation many years later. If Fu's translation of French literature only meets the reading needs of general literature lovers and the needs of the literary market, then his cross-cultural intersemiotic translation goes beyond the level of practice and rises to the level of theory, and provides a rare example for us to explore and construct a theory of cross-cultural intersemiotic translation from the perspective of visual culture today.

Many years later, when the cultural translation theorist Roger Hart discussed cultural translation from an anthropological point of view, he proposed the concept of "contextual turn".[25] This concept based on anthropology is then applied to the translation of art. As a matter of fact, the translation of art also goes beyond the context, and it should also have a "semiotic turn", so it can certainly contribute greatly to the revision of "intersemiotic translation" as described by Jakobson. Indeed, in this day and age, the traditional narrow definition of translation can no longer be adapted to the ever-changing development of contemporary culture, and the territory of translation is constantly expanding, especially in the translation of images and pictures. According to Wyatt MacGaffey,

> Translating art begins with framing and reframing the physical experience of encountering art, which for most people takes place in a museum or gallery. The style of the museum's building and its announcements of the kind of art within go far toward shaping the visitor's self-definition and his or her sense of the experience to come.[26]

Even so, the translations of art are still different from the translations of text, because the former "are always approximate, but good ones are best regarded as works of art in their own right".[27] However, the evaluation of the latter is more objective than that of the former because there are some obstacles in translating art:

> Impediments to translation in art include the art idea itself, which contains a set of invidious moral distinctions closely related to the ideological functions of art in modern society. Such distinctions are created, maintained, opposed and eventually changed by political action, including critical commentary, translation and retranslation. If elements of chauvinism, racism and condescension should be eliminated, translators still face the basic anthropological problem that societies (by definition) vary in their institutional structure—that is, the way they are organized to carry out basic social functions.[28]

In this way, the translation of art, as an aspect of intersemiotic translation, is far more complex than the translation of text, but at the same time, it is more open to theoretical contention and has a broader space for interpretation.

More than 80 years ago, when Benjamin discussed the relationship between originality and reproduction of artworks in *The Work of Art in the Age of Mechanical Reproduction*, he pointed out insightfully:

> Even the most perfect reproduction of a work of art is lacking in one element: its presence in time and space, its unique existence at the place where it happens to be. This unique existence of the work of art determined the history to which it was subject throughout the time of its existence. This includes the changes which it may have suffered in physical condition over the years as well as the various changes in its ownership. The traces of the first can be revealed only by chemical or physical analyzes which it is impossible to perform on a reproduction; changes of ownership are subject to a tradition which must be traced from the situation of the original.[29]

Of course, what Benjamin talks about here is the reproduction of works of art. Even if a work of art is a product of a particular historical period, it connotes a certain "translatability" or interpretability. The excellence of a good reader-translator lies in his/her ability to look beyond the surface and find this translatability, resonate with it, and finally translate it. Of course, as we all know, his/her translation cannot be 100% faithful to the original, but if it can grasp the spirit of the original and be close to the meaning of the original, it counts as a successful translation. If we do not deny that the emphasis on the faithfulness of translation is precisely like its reproductive feature, we can also apply it to the translation and interpretation of works of art: to translate from one language into another, no matter how different the translators are, the translation will not be very different at least in terms of quantity; but in the translation of art works, the art translator has the function of an interpreter, and the depth of his artistic attainment directly affects his discovery and interpretation of the profound meaning of the art work. A translator who lacks profound artistic attainments can only rely on the ready-made research materials on a work of art in the source language, sort and condense them, and then express them in the target language, without any originality. S/he will be helpless in the face of a newly created artwork without any social background or cultural information. Artists and translators like Fu, however, can at least translate and interpret its profound cultural implications with their own artistic intuition and attainments in the absence of background information. Therefore, while the translation of a text can have a relatively objective and comparable standard, the standard of art translation-interpretation is difficult to grasp, and its re-creative character is more obvious, which therefore places higher demands on the translator-interpreter.

When discussing the interpretation of images, contemporary British art theorist Gombrich points out:

> The reading of a picture again happens in time, in fact it needs a very long time. There are examples in psychological literature of the weird descriptions given by people of the same painting flashed on to a screen for as long as two seconds. It takes more time to sort a painting out. We do it, it seems, more or less as we read a page, by scanning it with our eyes. Photographs of eye movements suggest that the way the eye probes and gropes for meaning differs vastly from the idea of the critics who write of the artist 'leading the eye' here and there.[30]

Although Gombrich says these from the perspective of art psychology, the profound insights implied are at least as follows: the translation and interpretation of artworks depend largely on the translator-interpreter's own artistic training and writing talent, both being indispensable. However, there should be higher requirements for cross-cultural intersemiotic translation, as well as for the study of image translation. If the researcher himself does not have the ability to read pictures, his study of image translation will only be stretched to the limit and ultimately lead people astray.

7.5 Translation and interpretation beyond words

Martin Heidegger points out in his 1938 paper entitled "The age of the world picture":

> As soon as the world becomes picture, the position of man is conceived as a world view. To be sure, the phrase "world view" is open to misunderstanding, as though it were merely a matter here of a passive contemplation of the

world. For this reason, already in the nineteenth century it was emphasized with justification that "world view" also meant and even meant primarily "view of life." The fact that, despite this, the phrase "world view" asserts itself as the name for the position of man in the midst of all that is, is proof of how decisively the world became picture as soon as man brought his life as *subiectum* into precedence over other centers of relationship. This means: whatever is, is considered to be in being only to the degree and to the extent that it is taken into and referred back to this life, i.e., is lived out, and becomes life-experience.[31]

Of course, scholars still have disputes about the exact meaning of this "world picture", but Mitchell believes:

For Heidegger, the ancient Greeks and medieval man did not have a world picture in this sense, one which splits Being into a totalizing object, on the one hand, and a totally perspicuous subject, on the other, who "gets the picture" as if all the world were depicted "before" it, and yet also finds itself "in the picture", as its total situation.[32]

Mitchell here attempts to trace the pictorial description of globalization from Heidegger in order to emphasize the significance of a holistic pictorial portrayal for the present age. In addition, he also tries to demonstrate from a pictorial perspective that the presence of globalization is like a picture that makes people unconsciously feel that they are already in it. It should at least be regarded as one aspect of the study of cultural globalization.

Today, we can clearly feel the advent of this "world picture" era, and in the face of the global expansion of the pictorial world and its ubiquitous and great radiation, people who focus on writing and translation may inevitably feel the declining power of words. Although the use of words and characters has a history of thousands of years, we all know that its golden age will soon be over. One of the important consequences of globalization in this age is that its arrival has redistributed global cultural resources, making the former strong cultures stronger, the previously disadvantaged cultures becoming more insignificant. However, cultures with great potential for development may move from the periphery to the center and dissolve the already existing single "center", which paves the way for the formation of a real multicultural situation. Some kind-hearted intellectuals in China were very worried about the convergence effect that globalization may bring to Chinese culture. However, if we count from the late 1990s, globalization has been in China for more than 30 years. Chinese culture has not been homogenized but is becoming more and more powerful and playing an increasingly important role in a new world cultural landscape. The spectacular opening ceremony of the 2008 Beijing Olympic Games not only surprised the Chinese people but also shocked the Western media: the Chinese, once seen as the "sick men of East Asia", have stood up for themselves. China should become not only an economic and political power but also a cultural and sports power. All knowledgeable people have to realize that the globalization of Chinese culture, literature, and art is no longer a fantasy, it is gradually becoming a reality through the joint efforts of many literary artists and humanities scholars.[33] In this regard, the role of translation will become more and more important, and the demand for highly qualified and high-level translators will naturally become more and more urgent. It can be said that Zhang Yimou, the chief director of the opening ceremony of the Beijing Olympic Games, unconsciously played the role of an intersemiotic translator, but the path he took was the opposite of Fu Lei's translation: Zhang utilized all kinds of high and new technologies in the age of globalization to translate the ancient and indigenous Confucian concepts into colorful images, thus presenting the 5000-year history of Chinese civilization to people who had no idea of this history in just an hour or so. Here, globalization and localization, and tradition and postmodernism finally met and had fruitful exchanges and dialogues. There is no doubt that further in-depth study of the opening ceremony of the Beijing Olympic Games should become an important topic for scholars of cultural studies, and at the same time, it should attract the attention of scholars who study cross-cultural intersemiotic translation.

At present, Chinese language and script with Chinese characters as its basic components is facing a similar fate and future. An important impact of globalization on (language and) culture is that it redistributes global language resources and draws the map of a new global language system, which makes the former strong languages more powerful and the former weak languages more vulnerable. Under the tide of globalization, some languages that are seldom spoken are even dying out, while some languages with limited use but the potential for development are moving from the periphery to the center, and then to the ranks of the strong languages. The Chinese language is one of the direct beneficiaries of cultural globalization. The rapid development of China's economy over the past two decades has led many people outside the Chinese-speaking world to believe that in order to establish close political, economic, and cultural relations with China, they must first learn and master Chinese, and thus the global "Chinese fever" is always "heating up". However, some people are worried about the future of Chinese characters, especially the future of traditional Chinese characters used in calligraphy. Now that the United Nations has passed a bill to abolish traditional Chinese characters as one of the official written languages for the convenience of communication, and now that the popularity of the Internet has made many Chinese-learning foreigners and even some Chinese who have learned Chinese as their mother tongue accustomed to writing in *Pinyin* on the computer, but in real life, they can't write Chinese characters, are Chinese characters in danger of extinction in view of these two factors?[34]

In my opinion, we need not worry about the future of Chinese characters, but we should realize that the reform of Chinese characters is imperative. Otherwise, Chinese will never be mastered by the majority of the world's population, let alone become a major global language. In the tide of digitization and *Pinyin*, the communicative function of Chinese characters, especially traditional Chinese characters, will gradually shrink, but as an artwork, its aesthetic function will be greatly enhanced, and the ability to write beautiful traditional Chinese characters will become a symbol to test one's cultural cultivation and knowledge. Therefore, Chinese characters will not die in the future. Instead, their value will be enhanced. Of course, the cost of this is that fewer and fewer people will be able to write traditional characters and use them in the art of calligraphy. We should also be aware of this historical trend.

Calligraphy is a unique art in Chinese language and culture that combines Chinese characters and images. People who master this art have become fewer and fewer in number today. The popularity of computers has caused many educated people to feel even rusty in writing characters. Nowadays, fewer and fewer young and middle-aged intellectuals can read calligraphy, and even fewer can explain its profound meaning. On the other hand, foreigners interested in Chinese language and culture are more and more interested in calligraphy. Therefore, to make the art of calligraphy go to the world and let people outside the Chinese cultural context appreciate it, cross-cultural intersemiotic translation and interpretation is needed. This translation not only transcends simple textual conversion but at the same time it becomes a pictorial kind of interpretation: it is in the style of calligraphy that the meaning of the old Chinese saying "The writing mirrors the writer" (or: "The style is the man") is best expressed.

At present, iconographical writing and its research are emerging as a pioneering form of art and critical experiment. Image translation is still in its infancy, and many traditional translators and researchers do not even think it is translation. However, it is gradually invading the territory of traditional translation, and the research on it has already appeared in the writings of semiotic and pictorial scholars. Of course, it also, like all historical pioneers, still suffers from loneliness and "marginalization". Even in the Western context, there are few followers and practitioners. However, the rise of iconographical writing and intersemiotic translation poses a new challenge to our translation practitioners and researchers: if one day Chinese characters will become a work of art only for people to appreciate, just like calligraphy, will the intersemiotic translation within or between languages that render them into various languages, including modern Chinese, also become a major aspect of translation? With the rapid development of digitization in the age of globalization, cross-cultural intersemiotic translation will develop rapidly in China, because in the cultural context of China, there has always been a long tradition of pictograms, the unity of poetry and painting, and image writing. Its huge developmental space and potential will be more and more clearly understood. Although the creation of elite literature and art seems to be shrinking in globalization, even Terry Eagleton, who advocates that "[t]he golden age of cultural theory is long past",[35] also realizes:

> In any case, the avant-gardes did not fall because they were not radical enough or audacious enough, or because they were not doing things properly. In this sense, at least, art is absolutely not in control of its own fate. It does not determine its own destiny, as the word "autonomy" might suggest.[36]

Even so, intersemiotic translation and its research will also develop along with other emerging schools of translation studies, such as the postcolonial school of translation, the gender school of translation, the diasporic school of translation, and the ecological school of translation that originated in China,[37] and make great progress.

In discussing the necessity of intersemiotic translation, Jørgen Dines Johansen states bluntly:

> The content substance, however, is not of the nature of language, but of the nature of thought or of the nature of objects, states of affairs, events, and actions. Consequently, neither content nor meaning can be conceived and analyzed immanently, because content and meaning appear in the interplay between the structure of language and what Hjelmslev calls content substance. In other words, neither intralingual nor interlingual translation suffice to establish text meaning. *An intersemiotic translation is necessary.*[38]

It is true that when the words of a language express an imagery with rich connotation, they sometimes lack a vivid texture, and then when they are translated into another language, the connotation will be reduced again. Therefore, images can make up for the inadequacy of verbal expressions, and the role of the cross-cultural intersemiotic translator is what the traditional interlingual translator cannot play. S/he can express images in another language directly with his/her own artistic intuition and talent for verbal and written expression. Although something will be lost in this expression, it will be much less than in the former.

Of course, expressing images with language also involves the relationship between the symbolicity and the iconicity of images. In this regard, Johansen further points out:

> I have argued that the distinction between iconicity and symbolicity lies in the fact that iconicity is bound up with the sharing of perceptible properties between sign and object. Even if these are stereotyped or merely relational, some principle of translation exists that relates the qualities and structures of the sign-vehicle to those of the object, and *nota bene* a principle of translation that makes evident they share these properties. In other words, the important *articulatory fit* is between sign and object.[39]

In other words, just like the translation of language and text, there is a kind of translatability between the symbol and the object, but this translatability of the symbol has more interpretative tension than the single translatability of the text. Therefore, translators' skill in reading images should be as good as their ability to express themselves verbally. Otherwise, when they face an image, they will be at a loss.

Notes

1 Jakobson, R. 1992. On linguistic aspects of translation. In R. Schulte & J. Biguenet (eds.), *Theories of Translation: An Anthology of Essays from Dryden to Derrida*. Chicago, IL & London: The University of Chicago Press, 145.
2 Eagleton, T. 1997. The contradictions of postmodernism. *New Literary History*, 28(1): 1. The Chinese translation of this article was first published in the second issue of *Guowai Wenxue* [Foreign Literatures] in 1996.
3 The indirect citation here comes from Eagleton's keynote speech at "the International Conference on Cultural Studies: China and the West" (Dalian, China, August 1995).
4 The Chinese translation of this paper can be seen in the third issue of *Nanfang Wentan* [Southern Cultural Forum] in 2001.
5 Jameson, F. 1983. Postmodernism and consumer society. In E. Foster (ed.), *The Anti-Aesthetic: Essays on Postmodern Culture*. Seattle: Bay Press, 143.
6 For a review of Jameson's visit to China in 1985 and his lecture at Peking University, please refer to Chen, C. & Yin, X. 2007. A lecture and academic transformation in the new era: An interview with Wang Ning and Wang Fengzhen. *Zhongguo Tushu Pinglun* [China Book Review], (1): 76–79.
7 Cf. Jameson, F. 1991. *Postmodernism, or, the Cultural Logic of Late Capitalism*. Durham, NC: Duke University Press, 31.
8 For the English translation, see Baudrillard, J. 1988. *Selected Writings*. M. Poster (ed. & intro.). Stanford, CA: Stanford University Press, 29.
9 I should admit that I borrowed the word "iconography" from W. J. T. Mitchell, an American image theorist. He published in 1986 a collection of papers titled *Iconology*. On this basis, the author added the element of characters to form the term "iconography".
10 Cf. Mitchell, W. J. T. 1994. Introduction. *Picture Theory*. Chicago, IL & London: The University of Chicago Press, 5–6.
11 You can refer to the Chinese translation of Mitchell's speech: Mitchell, W. J. T. 2006. After theory is dead? P. Li (trans.). In X. Chen & Y. Li (eds.), *Beijing University Year's Selection 2005: Theory Volume*. Beijing: Peking University Press, 116–120.
12 Johansen, J. D. 1993. *Dialogic Semiosis: An Essay on Signs and Meaning*. Bloomington & Indianapolis: Indiana University Press, 98.
13 Fiedler, L. 1972. *Cross the Border—Close the Gap*. New York: Stein and Day, 80.
14 Remak, H. 1961. Comparative literature, its definition and function. In N. Stallknecht & H. Frenz (eds.), *Comparative Literature: Method and Perspective*. Carbondale: Southern Illinois University Press, 1.
15 Spivak, G. C. 2003. *Death of a Discipline*. New York: Columbia University Press, 16.
16 Iser, W. 2000. *The Range of Interpretation*. New York: Columbia University Press, 5.
17 Ibid., pp. 6–7.
18 Fu, L. 1997. *Twenty Lectures on Masterpieces of World Art* (2nd ed.). Beijing: SDX Joint Publishing Company, VI.
19 Translators' note: Cai Yuanpei (1868–1940) is an influential figure in the history of Chinese modern education. He was the president of Peking University.
20 Ibid.
21 Fu, L. 1997. *Twenty Lectures on Masterpieces of World Art* (2nd ed.). Beijing: SDX Joint Publishing Company, 26–27.
22 Translators' note: The "Carnival of Venice" is based on a Neapolitan folk tune called "O Mamma, Mamma Cara" and popularized by violinist and composer Niccolo Paganini.
23 Ibid., p. 29.
24 Ibid., p. 42.

25 Hart, R. 1999. Translating the untranslatable: From copula to incommensurable worlds. In L. H. Liu (ed.), *Tokens of Exchange: The Problem of Translation in Global Circulations*. Durham, NC & London: Duke University Press, 59.
26 MacGaffey, W. 2003. Structural impediments to translation in art. In P. G. Rubel & A. Rosman (eds.), *Translating Cultures: Perspectives on Translation and Anthropology*. Oxford & New York: Berg, 255.
27 Ibid., p. 257.
28 Ibid., p. 263.
29 Benjamin, W. 2006. *A Short History of Photography + The Work of Art in the Age of Mechanical Reproduction*. C. Wang (trans.). Nanjing: Jiangsu People's publishing house, 51. Translators' note: In translating this passage from the Chinese original we have consulted the English version from *Illuminations*, edited by Hannah Arendt, translated by Harry Zohn, from the 1935 essay. New York: Schocken Books, 1969.
30 Gombrich, E. H. 1989. *The Image and the Eye: Further Studies in the Psychology of Pictorial Representation*. J. Fan, S.Yang, Y. Xu, & C. Lao (trans.). Hangzhou: Zhejiang Photography Publishing House, 53. Translators' note: In translating this passage from the Chinese original we have cited the English original by Gombrich, E. H. 1982. *The Image and the Eye: Further Studies in the Psychology of Pictorial Representation*. Oxford: Phaidon Press Limited, 50.
31 Heidegger, M. 1977. The age of the world picture (1938). In W. Lovitt (trans. & ed.), *The Question Concerning Technology and Other Essays*. New York: Harper Torchobooks, 133.
32 Mitchell, W. J. T. 2007. World pictures: Globalization and visual culture. *Neohelicon, 34* (2): 55.
33 On August 9, 2008, the day after the opening ceremony of the Beijing Olympic Games, I was interviewed by a BBC reporter on the campus of Tsinghua University. From what the reporter said, I felt that most Westerners had realized that China is no longer a developing country in the Third World. In the future, only a few big countries can take turns to host the Olympic Games. In terms of the spectacle of the opening ceremony of the Beijing Olympic Games, the organizers of the next London Olympic Games could only look up to it.
34 Translators' note: *Pinyin,* abbreviated from *Hanyu Pinyin,* is the official romanization system for Standard Mandarin Chinese in the mainland of China and to some extent in Taiwan, and in Singapore.
35 Eagleton, T. 2003. *After Theory*. London: Penguin Books, 1.
36 Eagleton, T. 2004. The fate of the arts. *The Hedgehog Review*, 6(2): 13.
37 For Ecological translatology, please refer to my article: Wang, N. 2011. Eco-literature and eco-translatology: Deconstruction and construction. *Zhongguo Fanyi* [Chinese Translators Journal], (2): 10–15. In this regard, the Chinese scholar Hu Gengshen is a representative.
38 Johansen, J. D. 1993. *Dialogic Semiosis: An Essay on Signs and Meaning*. Bloomington & Indianapolis: Indiana University Press, 48.
39 Ibid., 139.

8 Translation and the relocation of cultures

According to the postcolonial theorist Homi Bhabha, translation, especially cultural translation, plays an important role in the location of culture.[1] Here, the word "culture" used by Bhabha is singular, but I express it in plural based on the pluralistic trend and diverse characteristics of culture in this age of globalization. In other words, an important function of translation is the relocation of different cultures in the era of globalization. This makes the task undertaken by the translator even more important. There is no doubt that Bhabha's view has widely influenced contemporary translation studies, especially translation studies from the perspective of culture, and greatly expanded the scope of translation. However, people can't help asking: to what extent can Chinese culture be "relocated" in the global cultural landscape? This is indeed an issue of interest to all scholars concerned with China and Chinese culture. In my opinion, cultural diversity in the age of globalization is significantly more pronounced than cultural convergence as a direct consequence of such cultural location and relocation. In this respect, translation has been playing a leading role: as a mediator and translator between different cultures. However, translation in this sense has long gone beyond its simple function of linguistic conversion. If we say that the large-scale literary and cultural translations in China in the first half of the twentieth century have brought Chinese literature and culture closer and closer to the mainstream of world culture and literature, then the practice of Chinese literary and cultural translations in the past decade or two has enabled Chinese literature and culture to engage in equal dialogue with the world. It can be said that the former is at the cost of "total Westernization" of Chinese culture and language, while the latter will lead to a greater contribution of Chinese literature and culture to global cultures and world literatures, because it is "relocating" global cultures with a positive attitude and playing its due role in remapping world literatures.

8.1 From global English(es) to global Chinese(s)

In a paper I published a few years ago exploring globalization and culture, I tried to describe the current situation of Englishes and Chineses in the plural form, aiming to emphasize the feature of diversity that globalization brings to contemporary culture.[2] There is no doubt that English and Chinese, as two major languages in the world, have both been in a state of fission: English evolved from a national language to a global lingua franca long ago, with different variants forming in different countries and regions; and under the impact of globalization, Chinese has also begun to change from a national language spoken mainly in the mainland of China, Hong Kong and Taiwan to a regional language, and is developing into a global language. In this part of the present chapter, I will first review this topic but mainly focus on the global characteristics of Chinese. In the past few years, there has been a so-called "Chinese fever" around the world. With the strong support of the Chinese government, hundreds of Confucius Institutes and more than 2000 Confucius classrooms have been set up around the globe. However, we should still acknowledge that the status of English as the lingua franca of the world today cannot be changed, at least in the near future. However, as has been noted,

> [t]he growth of the use of English as the world's primary language for international communication has obviously been continuing for several decades. But even as the number of English speakers expands further there are signs that the global predominance of the language may fade within the foreseeable future.[3]

That is to say, with the rise of other world languages, the hegemony of English will eventually be broken. Indeed, in the era of globalization, the hegemony of English, as a global lingua franca, has been strongly challenged by several other powerful languages. Among these powerful languages, Chinese undoubtedly occupies the most prominent position and will increasingly show its irresistible and powerful vitality.

As we all know, in the last ten or more years, the status of the Chinese language has been rising rapidly due to China's continued economic growth and rapid increase in comprehensive national power, but as one has to admit, "[s]ome 30 percent of the world's books are published in English (Chinese is second at 11 percent)".[4] Although Chinese language publications rank second, most of them are found in the Chinese mainland, Hong Kong and Taiwan, and rarely enter the world book market. As the "Chinese fever" continues to heat up, this percentage will change in the near future. In recent years, the popularity of Chinese books in international book fairs and the copyright export of Chinese books have proved this point. Therefore, as Bhabha insightfully pointed out, in today's world, there is an acceleration of globalization on the one hand, and a slow advance in the process of minoritization on the other, but the latter should be another form of globalization.[5] Thus according to Bhabha:

> …we are led to a philosophical and political responsibility for conceiving of minoritization and globalization in a dynamic, even dialectical relation, that goes beyond the polarizations of the local and the global, the center and the periphery, or, indeed, the citizen and the stranger. The most recent United Nations Educational, Scientific and Cultural Organization (UNESCO) report of the World Commission of Culture and Development suggests that the minoritarian condition is, indeed, a kind of global citizenship.[6]

Of course, this "minoritization" is a symbolic use of the term to refer to vulnerable groups that do not have hegemonic power. Despite its large size and population, China's international status has not been high for a long time, and the Chinese do not hold much of a voice in international affairs. However, in the globalization-minority confrontation, the world language system has been greatly "remapped". Some of the previously hegemonic languages, such as French, German, Russian, and Japanese, are gradually weakening and shrinking, while other newly emerging languages, such as Spanish, Arabic and Chinese, are becoming more and more popular. This leads to a new world cultural pattern. Therefore, it is quite appropriate for us to use the term "glocalization" to describe the developmental trend of world cultures in the future. That being the case, one might ask another question: in the era of globalization, since China's economy has grown rapidly in the past two decades, and the status of Chinese culture has also been greatly improved, what is the future orientation of Chinese? That's what I'll discuss later. In this section, I just want to describe the changes that have taken place in Chinese in the past ten years or so: it has changed from merely a national language to a regional as well as a major world language.

As a big country, both in size and population, China once had the title of "Middle Kingdom" in history. However, after the Opium War broke out in 1840, the weak and corrupt Qing government signed a series of unequal treaties with Western powers, Russia and Japan. Because of these disempowering treaties, large areas of Chinese land were ceded or placed under colonial rule. This situation naturally affected the status of the Chinese language. In Northeast China and Taiwan, people were forced to learn Russian and Japanese, respectively, and even communicated and worked using those foreign languages in their own country. In Hong Kong, all government officials must first learn and master English, because until its return in 1997, all government documents were first issued in English. The former Golden Empire was on the verge of disintegration and was gradually marginalized in the world. In order to restore the past glory and comprehensive national strength, some educated people in China had to look to the economically developed countries of the time and launched a massive translation campaign. After this attempt of "total Westernization", Chinese culture was almost reduced to a marginalized "colonial" culture. The large-scale literary and cultural translation and the introduction of Western academic thought have once led to the "Europeanization" or "colonization" of the Chinese language. Almost all Chinese intellectuals then believed that in order to keep up with the developed countries, they must catch up with them politically, economically and culturally. How to catch up with those developed countries? China could do so only by translating and introducing as many Western cultural trends, philosophical theories and literary works as possible. Therefore, China's political and cultural modernity emerged as an inevitable consequence of translation. It can be seen that the role of translation in the political and cultural enlightenment of modern Chinese history is unparalleled and goes far beyond mere language and text. Even leading intellectuals and writers such as Lu Xun spent a lot of time translating foreign literary works, and the number of words in his translated works even exceeded that in his own works.

On the other hand, Chinese culture travels around the world as many Chinese immigrate to different countries, but at a very slow pace, and many have to temporarily abandon their native language in favor of the local language in order to assimilate into the country where they have settled. They also played the role of coordinator and translator between the two languages and cultures concerned at first, but later, many of them became localized. Nevertheless, the values and aesthetic sentiments of Chinese culture are still hidden in the depths of their memories. Although this large-scale migration did make some Chinese cultural conventions spread abroad, the Chinese language itself has not had much influence in the world. Among the Chinese immigrants abroad, many people first consider how to enter the mainstream culture of the country where they live. They are aware that to be in the mainstream cultural circle, they must learn and master their language first. If you want to master the essence of a foreign language, you must think and express ideas in that language, and sometimes even forget your native language for a while. This ironic phenomenon often appears in the works of many Chinese American writers. Many of them do not want to be called "Chinese" American writers. They insist on writing in English, but the idea from Chinese culture which is inherited and hidden in their deep memory often manifests itself in their writing in a circuitous way. Therefore, they also play the role of cultural "translator" and "coordinator": constantly reconstructing and relocating Chinese culture. However, what many people do is to adapt Chinese culture to the cultures and customs of the countries where they live, so as to cater to the local readers and audiences.

Many other Chinese immigrants continue to promote the Chinese language and culture in the countries where they have settled. They insist on writing in Chinese and publishing Chinese newspapers, books, and magazines in their host countries. Take North America as an example. In many North American universities today, many children of second or third-generation Chinese immigrants are taking Chinese language and culture courses in the Department of East Asian Languages and Literatures in order to find their own national and cultural identity, which is also the personal experience of many Chinese American writers and intellectuals.[7] Many of them are often in a state of contradiction: on the one hand, they try to express ideas from Chinese cultural experience in English; on the other hand, in order to cater to the appreciation of mainstream culture, they have to describe Chinese cultural conventions in a critical or even distorted way, showing some ugly things of Chinese people in their works. In any case, their "translation" and then dissemination of Chinese culture have promoted Chinese culture all over the world. We must not underestimate this effect.

In fact, driven by the wave of globalization, Chinese has gradually become another major global language, which is of great significance for us in disseminating and popularizing Chinese literature and culture around the world. If Chinese could really become as inclusive and hybridized as English, it would be made the second most used language in the world next to English, because it can play a role that English sometimes does not, and in more ways than one, it can also interact with and complement English as a major world language.

Of course, it is undeniable that the Chinese government has made great efforts to popularize and promote the Chinese language and culture, and is beginning to see results. Just as the British Council has spared no effort to promote English teaching and cultural communication overseas for decades, the Chinese government has also set up hundreds of Confucius Institutes abroad, and through this intermediary promote Chinese and spread Chinese culture. The difference between the two is as follows: the former has long reaped huge benefits, including lucrative economic benefits, while the latter has invested heavily and was just beginning to see the first results when in some countries in Europe and America Confucius Institutes were forced to close down. Nevertheless, we can still foresee that in the coming years, these Confucius Institutes will make remarkable achievements in terms of cultural influence and economic benefits.

Thus, the process of cultural globalization has broken down the ethno-national boundaries and at the same time extended the borders of the world's major languages. On the one hand, Chinese as a regional-global language advances the process of cultural globalization, and on the other hand, cultural globalization promotes the spread and popularization of Chinese around the world. In this process, some minor languages have fallen victim to cultural globalization, while the previously popular and frequently used languages, such as English, Chinese and Spanish, have become more and more popular. This helps not only to reconstruct the layout of the world language system but also to set up a new pattern of global cultures. In this new pattern, Chinese will play an increasingly important role.

Therefore, we can predict that under the influence of globalization, a new world cultural framework will soon be formed, which remains largely bounded not only by nation-states, but also by languages, i.e., not just one English culture, but multiple cultures written and recorded in English, and in this regard, both cultures and Englishes should be plural. Similarly, in the new framework of coexistence of different cultures in the future, Chinese culture will become increasingly important as the "Chinese fever" continues to rise worldwide. As translators and scholars of translation studies, we should also answer the question: since the functions of translation are constantly changing, how can we relocate Chinese culture in the context of globalization? This is exactly what I will discuss in the next section.

8.2 Translating China and publishing in international academic circles

There is no doubt that translating China and publishing internationally cannot be done without the mediation of translation, which are, in fact, two different forms of translation. Even when we write directly in English, we cannot do it without translating Chinese materials, experiences, perspectives, and viewpoints into a language that readers in the English-speaking world can understand. Therefore, this is much different from our long-standing practice of translating foreign language writings into Chinese, and it is much more difficult. As we all know, in the history of modern Chinese literature and thought, translation has played a huge role. Through translation, the latest cultural trends and theories as well as excellent literary works from abroad have entered China, bringing Chinese culture and literature closer to the mainstream of world culture and literature. In many people's eyes, the history of modern Chinese literature is almost a "translated" literary history, and the influence of foreign countries, especially from the West, is evident. However, when we reflect on the great achievements of literary and cultural translation, we can't help but feel a certain regret: when we translated foreign academic thoughts and literary works, especially Western ones, into Chinese on a large scale, we seldom translated China's own cultural theories and literary works into major world languages. Even though excellent translators like Yang Xianyi and his wife Gladys Yang spent a lot of time and energy translating excellent works of Chinese literature into English, the circulation channels of these works are far from satisfactory, and many translated Chinese literary works are only occasionally consulted by scholars engaged in Sinology or translation studies, and are far from entering the English book market, let alone being read by the general English-speaking world. Therefore, many people believe that the translation of Chinese culture and literature is mainly the task of translators in the target language, which of course makes sense. However, if we look back carefully, how many of those sinologists who are proficient in Chinese are willing to spend their whole life on translating and introducing Chinese culture and literature? It can be said that there are only a handful, so only a few lucky authors have benefited so far. The reason why Gao Xingjian, a Chinese French writer, won the Nobel Prize for literature in 2000 is largely due to his English translator Mabel Lee, who translated Gao's masterpiece *Ling Shan* (Soul Mountain) into beautiful English, which was then recognized by the English-speaking world and the Nobel Prize Committee for literature and won the prize. Similarly, Mo Yan, the Nobel laureate in 2012, has even benefited more so: if there had been no sinologists Howard Goldblatt and Anna Gustafsson Chen who translated his main works into beautiful English and Swedish, Mo Yan's award would have been delayed for at least ten years, or maybe he would have missed out on this award during his lifetime. Such examples are not uncommon in the history of world literature in the twentieth century. We can see how important the role of translation is! Of course, there is no shortage of contemporary Chinese writers who are as good as Mo Yan—at least such authors as Jia Pingwa, Yan Lianke, Wang Anyi, Yu Hua, Liu Zhenyun, and Can Xue are comparable to him, but Mo Yan is indeed very lucky that Goldblatt's translation not only retells his story in English to a certain extent but also enhances the language level of the original, making it aesthetically appealing and moving to readers. It can be seen that an excellent translator can not only faithfully convey the meaning of the original, but also enhance the aesthetic form of the original, while in contrast, a poor translator can even make an otherwise good work pale in the target language. There are many such examples in the history of literature and translation. I will discuss this later.

Just as what the deconstructive theorist Hillis Miller summarizes:

> A work is, in a sense, "translated," that is, displaced, transported, carried across, even if it is read in its original language by someone who belongs to another country and another culture. In my own case, what I made, when

I first read it, of Georges Poulet's work and, later on, of Jacques Derrida's work was no doubt something that would have seemed more than a little strange to them, even though I could read them in French. Though I read them in their original language I nevertheless "translated" Poulet and Derrida into my own idiom.[8]

Here, I would like to emphasize that writing academic papers and monographs in English is another form of translation, especially for our Chinese humanities scholars, because when we write and publish about Chinese humanities research in the world's major languages or examine and analyze issues from our unique Chinese perspective, this is itself a form of cultural translation in the broad sense. However, the importance of this form of translation is not yet recognized by many Chinese scholars. They are still stuck in the debate between the so-called "external study of translation" and the "ontological study of translation".

We still remember that the Indian American postcolonial theorist Gayatri Spivak, in a famous paper entitled "Can the subaltern speak?", tried to defend those from the lower classes of the Third World who have been unable to make their voices heard in international forums for too long. Even if they intend to speak, they cannot be "heard" or "recognized" by others.[9] All they can do is find some sort of intermediary through which to make their voices heard. As we know, despite the attention China has received from the world because of its economic takeoff, it has long been a third world country after all. Therefore, if we follow Spivak to reflect on the current situation of international China studies, we will find that Chinese domestic scholars have little voice in international China studies, especially in the humanities. Therefore, can we change the title of Spivak's article to "Can the Chinese speak at international forums?" I think the answer should be yes. Even in the past, they were able to speak, but they did not have the opportunity to do so, or rather, no one wanted to listen to them. That is, even if they had such an opportunity, the voice they made is difficult to be heard, or others simply did not want to hear them speak. I think this is partly due to the absence of translation, and partly due to the fact that our domestic scholars have paid little attention to the importance of writing directly in a foreign language (another form of translation).

Now let us review the situation of China studies in the West. In those early days, when we picked up an English journal of China studies, it was almost difficult to find the names of Chinese authors. Even if you occasionally saw a Chinese name, you would find that he or she was either from Hong Kong or Taiwan or was a Chinese scholar who lived in the West. Indeed, it was very difficult for domestic scholars of the humanities and social sciences to have the opportunity to publish papers in such journals. In contrast, their domestic counterparts in the natural sciences had already targeted cutting-edge international academic topics and started publishing in those top academic journals.

As we all know, in the 1980s, China was a very open country, and almost all of the leading Western academic and theoretical works as well as literary works were translated and introduced into China. At that time, many of these translators were novices, and I myself had the audacity to translate world literary and academic classics. As a result, there was an imbalance in the cultural and academic exchanges between China and the West: an open China was eager to learn about what was happening in the outside world, especially the latest developments in Western academic circles, while the outside world knew little about China, or was less concerned with what was happening in China and was especially reluctant to listen to what the Chinese themselves had to say about Chinese culture. Obviously, there are various reasons behind this. Of course, China was still economically lagging behind at that time, and a country that lags behind is not considered to be qualified to serve as a good model to the world. In the past, some people said that "weak countries have no diplomacy". In academic circles, this would be "weak countries have no scholarship" or "weak countries have no culture". Another important reason is that most Chinese scholars did not learn English well enough to communicate orally, much less to publish. Therefore, in the international academic circles then, Chinese scholars indeed suffered from "aphasia". The only thing they could do was to wait passively for foreign sinologists to "discover" them, like "waiting for Godot", but even so, most of them couldn't have their works translated into foreign languages and published abroad.

In the years when Chinese scholars "lost their voices", the international academic circles' understanding of China has depended largely on the description of sinologists, and they seem to be speaking for China and publishing works on Chinese studies in international academic journals. Frankly speaking, most sinologists are friendly to their Chinese counterparts. They love China and most of their research results published are based on their long-term in-depth research and serious thinking. However, due to the limitations and prejudice of Orientalism for a long time, the image of China in the eyes of Westerners has always been illusory and untrue, which unavoidably affects the research of these sinologists. As a result, a few of these sinologists think highly of themselves and simply despise domestic Chinese scholars, believing that only they can speak and describe China in the international academic community. Ironically, what they speak or write about China is mostly based on misunderstandings or misinterpretations of China, and the information they have is not very comprehensive, which cannot show the real China to the world. Of course, in those closed years, their words and writings were more or less convincing to the outside world, but in essence, they are by no means representative of international China studies as a whole.

Some 40 years have passed, and the humanities and social sciences in China have undergone tremendous changes. We are very pleased to see that in the library of any research university in the world today, we can easily find academic works and journals on China issues. We are even more glad to find that in almost all journals on Chinese studies, we can easily see the names of some Chinese authors, and some of them are scholars from universities or research institutions in the mainland of China. As far as I know, the editors of almost all these journals are very eager to hear the voice of Chinese scholars, and some of them also ask me to recommend excellent papers of Chinese scholars to them. Even if these papers are written in Chinese, they can organize manpower to translate them into English. One may ask, is the English proficiency of the Chinese authors who published papers in international journals really better than that of the scholars in the 1980s? I don't think so. When I was engaged in postdoctoral research at Utrecht University in the Netherlands from 1990 to 1991, I published my first English paper in the sinological journal *China Information*, discussing the reception of Freudianism in modern Chinese literature. What I still remember is that I made a related speech at the Sinological Institute of Leiden University. The editor of the journal listened carefully to my lecture and then wanted me to give her the manuscript to see if it was suitable for publication in the journal. She read my article with a friendly and serious attitude, made some major modifications and refinements, and then sent me the proofs for review. It was through my English paper published in that international journal of Chinese studies that I became familiar with some of the knowledge and norms of academic writing in English, which laid the foundation for my subsequent successive publications in international humanities and social science journals.

In any case, in this era of globalization, this is already a big step forward. China can be said to be one of the countries that have benefited most from globalization in the world today, which is not only reflected in economy and politics, but also in culture. With the rapid development of China's economy, its international image as a political and economic power is no longer under any doubt, but we still have to work hard to build up the image as a cultural power. In this regard, translation will play a unique and decisive role. The advent of globalization has indeed provided us with a broad platform for scholars from different countries to have equal dialogue and to exchange and discuss their views on issues of common concern. In this respect, natural scientists are really ahead of us. They have already put much effort into publishing their works in the international academic community. What are our humanities and social science scholars doing about it?

As an emerging scientific and technological power, China's role has been increasingly recognized by the international community, but what is the international position of China's humanities and social sciences? Although many domestic scholars have realized the importance of publishing works in international journals, they are not optimistic about the results. Since in many fields of the humanities and social sciences, only a very few Chinese scholars have been able to publish in major international academic journals, how can we make our voices heard in the international community? Take the humanities in my field as an example. In the mainstream international journals of philosophy and social sciences, we hardly see papers by Chinese scholars, not to mention equal exchanges and dialogues with international peers. In my opinion, in addition to the lack of the necessary training in professional English writing, many scholars even lack the basic academic training in thinking and writing. They can only relay the theoretical views of international academic masters to domestic readers in Chinese, but they cannot communicate and engage in dialogue with their international counterparts. That is to say, when discussing issues with international counterparts, they lack the fundamental awareness of problems and the power to speak. Nevertheless, many editors of international academic journals, including journals on China studies, still want to read the works of Chinese scholars. They know that when discussing some basic theoretical topics, they need to hear the voices of all the scholars, whether they are from the East or the West. The editors of some of these journals even invite influential Chinese scholars to edit special issues by inviting distinguished scholars in related disciplines to contribute to the special issues. In this way, these editors get to hear from real Chinese scholars on cutting-edge topics of common concern. For the excellent papers of Chinese scholars who have profound academic attainments but have an inadequate command of or do not understand English, they even organize efforts to translate them into English and publish them in their journals. In addition to inviting scholars to write directly in English, some major international academic publishing institutions have also organized efforts to translate outstanding works of Chinese scholars into English for publication in the English-speaking world.[10] To be fair, however, few Chinese scholars have been chosen by these publishing organizations to have their works translated and published. It is in sharp contrast to the domestic publishing industry, which is scrambling to translate and publish Western academic works.

I have been invited to edit special issues for some international academic journals since the late 1990s. Although only a very few of the special issues I have edited have been published in China studies journals, one can easily find that almost all of them are relevant to China studies or address fundamental questions of common interest to Chinese and Western scholarship from a global or comparative perspective. That is to say, when we publish internationally, Chinese scholars should focus on Chinese issues, especially contemporary ones. This is exactly what foreign researchers of China studies can hardly do well, but our domestic scholars are good at. In writing and publishing in English, we actually play the role of translators: it is not translating our ready-made Chinese works into English word by word but expressing our thoughts directly in English. I always believe that in order to promote Chinese culture around the world, we can rely on the help of sinologists to some extent, but we should rely more on our own efforts. In particular, it is important to rely on one's own strength and to adopt a Sino-foreign cooperation approach in bringing the research results of humanities to the world. Sinologists are after all very limited in number and the excellent ones who are proficient in more than two languages and cultures are rare. Even if they attain this level, they tend to be more concerned, as we are, with publishing their own research and less inclined to take the time to translate what others have done into their own native language. I believe that with more and more domestic scholars beginning to focus on writing or publishing in English, international journals on China studies will also play an increasingly important role in publishing outstanding works of Chinese scholars. In this way, Chinese scholars can really make their own voices heard in international forums.

8.3 Translation and the future of Chinese

On October 11, 2012, the Swedish Academy announced the award of that year's Nobel Prize in Literature to Chinese author Mo Yan (penname of Guan Moye) "who with hallucinatory realism merges folk tales, history and the contemporary" in an achievement that is difficult to replace. According to the Swedish Academy's permanent secretary Peter Englund, "[h]e has such a damn unique way of writing. If you read half a page of Mo Yan you immediately recognize it as him".[11] This is indeed very high praise, which is not without exaggeration, but one wonders whether Englund read Mo Yan's works in the original, or Howard Goldblatt's English translation or Anna Gustafsson Chen's Swedish translation. The answer to the puzzle is obviously the latter two, because we all know that among the 18 members of the Swedish Academy of Letters, the only one who knew Chinese was Göran Malmqvist, but he did not say this. It can be seen that successful translations have reached the point of helping literary works to achieve "canonization", which is precisely the advanced state of "re-creation" that literary translations should reach. Likewise, it was thanks to Goldblatt's English translation and Chen's Swedish translation that Donald Morrison, a journalist for *Time* magazine, was able to call Mo Yan one of the most famous, often banned and widely pirated of all Chinese writers.[12]

There is no doubt that Mo Yan's winning of the Nobel Prize in Literature has had a great impact on domestic and international literary and cultural circles, and the vast majority of Chinese writers and readers consider it a welcome start for Chinese literature to be truly recognized by international authorities. In fact, as far as I know, Mo Yan's award is no accident. As early as the early 1990s, Goldblatt began to translate Mo Yan's works and published his first translation, *Red Sorghum*, in 1993, while Mo Yan was just emerging on the domestic literary scene, and his popularity was far behind many contemporary Chinese writers. Although Mo Yan's literary achievements were not fully recognized by domestic literary authorities at the time, some visionary literary critics and scholars in the West had already discovered that he was an excellent writer with great creative potential. Douwe Fokkema, a Dutch comparative literature scholar and sinologist, reread Mo Yan's work a decade later from a Western and comparative perspective. In a paper he published in 2008 on postmodernist fiction in China, he discussed some of the representative writers, with Mo Yan being the first one.[13] I think it's probably not a coincidence either.

Indeed, from the very beginning of his literary career, Mo Yan had a broad vision of world literature. He wrote not only for the folks of his own hometown in Gaomi County or for readers in China but also for readers all over the world, so his works were already somehow "translatable" at the beginning of his career, because he explored issues that are common to all of humanity. Of all the Western writers he had read, he most admired the modernist writer William Faulkner and the postmodernist writer Garcia Marquez, and he unapologetically admitted that his writing was inspired and influenced by these two masters of literature. Indeed, just as Faulkner's work was devoted to a small town the size of a "postage stamp" in Lafayette County, Mo Yan focused much of his work on his hometown of Gaomi County, Shandong Province. Similarly, like Garcia Marquez, Mo Yan created in many of his works an absurd, even almost "hallucinatory", atmosphere in which the mystical and the real are intertwined, and violence and death reveal themselves as uncanny grotesques. In fact, he was not so much interested in the content of the stories he told as in how to mobilize all the artistic and narrative techniques to tell his stories well, so for him, the novelist's strength lies in putting those fragmentary events into his narrative space, thus making an unbelievable story believable, as if it were a real event that happened around him. It is largely due to his mastery of narrative craft that Mo Yan has become one of the very few contemporary Chinese writers with a wide international reputation and a large readership, and almost all of his major works have been translated into major world languages such as English, French, German, and Spanish.[14] There are also some critical essays discussing his works published in international literary and academic journals, while few contemporary Chinese writers get their works discussed in international journals. This proves once again that translation can make an already well-written literary work better and accelerate its classicization, while poor translation may destroy the form of an otherwise good work, leaving it in a state of "death" in another context. It is in this sense that we say that an excellent translation should have the same value as the original work, and an excellent translator should be given the same respect as an exceptional author.

At this point, I have to think about this phenomenon: if Mo Yan's works had not been translated by such excellent translators as Goldblatt and Chen, would he have won the 2012 Nobel Prize in Literature? I think the answer would be most likely no. We can say that if they had not translated these works, other translators would still have translated them, which is fine, but as far as I know, there are really only a few sinologists in the world today who love literature as much as these two translators do, and those who are so dedicated are even more rare. It is certain that if they had not translated Mo Yan's works, his award would have been delayed for at least a few years or even decades, and it is likely that he would not be honored with the Nobel Prize in his lifetime. Are such examples rare in the history of world literature in the twentieth century? We cannot expect all literary translators to have a masterly command of Chinese and willingly devote most of their time and energy to translating Chinese literature into a major world language, so for this matter, we should decisively shift the focus of the current Chinese translation community: from foreign-to-Chinese translation to Chinese-to-foreign translation, that is, to devote ourselves to translating the best works of Chinese culture and literature into the world's major languages, especially English. Nevertheless, the translation of excellent foreign literary works into Chinese will remain necessary for a considerable period of time in the future, only that the emphasis should shift. This will be more conducive to the really effective globalization of Chinese culture and literature. Obviously, the latter should be greatly strengthened in terms of accelerating the process of internationalization of Chinese literature and humanities research. On the other hand, we should not ignore the importance of promoting and popularizing the Chinese language overseas, even though it seems to be much more difficult for foreigners to master Chinese than for Chinese people to master English. If we strengthen our cooperation with our international counterparts, we can certainly succeed in raising the status of Chinese as the second most spoken language in the world after English. However, this in turn cannot be done without the mediation of translation, and we cannot accomplish this historical mission without the participation or intervention of translation, because it can help us relocate world culture both at present and in the near future. In this regard, it is the exceptional translators and sinologists such as Goldblatt and Chen who have given Mo Yan's works a "continuous life" and "afterlife" outside China.

Notes

1 Bhabha, H. K. 1994. *The Location of Culture*. London & New York: Routledge, 1994.
2 Wang, N. 2010. Global English(es) and global Chinese(s): Toward rewriting a new literary history in Chinese. *Journal of Contemporary China*, 19(63): 159–174.
3 Kinnock, H. L. N. 2006. Foreword. In D. Graddol (ed.), *English Next*. London: British Council, 1.
4 Tonkin, H. 2007. World language system. In R. Robertson & J. Scholte (eds.), *Encyclopedia of Globalization*. Vol. 4. London & New York: Routledge, 1288.
5 Please refer to "The black savant and the dark princess", a keynote speech delivered by Homi Bhabha at the Tsinghua-Harvard Advanced Forum on Postcolonial Theory on June 25, 2002.
6 Bhabha, H. K. 2002. Afterword: A personal response. In L. Hutcheon & M. Valdés (eds.), *Rethinking Literary History: A Dialogue on Theory*. Oxford & New York: Oxford University Press, 201–202.
7 Indeed, many Chinese American writers, such as Maxine Hong Kingston, have even lost their ability to communicate and write in Chinese. Their purpose of writing and communicating in English is to quickly identify themselves with the mainstream American writers.
8 Miller, J. H. 1993. *New Starts: Performative Topographies in Literature and Criticism*. Taipei: Academia Sinica, 3.
9 Cf. Spivak, G. C. 1988. Can the subaltern speak? In C. Nelson & L. Grossberg (eds.), *Marxism and the Interpretation of Culture*. Basingstoke: Macmillan Education, 271–313.
10 Only a few of these series are mentioned here: the series edited by Zhang Longxi and Axel Schneider and published by Brill in the Netherlands, the series of studies on contemporary China edited by Daniel A. Bell and published by Princeton University in the United States, and the series on contemporary China studies edited by Wang Ban and published by Macmillan in the United States. The first two aim to translate influential Chinese works already published in China into English and publish them, while the last one publishes humanities and social science works written directly in English.
11 See "Chinese Writer Mo Yan Wins Nobel Prize". *The Irish Times*. 11 October 2012. http://www.irishtimes.com/newspaper/breaking/2012/1011/breaking27.html. Retrieved 11 October 2012.
12 See Donald Morrison (14 February 2005). "Holding up Half the Sky". *TIME*. http://www.time.com/time/magazine/article/0,9171,501050221-1027589,00.html. Retrieved 14 February 2005.
13 Fokkema, D. 2008. Chinese postmodernist fiction. *Modern Language Quarterly*, 69(1): 151.
14 Mo Yan's works that were translated by Howard Goldblatt include *Red Sorghum*, *The Garlic Ballads*, *The Republic of Wine*, *Shifu, You'll Do Anything for a Laugh*, *Big Breasts and Wide Hips*, *Life and Death Are Wearing Me Out*, and *Sandalwood Death*.

9 The role of translation in the Chinese revolution

As mentioned above, the cultural turn in translation took place a long time ago in China. It played an important role in the Chinese revolution and the process of modernization. As far as modern nations are concerned, translation is indispensable if a country is to play an important global role. During the Chinese revolution, translation all along played a very important role, not only in introducing the world's advancements in science and technology and the concept of democracy into China at the turn of the twentieth century but also in enabling China to join the socialist group headed by the former Soviet Union. Even after the founding of the People's Republic of China, it continued to have a huge and practical function to a large extent, during the socialist revolution and construction led by Mao Zedong and during the reform and opening-up policy launched under the leadership of Deng Xiaoping. In the four decades of the reform and opening-up policy, China has long established a national policy with economic development as its top priority to safeguard national stability and a flourishing economy in accordance with the will of the people. As a result of the construction and development in past decades, China has become the second largest economic power in the world, and it is currently undergoing a process of "depovertizing" and "de-third-worldizing". At this stage in history, Chinese culture and literature are making an effort to reach out to the world in an attempt to make greater contributions to global culture and the remapping of world literature. In this sense, translation will play an even more important role in promoting Chinese culture and humanistic thinking to the world. Therefore, my argument in this chapter is that translation is closely related to the Chinese revolution in the twentieth century: this was true during the democratic revolution before 1949, and even more so after the establishment of the People's Republic of China and in the years since the reform and opening up. These revolutions and constructions could not have been completed successfully without the contribution of translation. This chapter will divide the function performed by translation over the course of the Chinese revolution into four stages and discuss the different roles it has played in each historical stage in the twentieth century and the new century.

9.1 Translation as an instrument of cultural enlightenment

Historically, China is known as the "Middle Kingdom", and its culture was seldom influenced by other cultures because of the autocratic rule by its feudal dynasties. For a long period of time, China was isolated and self-complacent, and seldom tried to learn from other countries. Eventually, it was translation that helped China to become a modern country that developed towards democracy. It is common knowledge that translation has been in existence since human beings started communicating, and the interest in translation can be traced back to Cicero in the first century BCE in the West, and even earlier in Asian countries like China, where Chinese translations of Buddhist sutras into Chinese played an important role in the prosperity of Chinese religious culture. In this section, I will illustrate how large-scale translation in the twentieth century has helped to form the modern Chinese literary tradition, and how literary translation has made the Chinese language almost "Europeanized" or modernized. In this light, the attempt to conduct a comparative study of literatures from cross-linguistic and cross-cultural perspectives involves both an interlingual translation and a cultural translation. According to the definition of Mark Shuttleworth and Moira Cowie, "[t]ranslation is frequently characterized metaphorically, and has—amongst many other things—been compared to playing a GAME or making a MAP".[1] Since translation is closely related to the Chinese revolution, especially in its modern sense, the term "translation" discussed here is more about cultural and metaphorical rendering rather than linguistic rendition, because in my opinion, translation has indeed inspired Chinese intellectuals to carry out the revolution. Of course, the nature of this revolution was not only political and cultural but also linguistic and literary.

It is well known that the Chinese revolution is closely related to the issue of modernity. Throughout the twentieth century, modernity has been a heatedly discussed topic that even led to arguments in Western and Chinese academic circles. In the Chinese context, modernity is both a "translated" concept and a recourse to its internal development. Here I will only look at modern Chinese literature and culture to illustrate how translation brought advanced science and culture to China around the time of the New Culture Movement (1915–1923), which undoubtedly heralded the democratic revolution led by the Chinese Communist Party (CCP) later on.

During the New Culture Movement, such important thinkers and humanities scholars as Hu Shi, Chen Duxiu, Lu Xun, Cai Yuanpei, Qian Xuantong, and Li Dazhao, who were either educated in the West or Japan, or had a profound attainment of Western learning, took the lead in launching the ideological and cultural movement of "anti-tradition, anti-Confucianism and anti-classical Chinese" to modernize China in a comprehensive manner. They used translation as an efficient tool to introduce new Western political and cultural trends to China, hence greatly accelerating its modernization. During or even before this movement, those intellectuals helped to initiate a large-scale project of translating Western learning. European thinkers and philosophers such as Nietzsche and Marx were revered in

Chinese academies, their writings were frequently quoted and discussed in the Chinese context and their works influenced or inspired almost all the major Chinese philosophers and literary figures back then. The introduction of "Mr. Democracy" and "Mr. Science" influenced the development of the Chinese science and democratic revolutions throughout the twentieth century. Chen Duxiu, an early leader of the CCP founded the influential progressive magazine *Xin Qingnian* [New Youth], which published articles introducing or translating advanced Western ideas of the time, aiming to enlighten the Chinese people and promote the development of science and technology, as well as humanistic thought in China. Their efforts laid an important foundation for the introduction and dissemination of Marxism in the country. In addition, the New Culture Movement also witnessed the founding of the CCP in 1921, which later led to the victory in the democratic revolution and the establishment of a new socialist China in 1949. Therefore, in this regard, I would like to argue that translation indeed served as a tool of enlightenment to liberate the Chinese people from darkness and ignorance.

This shows that modernity in China is a theoretical concept or a cultural and literary discourse that was "translated" from the West, which has been transformed and undergone various forms of construction and reconstruction since its introduction to China. In the Chinese context, modernity has undergone three stages:

1 Early twentieth century until the 1970s: modernity was translated into China as a literary and cultural grand project to help rebuild Chinese modern literature and culture;
2 The late 1970s until the early 1990s: postmodernity was translated into China as simultaneously a rebellion against, and an extension of, modernity, with the aim of laying the foundations for the formation of either an alternative modernity, or an extended and "transformed" pluralistic modernity with Chinese characteristics;
3 The entry of globalization into China has led to the connection of modernity with postmodern discourse.

As a direct result of these three stages, China's alternative modernity has finally integrated into the grand discourses of global modernity. However, as noted above, the unique characteristics of Chinese modernity have distinguished it in the pluralistic orientation of global modernity. Lu Xun, who was the pioneer to introduce modernity into China, played a leading role in the literary revolution. When he spoke about his own fiction writing, he frankly claimed that the inspiration for his creative writing "totally depended on hundreds of foreign literary works plus a little knowledge of medicine",[2] without any other preparation. In other words, he believed that his inspiration was drawn from foreign literature rather than from classical Chinese literature and culture. Therefore, in addition to his own literary writing, he also translated a large number of foreign literary works. He believed that only by translating foreign literature and academic works of the humanities on a large scale can modernity be introduced into China and Chinese literature and culture be closer to the world.

Other thinkers and writers in the May Fourth Movement, including Hu Shi and Guo Moruo, also vigorously deconstructed traditional Chinese literary discourse by translating a large number of Western literary and theoretical works into Chinese. Interestingly, both Hu and Guo had done a great deal of translation before they became political figures: Hu was the first to introduce Henrik Ibsen and his plays to China by editing a special issue on Ibsen for *New Youth* in 1918 and he also translated some of his plays, while Guo translated important works by such influential Western authors as Goethe and Whitman into Chinese. They made full use of translation as a tool for enlightenment during the New Culture Movement and made outstanding achievements in their respective fields.

During the course of the Chinese revolution, translation itself also evolved considerably from a purely technical rendering that sought to faithfully convert texts from one language into another, to another form of translation at the political and cultural levels with a much stronger function. Scholars have paid attention to translation because it is not merely a linguistic skill but rather a strategy for cultural change and a political weapon with which to advance the revolutionary cause. Even in China today, translation is still closely related to politics and ideology: the CCP and government leaders, as well as leading scholars, attach great importance to using the medium of translation to introduce Chinese political, economic, cultural, and literary achievements to the world. Therefore, in present times, the function of translation has by no means been weakened but has become increasingly important and essential. If we acknowledge that globalization has a major impact on national literature, then it has also promoted the study of comparative literature and world literature. Let us take the translation of Chinese literature as an example. Over the past century, Chinese literature has, under the influence of the West, constantly been moving closer to the world by means of translation. In this regard, the May Fourth Movement started the process of Chinese modernity, while undermining the mechanism of China's long-lasting national isolation. Even the Chinese language was largely "Europeanized" or "Westernized" in this "colonization" process. Nevertheless, there is no doubt that this is the inevitable result of the difference between Chinese and Western modernity.

As we can easily see from the above description, modern Chinese literature has been moving gradually closer to world literature thanks to the large-scale translation movement. As a direct result, a modern Chinese literary canon or tradition has emerged, which can carry out dialogue not only with modern Western literature on an equal footing but also with its own traditional classical literature. Translation has undoubtedly played an important and indispensable role in the history of modern Chinese literature and thought, but this kind of translation is a kind of cultural change through the medium of language rather than the traditional linguistic rendering from one language to another. It is through this kind of cultural translation that a new literature and culture was born, which is both different from its own tradition and from its Western counterpart of the same period. It should be seen as a product of the cultural and literary exchange and collision between China and foreign countries.

9.2 Translation as an instrument of ideology

As mentioned above, translation has played an important role in enlightening people during the course of the political and cultural revolution of China. On the other hand, we cannot ignore the fact that China's large-scale translation of Western and Russian literary works has given translation a more pragmatic function and ideological quality.

It is well recognized that China is a socialist country with Marxism as the theoretical foundation that guides our thought. Over the past decades, the CCP spent much time and effort translating the works by Marx, Engels, Lenin and Stalin, eventually introducing all of the works of the founders of Marxism to China in a comprehensive manner. However, it must be noted that Marxism had been introduced into China long before the founding of the CCP. The earliest translations of Marx's works were not done from the original German into Chinese but via the intermediary language of Japanese or Russian. Among the earliest translators of Marx's works was Xiong Deshan (1891–1939), who studied in Japan in his early years and later translated some of Marx's works from Japanese into Chinese. On 15 February 1922, he founded the magazine *Jinri* [Today] which was published by Beijing Xinzhi Shushe [New Knowledge Publishing House]. He himself also wrote many articles including "Refuting the Fallacy of Public Wife", "The Future State of Socialism", "Socialism and Population Theory", "The Due Attitude of the Proletariat toward Politics", and "The Discussion of Name and Reality", to refute the bourgeois slanders of the communist "Public Wife". In critiquing the Malthusian population theory, he explained the proletariat's aims and means for socialism. Around this time, he translated Marx's works including *Critique of the Gotha Program*, *Marxist Socialism*, and the *History of the International Labor Alliance*. He also published translations by Ruo Fei, Kuang Mohan, and others, as well as numerous articles that propagated scientific socialism. In the same year, he became a member of the CCP but soon afterwards he left the party.[3] Another early translator was Zhu Zhixin (1885–1920), one of the first bourgeois revolutionaries to introduce Marxism to China. As early as 1906, he translated from Japanese the classical texts *Communist Manifesto* and *Das Kapital*. He had his own unique understanding of Marxist theory about class struggle, social and political revolutions, and the historical position of the masses. At the same time, he introduced the basic principles of Marxism to Chinese readers based on his own dynamic understanding and interpretation.[4]

As one of China's earliest Marxists and one of the earliest leaders of the CCP, Li Dazhao actively participated in the editorial work of the magazine *New Youth* and passionately helped spread Marxism in China. He edited a special issue on Marxism for the magazine (No. 5, Volume 6, September 1919), where Li published the long article "My View on Marxism" that provided a comprehensive introduction to the basic principles of Marxism and generated strong reactions among its wide audience. The young Mao Zedong, who was working in the university library at the time, was inspired by these early efforts by Li Dazhao and others which provided access to Marx's works to Mao and his young companions who could not read the originals in their foreign language. Therefore, we should say that the Marxism that Mao received is a kind of "translated" version or a "sinicized" Marxism through translation. It was characterized by combining orthodox Marxist doctrines with some of the teachings of Confucianism to a certain extent to form this "sinicized" Marxism. Mao himself was against adopting a dogmatic attitude toward Marx's works. Instead, he called for a creative understanding of the fundamental principles of Marxism and their integration with the specific practice of the Chinese revolution. Therefore, Mao developed Marxism into a kind of "sinicized" Marxism called "Mao Zedong Thought", also known as "Maoism" in the West. It is not difficult to find that the early translations of Western learning, including the translations of Marxist works, demonstrate distinctive features of pragmatism during the course of the Chinese revolution. In other words, as Lu Xun said, as long as it is useful for the process of China's modernization, we will use it all for our own purpose.

Moreover, Mao Zedong was also passionate about literature, especially classical Chinese poetry, and he wrote many poems during the long revolution and war. Unsurprisingly, he developed Marxist literary theory and applied it to the study of Chinese literature and art, while leading the Chinese revolution. In his guiding work, "Talks at the Yan'an Forum on Literature and Art", he tried to answer the closely related questions for Chinese literature and art: for whom are literature and art created? What is the function of literature and art? In Mao's view, Chinese literature and art should first of all serve the general public, in particular workers, peasants, and soldiers: they should be created for them and used by them. Thus, it should "become an integral part of the entire revolutionary machine, functioning as a powerful weapon to unite and educate the people, and to combat and destroy the enemy, and helping the people to fight against their enemy with one heart and one mind".[5] Therefore, the political and practical function of literature and art was more important than its aesthetic and appreciative function.

Although Mao was primarily a nationalist, he did not deny that the new culture should inherit and develop ancient and foreign progressive cultures, while stressing the construction of revolutionary culture. Mao was never against the study of foreign literature, but he was concerned about what kind of foreign literature China should be introduced to. He did not read foreign literature as extensively as Marx, Engels, Lenin, and Stalin did. He had to rely on translation to read foreign literary works because of his limited knowledge of foreign languages. In fact, he did not even read many of those translated works. In the entire text of the "Yan'an Talks", he only mentioned one Russian-Soviet novel, namely *The Rout* by Alexander Fadeyev:

> Fadeyev's *The Rout* only describes a small guerilla band, with no thought at all of appealing to the taste of old world readers, but its influence has spread throughout the world, at least in China, as is known, it has had a great impact.[6]

Obviously, since Mao's foreign language skills were limited and he really did not read many foreign literary works, so he seldom cited foreign literary works in his writings but quoted extensively from ancient Chinese literary and historical works and allusions. Even so, he insisted on critically inheriting all the outstanding literatures and arts of the past and present. His attitude was: "Make the past serve the present and foreign things serve China".[7] There is no doubt that this has been inherited and carried forward by Chinese leaders today.

In the Chinese context, certainly influenced by Soviet literary thought, the relevant domestic departments also have distinct subjectivity and initiative in the selection of world literary classics. The relevant government departments and publishing houses cooperate to select in an organized and planned manner the foreign works that we ourselves consider to be the classics of foreign literature and then invite outstanding translators to translate them into Chinese. The result of these procedures is that the classics of world literature in China are different from those identified in the West or the former Soviet Union. Of course, the focus of translation is sometimes appropriately adjusted to the needs of the political situation and the guiding principles of Marxism. Since Marx and Engels highly appreciated authors such as Homer, Dante, Shakespeare, Goethe and Balzac, their representative works should be translated and undergo critical and academic discussion. Since Lenin considered Tolstoy the "mirror" of the Russian revolution, Tolstoy continues to be highly regarded in China by the academic community to this day and is listed as an important research topic for Chinese scholars of foreign literature. Lenin and Stalin highly valued the Soviet author Maxim Gorky and had close relations with him, so all his major works have been translated into Chinese and they have become the focus of study and discussion by Chinese scholars.

Sometimes authors whose work is not considered canonical in the West but were translated and promoted in China would become very popular or even canonical in China for political reasons. The novel *The Gadfly* about the Italian revolution written by Irish author Ethel Lilian Voynich (1864–1960) in 1897, for example, became very popular in China for political reasons. The same happened with *Mother* by Gorky and *How Steel Was Tempered* by another Soviet writer Nicolas Alexyevitch Ostrovsky (1904–1936). Both have become canonical works in the Chinese context and once had tens of millions of readers. It is not surprising, therefore, that during the Cultural Revolution, while most Western literary works and Chinese classical and modern works were condemned,[8] the three aforementioned works were popular among a large group of readers, especially young readers.

In sum, in the revolutionary era, translations were planned, selected, and organized mainly according to the instructions of the ideologically dominant party. In the old society when China was poor and underdeveloped, Chinese culture and literature were also regarded as backward and did not have a place on the map of world literature.[9] Therefore, Chinese writers called for a large number of foreign works to be translated into Chinese, so as to promote the movement of modern Chinese literature from the periphery to the center and eventually to the world. Now that China is economically and politically strong, the priority for Chinese intellectuals is to rebuild the soft power of Chinese culture. Translation, therefore, plays an even more important role in bringing Chinese literature and culture closer to the mainstream of world literature and global culture. The difference, however, is that the focus has shifted from translating Western literature into Chinese to translating Chinese literature into the major languages of the world. Therefore, translation, to some extent, served as an ideological tool at different stages of the Chinese revolution.

9.3 Translation as a way of opening up to the world

As we all know, in the first two years after the Cultural Revolution ended, China did not immediately implement the policy of "reform and opening up", although the door to translation was open. Not until 1978, when the Third Plenary Session of the Eleventh Central Committee of the CCP was held, did China really start to reform and open up. It was then that the second peak of cultural and literary translation occurred in Chinese cultural and intellectual circles. Many Western modern and postmodern authors were translated one after another, including T. S. Eliot, William Faulkner, Marcel Proust, James Joyce, Ernest Hemingway, V. S. Naipaul, Gabriel García Márquez, and Milan Kundera, which greatly influenced the prosperity of contemporary Chinese literature. In the humanities and intellectual circles, many important works of Western philosophers and thinkers, such as Arthur Schopenhauer, Henri Bergson, Friedrich Nietzsche, Sigmund Freud, Martin Heidegger and Jean-Paul Sartre, were also translated into Chinese, which had a great impact on the prosperity of scholarship in the humanities in contemporary China.

In the early 1990s, with China's reform and opening up, globalization also came to China, making great contributions to China's economic and cultural development. Since the term "globalization" was also introduced via translation from the West, it had a distinctive connotation of Western-centrism. For a relatively long time, the term "globalization" was simply perceived as "Westernization" which in turn was essentially equal to "Americanization" because the United States was a Western power with the strongest economy and the greatest influence in politics and culture in the world today. This of course is true to some extent, but those who hold this view overlook another obvious factor: in the process of globalization the hegemonic ideology and culture of the empire quickly infiltrated into non-Western societies through translation, and on the other hand, the cultural concepts and standards of value of non-Western countries have slowly seeped into the center of the empire through translation, mixing Western values and cultural concepts. While it is true that modern Chinese culture and literature have been greatly influenced by Western culture and literature, they are also constantly trying to engage in dialogue with them. In this regard, translation plays an indispensable role. It was very effective in introducing Western culture into China, but it appears rather ineffective when it comes to the introduction and promotion of Chinese culture. A direct result is that modern Chinese literature and culture are not widely known in the world. Some of China's most famous authors and scholars in the humanities are little known outside the Chinese context because their works have not been translated or have been translated poorly, so it goes without saying that they lack any wide global impact.

The development of classical Chinese literature was virtually free of Western influence because China was isolated from the outside world for a long time, and it was resistant to foreign influence. By contrast, the unique tradition of modern Chinese literature was formed under Western influence. In today's discussion of global modernity and world literature, it is impossible to ignore Chinese modernity and modern literature because modern Chinese literature has taken part in the practice of "glocalization" [global localization] of modernity. As a result, different types of modernity have emerged in China: political, cultural, literary and aesthetic. Together they constitute an alternative concept of modernity different from the Western model. This alternative concept forcefully deconstructed the "metanarrative" (grand narrative) of the so-called "singular" (monolithic) modernity dominated by Western culture. Translation has thereby played a unique role. It is thus clear that translation makes the concept of modernity appear differently and distinctly in different places. Even in the same country or region, modernity can take different forms. As such, translation in fact acts as a mediator between different cultures.

Since we live in the era of globalization, where literature has gone far beyond fixed national and linguistic boundaries, it is necessary to re-examine twentieth-century Chinese literature which has been influenced by the West from cross-cultural and global perspectives. We can't help noticing that translation has indeed played a very important role. If modern Chinese literature is examined in a broad cross-cultural context of world literature, it appears that it has in fact been moving toward the world and trying to identify with world literature in the course of cultural globalization. In this regard, translation does not necessarily imply word-for-word rendition at the linguistic level, but rather a sort of cultural translation or transformation, through which global cultures are "relocated".

From historical perspectives, since the twentieth century, Chinese scholars of literature have become increasingly aware of the "marginal" status of Chinese literature on the world literature map. To restore its former glory, Chinese literature needs to move from the periphery to the center by identifying with the world's most dominant literature: the modern literature of the West. That is exactly why Chinese scholars strongly supported the translation of Western literature and works in the humanities on such a large scale. In their view, translation was the best way to bring China out of its isolation. Indeed, large-scale translation introduced to China all the major cultural trends or literary movements, such as romanticism, realism and modernism that had dominated Western literary circles for more than a century, as well as representative authors and their works. This had a profound impact on twentieth-century Chinese literature at the threshold of cultural modernity. In the same vein, the efforts of translating Western literature accelerated and promoted the internationalization of modern Chinese literature, leading to a modern turn. Hence, under Western influence, modern Chinese literature formed its own unique tradition: it can engage in dialogue with both modern Western culture and classical Chinese literature. In the process of bringing modern Chinese literature to the world, translation played an essential and practical role. The literary and cultural revolution on a large scale, as we can say, has made translated literature a part of Chinese literature, and contemporary Chinese writers acknowledge that the external influence on them is even much greater than the influence of the older generation of Chinese writers.

Yu Hua is one of the few contemporary Chinese novelists whose works have been taken seriously by mainstream scholars, such as the American Marxist theorist Fredric Jameson. Although Jameson does not understand Chinese, he has shown a keen interest in Chinese literature. He has read translations of modern and contemporary works by Chinese authors, such as Lu Xun and Yu Hua, and tried to interpret them from the perspective of Western Marxism. There is no doubt that Yu Hua was influenced and inspired by modern and postmodern Western literature since the beginning of his literary career. In a personal letter dated September 16, 1990, he wrote to me without reservation that he was more influenced by modern and postmodern Western literature than by Chinese literature, and therefore, he sincerely appreciated the excellent translators who translated outstanding foreign literary works into Chinese. Nevertheless, Yu is convinced that if a writer aims to write a masterpiece of eternal artistic value, he must "endure loneliness like Kafka and Joyce".[10]

When foreign literature and academic works of the humanities are translated into Chinese, the quality of the translation cannot always be guaranteed because many translators are engaged in such a difficult task with only a minimal knowledge of the foreign language. If we look at the current situation of translation practice in China, especially literary translation, there are three types of translator/author relationships: (1) the expressive language skills of the translator are superior to the author's; (2) the translator's literacy level is equivalent to that of the author; and (3) the translator's level is lower than the author's. Obviously, in the first type, it is entirely possible that the translator is too much engaged in rewriting the original text. Not unlike the translation practices by Chinese translator Lin Shu, who was active at the turn of the twentieth century and was convinced that he had a good command of classical Chinese, and therefore was able to rewrite all the original texts in his own style of classical Chinese. The second type is more ideal, in which the translator completely understands the original text, renders the meaning between the lines and even reproduces the original's style. Fu Lei's translation of Balzac's works in the 1950s and 1960s is a typical example. It is due to Fu's unparalleled translation that Balzac became the most famous French classic writer in China, and his popularity in China greatly exceeded that of Victor Hugo. The third type is the most common in today's translation circles, in which many novices with poor knowledge of foreign languages and a lack of Chinese language skills are engaged in the translation of literary masterpieces and academic masterpieces in the humanities. As a result, these translations are simply unreadable.

It cannot be denied that the literary translations as discussed above enabled Western discourse to shape the direction of Chinese literature in the broad context of world literature. As a result, the opening up of Chinese literature to the world is in fact a process of Westernization, much like the cultural globalization that took place initially. Even contemporary Chinese language is full of "translated" jargon and expressions. Yet in the process, Chinese culture develops unevenly in interacting in a kind of global localization, or "glocalization".

On the other hand, since China has opened up, it should also embrace global culture and world literature, which is impossible without the intermediary of translation. For example, in the discussion about modernism at the start of reform and opening up, China clearly lagged behind the pioneers of international academia. Many authors and their works that we thought belonged to modernist literature were actually postmodernist. It was not until the late 1980s and early 1990s, that postmodernism was critically discussed in China. The translation and introduction of postmodernism deconstructed the grand narrative to a certain degree, weakened the power of elite culture, and helped Chinese literature and culture develop in a pluralistic direction. In the last two decades, the introduction of "globalization" as a new theoretical discourse to China has brought a connection between modernism and postmodernism. Chinese intellectuals have become increasingly aware that besides contributing to the global economy, China should also contribute to the task of remapping global culture and world literature. In this regard, translation has once again been given an important task and historical mission.

9.4 Translation as a way of remapping global culture and world literature

Since the start of the twenty-first century, China's reform and opening up has entered a deepening stage, and the role of translation has not been neglected, but has been increasingly emphasized. However, the focus of translation has changed: unlike before when the emphasis was on translating from foreign languages into Chinese, or more specifically from foreign cultures into Chinese, now the focus is on translating Chinese thoughts, theories, and literary works into the major languages of the world with the aim to engage in equal dialogue with Western or international academic circles on some basic theoretical issues.

When we review and examine the current status of Chinese translation, we cannot help but be surprised at discovering an imbalance: the understanding of the West by Chinese scholars greatly surpasses the understanding of China by Western scholars. Take knowledge of literature and culture for example: if Chinese secondary school students had not heard of the Western cultural giants Plato, Aristotle, Shakespeare, Goethe, Mark Twain, James Joyce, T. S. Eliot, William Faulkner, and Ernest Hemingway, they would feel ashamed; but it is quite common for Western literary scholars, let alone general readers, not to know the names of famous Chinese writers such as Qu Yuan, Tao Yuanming, Li Bai, Du Fu, Su Shi, Wang Yangming, Lu Xun and Qian Zhongshu. As Chinese-American scholar Ming Dong Gu argues:[11] "Due to the radical differences between Chinese and Western languages, Chinese-Western translation has been dominated by an overwhelmingly one-way flow, especially in the domains of literature, art, and cultural studies".[12] As a result of this imbalance, though Chinese literature has been making ongoing efforts to move to the center of the world, there is still a certain distance ahead to the mainstream of world literature.

China is indeed one of the very few countries in the world that has benefited directly from globalization not only economically but also politically and culturally. Thanks to the rapid economic development, the Chinese government was able to set up more than four hundred Confucius Institutes and more than two thousand Confucius classrooms worldwide to promote Chinese language and culture. It can be said that China is currently undergoing a process of "depovertization" and "de-third-worldization", aiming to transform itself from a "theory consuming" to a "theory producing" country. Since literature is primarily a form of art expressed in language that conveys the spirit of a culture, Chinese literature should be valued. No matter what, any objective and complete history of global comparative literature should include the works of modern Chinese literature, its theory and criticism, otherwise that history is incomplete and deficient.

In the same way, the impact of globalization can also be detected in two opposites: its impact from West to East and at the same time from East to West. In this era of globalization, "all identities are irreducibly hybrid, inevitably instituted by the representation of performance as statement",[13] which makes it even more challenging to conduct comparative studies in literature and culture between East and West. This is to a certain degree a matter of translation. In this respect, translation will contribute immensely to the reconstruction of national literature and the re-mapping of world literature. From this angle, translation becomes increasingly indispensable, not only as a medium of communication but also as a tool for literary exchange. It goes far beyond the superficial level of linguistic conversion, hence scholars in the humanities should pay even more attention to the cultural dimension of translation when studying translation. As Laurence K. P. Wong and Chan Sin-wai point out, the relationship between the translator and the translation is

> similar to that between the dancer and the dance, especially in view of the fact that what goes on in the translation process—the synapse, as it were, that connects the translator and the translation—is determined by a myriad of inexplicable factors: linguistic, cultural, ideological, psychological, and idiosyncratic.[14]

In other words, it is entirely possible for an ideal translator to improve an originally well-written work and even make it become a classic in the target language, whereas a poor translator will not only destroy an originally well-written work but even causes it to lose its canonical status and the wide readership it would otherwise have in the target language. Many such examples can be cited throughout the history of translation at all times, both at home and abroad.

Reading literary works is like a window through which the reader can see the development of China: its history in the past and reality at the moment. When Mo Yan won the Nobel Prize in Literature in 2012, it gave other Chinese writers and scholars in the humanities more confidence to reach out to the world. The role of translation in this regard is indispensable. Here again, literary creation and criticism can serve as an example. Along with globalization in culture, the highest stage of comparative literature today should be world literature. As we all know, in terms of classicization of world literature, the most authoritative institution of the twentieth century is undoubtedly the Swedish Academy and its Nobel Prize in Literature that they award, because it can manipulate the reputation of a writer, making a relatively unknown writer become a canonized writer in a short time. This is, of course, directly related to translation: it was sheer luck that the novel

Soul Mountain by Gao Xingjian, for which he was awarded the Nobel Prize, was translated into English by the excellent translator Mabel Lee, while many other overseas Chinese authors have not been so fortunate. The case of Mo Yan is an even better example: without the incomparable translation of the excellent English translator Howard Goldblatt, Mo Yan would have probably missed the chance of winning this prestigious award, like so many of his international peers. If it had not been for Goldblatt's beautiful and authentic English to retell Mo Yan's story, it would not have gained new life in the Anglophone world. Many of Mo Yan's peers back at home in China do not have such excellent translators and never even get the chance to be nominated. Of course, the objectivity, impartiality and authority of the Nobel Prize can be questioned. Yet, as long as there is no similar literary award with worldwide influence in the Chinese-speaking world, it must be acknowledged that the Nobel Prize—with its relatively authoritative and serious and objective method of selection—is unmatched by other international awards.

In short, the function of translation has never weakened in the era of globalization. On the contrary, it has become increasingly important and indispensable. Chinese scholars in the humanities are fully aware that over the past hundred years, Chinese literature has come into closer contact with and gained a better understanding of the rest of the world through the medium of translation. To conservative intellectuals, this opening up to the outside world and modernizing is merely a process of "colonizing" Chinese culture and literature; to a certain extent, the result of this one-way translation has led Chinese literature to lose its own national characteristics and form of expression. Therefore, the May Fourth Movement initiated the process of modernism in China and undermined the mechanism of Chinese nationalism formed a long time ago. However, it is undoubtedly a direct result of Chinese modernity, one of the obvious phenomena being the flood of foreign literary works and theoretical trends into the Chinese context through translation, which powerfully stimulated the creative imagination and writing motivation of Chinese writers and humanities intellectuals.

Obviously, if the positive and negative consequences of the May Fourth Movement are re-examined today, the following conclusion can be tentatively drawn: the May Fourth writers and scholars in the humanities have purposefully or accidentally neglected introducing Chinese culture and literature to the world while translating into Chinese large numbers of Western literary thoughts and theories. Currently, in addition to the need for translators dedicated to translating foreign works into Chinese such as Yan Fu, Lin Shu and Fu Lei, there is even a more urgent need for translators who translate from Chinese into foreign languages such as Gu Hongming,[15] Lin Yutang and Yang Xianyi. Thanks to their efforts and hard work, Chinese culture and literature have become known to the world. This should also be a research topic for Chinese scholars in comparative literature because translation is also an important issue for scholars in comparative literature. However, when it comes to how to translate Chinese literature to the world, especially the West and the Anglophone world, different views prevail. Some people believe that the translations done by Chinese translators are not authentic or idiomatic and full of foreignizing elements, which are difficult to be accepted and appreciated by the target language readers.[16]

This is of course true, but it cannot be generalized. To introduce Chinese literature and culture to the world, should we just wait for foreign translators to translate it into their languages? What if no one is willing to translate Chinese literature? If there were no good translators such as Howard Goldblatt and Anna Gustafsson Chen, what could Chinese writers and intellectuals do? Could they only wait passively for Godot who never shows up, like those characters in *Waiting for Godot*?[17] To solve this problem, my tentative suggestion is for a Chinese translator to collaborate with a native speaker and produce high-quality translations for publication by internationally renowned publishers so that they can be distributed and read by many readers. This is the only way for Chinese literature and critical theories to reach an international readership, and this is the only way to thoroughly redress the imbalance that exists on the contemporary Chinese translation scene.

Notes

1 Shuttleworth, M. & Cowie, M. 1997. *Dictionary of Translation Studies*. Manchester: St. Jerome, 181.
2 Lu Xun. 1981. *The Complete Works of Lu Xun*. Vol. 4. Beijing: Renmin Wenxue Chubanshe [People's Literature Publishing House], 512.
3 See Hu, W. 2013. A century of translating and disseminating Marxist works in China. *Zhongguo Yan'an Ganbu Xuexiao Xuebao* [Journal of China Executive Leadership Academy Yan'an], (2): 75–82.
4 Ibid.
5 Mao, Z. 1991. *Selected Works of Mao Zedong*. Vol. 4 (2nd ed.). Beijing: Renmin Chubanshe [People's Publishing House], 848.
6 Ibid, p. 876. Translators' note: Fadeyev is a Soviet revolutionary author. *The Rout* is also translated as *The Nineteen*. For the English translation, the translators consulted Bonnie McDougall's rendering entitled *Mao Zedong's "Talks at the Yan'an Conference on Literature and Art": A Translation of the 1943 Text with Commentary*. Ann Arbor: Center for Chinese Studies, The University of Michigan, 1980, p. 85.
7 Translators' note: This phrase has in fact become such a commonly used phase in Chinese that it can be found as an entry in modern Chinese language dictionaries.
8 Translators' note: They were condemned and labeled as "poisonous weeds" of feudalism, capitalism and revisionism.
9 Translators' note: The old society here refers to the pre-modern China before the founding of the People's Republic of China in 1949.
10 See Wang, N. 1992. Reception and transformation: Postmodernism in Chinese contemporary avant-garde novels. *Zhongguo Shehui Kexue* [Social Sciences in China], (1): 147.
11 Translators' note: Professor Gu is known in the West as Ming Dong Gu.
12 Cf. Gu, M. D. & Schulte, R. (eds.). 2014. *Translating China for Western Readers: Reflective, Critical and Practical Essays*. Albany: State University of New York Press, 1.
13 Spivak, G. C. 1999. *A Critique of Postcolonial Reason: Toward a History of the Vanishing Present*. Cambridge, MA: Harvard University Press, 155.
14 Wong, L. K. P. & Chan, S. (eds.). 2013. *The Dancer and the Dance: Essays in Translation Studies*. Newcastle: Cambridge Scholars Publishing, ix.
15 Translators' note: Aka Ku Hung-ming in the old Wade-Giles romanization system used before *Hanyu Pinyin* was introduced.
16 Huang, Z. 2015. Who is the main translator in cultural translation? *Dushu* [Reading], (10): 66–68.
17 Translators' note: *Waiting for Godot* is Samuel Beckett's two-act stage drama.

10 The future of translation studies in the age of globalization

The previous chapters of this book have each given a cursory view of the cultural turn in translation studies. Of course, it would be impossible to cover all contemporary translation theories in such limited space and therefore the focus is only on some theoretical trends that have had a major impact on and considerably advanced the cultural turn in translation studies. In addition, we have also incorporated some Chinese elements by introducing the translation practice and studies in modern China. There is no doubt that discussing translation issues in the era of globalization from a cultural perspective has become a subject of great interest in all disciplines of the humanities and social sciences today. Not only traditional translation studies scholars have begun to pay attention to translation in the era of globalization and the cultural turn in translation studies,[1] but even scholars outside the field of translation studies have also started to place focus on translation issues.[2] Therefore, this kind of turn is still in progress and its gains and losses should naturally be summarized by future researchers, while we will continue to closely follow the prospects of its future development and promptly put forward our countermoves.

It should be explained here that since I have had close academic exchanges with several representatives of cultural translation in the West, their influence on me is inevitable, so my inclination is from time to time revealed in discussions in this book. On the other hand, the reason why the cultural turn in translation has been developed and promoted in China is inseparable from my own efforts, so I have become China's representative in this respect in the view of international colleagues. Nevertheless, as a Chinese scholar, I have never forsaken my Chinese perspective and viewpoint, and I have always used every opportunity to make my voice heard on behalf of the Chinese academic community in international forums. Therefore, from the perspective of a humanities scholar, emphasizing the cultural turn in translation studies is by no means intended to exclude other research methods, and the reason why the author was able to undertake this research project to study the cultural turn of translation studies funded by the National Social Science Fund of China is that it was to great extent supported by domestic language and literature scholars. Some scholars, who are open-minded and enthusiastic about the frontier of international scholarship, hope that scholars outside the traditional field of translation studies from a linguistic perspective will make an impact on it and thus stimulate it to update its research methods. It should be acknowledged that the reason why translation studies is so highly valued today lies exactly in the openness of this burgeoning discipline and its inclusiveness of various research methods and theoretical perspectives. Since the cultural turn in translation and translation studies is an international phenomenon, it is evident that people in the present era are inseparable from translation, just as we are equally inseparable from language and culture. Every day we encounter translated culture in one way or another, and thus it has already invaded our daily life and permeated all aspects of contemporary culture. On the other hand, translation has to be involved in the study of the humanities and social sciences from a broad cross-cultural perspective. For example, for various types of international academic conferences held in China, we always need translation. Even if all the participants present their papers in English, those whose mother tongue is not English, including us, still need to translate (or write) their own papers into English because they need to express in English the issues that were originally thought out in their mother tongue. Even if we are fully equipped with the skills of thinking and writing in English, our starting point and angle of thought are inseparable from our mother tongue and the culture of our motherland. This may be one of the reasons why scholars in various disciplines of the humanities and social sciences are quite interested in translation today. For scholars who specialize in translation studies and theoretical construction, our task is not only to make due contribution to the construction of our discipline but also to make contributions to the entire humanities with our own theoretical innovation and construction. Since translation theory has borrowed many existing theories from other disciplines, why can't translation studies offer its own theories or new research paradigms to those disciplines? Since translation is extremely important and essential for our time, what are the current status and future prospects of translation studies as a study of the phenomena of translation? This is precisely what I will describe in the last chapter of this book.

10.1 Translation studies from the perspectives of the new humanities[3]

The once dynamic cultural turn in translation studies has become history and leaves many questions worthy of reflection, including: what is the status quo of translation studies after the cultural turn? What are its prospects for the future? Recently, articles discussing the new humanities in the Chinese context have appeared in academic journals and mass media from time to time. I myself have actively participated in this discussion and published a few articles. People might ask: what exactly is the new humanities? How does it differ from the traditional humanities? Why is the concept of the new humanities proposed? How will it contribute to the development of disciplines in colleges and universities? What is its direct impact on and significance for translation studies in China today? Of course, we cannot answer these questions in general but should start with a specific case. In my opinion, the key lies in the word "new" in "new humanities". The concept of the new humanities, just like different disciplines such as the new medicine and new engineering, is bound to challenge the conventional definition of the humanities and its evaluation system.

I have written an article discussing the construction and development of the discipline of foreign languages from the perspective of new humanities.[4] In my opinion, since translation studies is a secondary discipline practiced mainly by scholars of foreign languages, it has a close relationship with the discipline of foreign languages and literatures. Therefore, compared with the traditional humanities, the new humanities in China should embody the following four characteristics: international, interdisciplinary, cutting-edge, and theoretical. This should be the difference between the new and the traditional humanities. This applies especially to the discipline of foreign languages in China. If we make further inferences, we can see that the concept of new humanities is highly suitable for translation studies, because the four characteristics mentioned above are all directly related to translation.

Let us first look at its international nature, which is related to the concept of "global humanities" which I proposed.[5] According to this concept, Chinese scholars in the humanities should not only speak out on China issues internationally but also at the same time should contribute Chinese wisdom and propose Chinese solutions to issues of universal significance that are common to all mankind. Global humanities is not a collection of the humanities of all countries and nations put together, but rather a global view on fundamental issues that are of common concern to mankind. Some global topics of universal significance that are closely related to the discipline of foreign languages and literature include cosmopolitanism, world literature, world philosophy, general world history, global culture, world images, world language systems, etc. These are all topics that scholars in the humanities should address and pay attention to. Chinese scholars in the humanities are particularly influenced by Confucian philosophy and have always had a view of "tianxia" [literally: under heaven] or world view, meaning that they are concerned with what is happening in the world. In this regard, translation scholars have contributed a lot. It is precisely because Chinese and overseas Chinese scholars have translated the Confucian view of "tianxia" into the English-speaking world and have expounded and discussed the concept at international events that the discussion of cosmopolitanism in international academic circles finally began to have a Chinese voice.[6]

As such, it naturally leads to the second characteristic of the new humanities: interdisciplinarity. This interdisciplinarity is not only reflected in its crossover and mutual infiltration with other branches of the humanities but also in its mutual influence, infiltration and intersection with the social sciences. It once again reflects the characteristics of the classification of the disciplines in China. As we all know the humanities in China were for a long time included in the broad framework of the social sciences, and until now projects in the humanities at the national level fell under the general framework of the National Social Science Fund of China. This is not quite the same as the situation of disciplines in the United States.

This happens to be another feature of the humanities in China: it has a close relationship with the social sciences. It is especially evident in the large number of translation practices and translation studies in modern and contemporary China. In practice, translators have translated numerous Western and Russian social science documents since the early twentieth century, which has greatly advanced the process of Chinese modernity. As I pointed out in an article commemorating the centenary of the New Culture Movement: without translation, the New Culture Movement would not have erupted, and without translation, it would have been impossible for Marxism to enter China, and the establishment of the Communist Party would be out of the question.[7] It shows that the role of translation far exceeds the conversion between two languages, and it can even trigger a (cultural) revolution and give impetus to social change.

It is well known that the Chinese revolution is closely related to the subject of modernity. Throughout the twentieth century, modernity has been a topic of heated discussion and even debate among Western and Chinese academic circles. In the Chinese context, modernity is both a "translated" concept and a concept that appeals to its inherent logic to development, so it is a kind of "alternative" modernity or modernities. I once revealed how translation brought advanced science and culture into China around the time of the New Culture Movement from the perspectives of modern Chinese literature and culture.[8] It is exactly the translation of these Western ideas introduced into China that to some extent heralded the democratic revolution led by the the Chinese Communist Party (CCP). This proves once again that translation is far more than just a conversion skill between two languages, it has a more important function, and in fact it has indeed played an important role in modern Chinese history.

It can be seen that cross-linguistic and cross-cultural translation of literature and humanities is both an interlingual and a cultural translation. Since translation is closely related to the "sinicization" of Marxism, especially in the modern sense, the term translation as discussed here has more cultural and metaphorical traits, and is less about linguistic transformation, because it has inspired the progressive intellectuals of China to carry out revolution. Of course, this revolution was not only political and cultural but also linguistic and literary.

In addition, the interdisciplinary nature of the new humanities is also reflected in the mutual infiltration and correlation between the humanities with the natural sciences and technology. For example, during the new coronavirus pandemic, many of our in-person academic and cultural activities are carried out online. Even the lectures in the humanities and the postgraduate oral defenses can be conducted online. The comparative study of the spread of the pandemic in different countries requires the analysis of the data of epidemic cases in different countries, which, of course, cannot be done without the mediation of translation. Therefore, this poses a severe challenge to scholars in the traditional humanities. As scholars in the humanities, we need to master not only multidisciplinary knowledge but also certain presentation and dissemination techniques, in order to ensure the smooth dissemination of our knowledge.

Again, this has to be done with the help of translation and translation studies. I once created a new definition for the contemporary form of translation studies. It seems to me that, along with the rise of modern translation studies and the impact of the cultural turn in translation studies, there is a growing sense that it is clearly not enough to define translation only at the level of language alone. At this point, the study of translation, especially literary translation, takes on a cross-cultural and interdisciplinary perspective. This is the "cultural turn" in translation and translation studies that we often refer to. However, this "cultural turn" in translation studies in the end failed to rescue translation from the stigma of "linguo-centrism" that it carried. What kind of turn will come after the "cultural turn"? It is the technological turn. This is especially reflected in image translation and artificial intelligence translation that are popular topics of conversation nowadays. These are exactly the two key topics that I will discuss in this section. Now first I want to revise and add to my definitions of translation:[9]

> A conversion of an ancient form into a modern one within the same language;
> A conversion between two written texts that crosses linguistic boundaries;
> The deciphering and interpreting of codes or signs into text;
> The cross-cultural interpretation of images that crosses linguistic boundaries;
> A mutual conversion of images and language that crosses linguistic boundaries;
> A kind of adaptation and reproduction of a reading text into performance scripts for film, TV, and drama;
> A kind of cross-media interpretation with language as the main medium;
> A conversion between two languages by machine and artificial intelligence.

From the above definitions, it is fully clear that the current interdisciplinary form of translation and translation studies has gone beyond the barriers of "linguo-centrism": it not only crosses the boundary between language and culture but also the boundary between languages and other branches of the humanities and the boundaries of languages and the social sciences, the natural sciences and technology. Regarding this point, I will discuss it in more detail later on from the perspective of the discipline's current status and future prospects under the challenges of image translation and artificial intelligence translation.

Now I will go back to review the cutting-edge and theoretical nature of the new humanities. Why do I put these two features together? The reason is that the cutting-edge nature of the new humanities breaks through the artificial and subjective nature of the traditional humanities, adding some elements of science and technology to make it a veritable academic discipline that can stand up to evaluation, and at the same time also paves the way for theorists to put forward some theoretical topics of universal significance that transcend disciplinary and national boundaries. Since this cutting-edge and theoretical nature is prominent in the global context it cannot be separated from the medium of translation.

Therefore, the concept of the new humanities laid the foundation for theoretical innovation for scholars in the humanities. Under the broad vision of the new humanities, there is no need to worry about the disciplinary attributes of our theoretical concepts, and we can put some new theoretical concepts in a broader context, so as to give them the significance of guiding research in all branches of the humanities. To achieve this, the help of translation is needed. Therefore, it is no wonder that the French deconstructive philosopher and translation theorist Derrida believes that the history of Western philosophy is in a certain sense also the history of translation.

Below I will briefly discuss two central issues. The first is the "pictorial turn" caused by the disintegration of linguistic-centralism in translation. In recent years, the rapid development of high technology and the Internet brought major changes to reading habits, especially in the present age among young people who are no longer accustomed to quietly enjoying the pleasure of reading in libraries. They are more used to downloading various images from the Internet to read and enjoy on their mobile phones and tablets. Therefore, some intellectuals in the humanities who adhere to their traditional reading habits involuntarily sigh that the era of reading has passed, or more specifically, the era of reading physical books has had its day, with the arrival of an era of reading images.

Since many images and texts that we are now exposed to are not expressed in Chinese, issues of cross-linguistic and cross-cultural translation are involved. If we look at the history and modern form of the word "translation", it is easy to see that its traditional meaning has undergone major changes, including not only the conversion between two languages but also the interpretation and deciphering of various codes, and even the adaptation of works of literature and drama. The construction of national images as discussed in the academic circles of international politics today is also inseparable from the medium of translation, so it can be fully included in the framework of translation in the broad sense.

Thus, it is clearly insufficient to adhere to the definition of "linguo-centric" translation as put forward by Jakobson more than 60 years ago. Therefore, I will start by questioning the three elements of translation by Jakobson and focus on another form of contemporary translation: the translation of images and their conversion to language and texts. I believe that this is an expansion of the traditional field of translation and an improvement of the status of translation, and it also helps translation studies to become an independent branch of the humanities and social sciences.

The discussion of the phenomena of visual culture in the era of globalization has become a key issue in the circles of literary theory and cultural studies in the last decade or so. People will inevitably associate this with a kind of "pictorial turn" that has recently emerged in contemporary cultural and art criticism. Since this kind of image, which contains the meaning of language, cannot be separated from the specter of language, and to a large extent also bears the function of the original language and writing, we can also call it the "iconographical turn" so that it can combine the linguistic signs of the text and the images of the picture. This should be a new point of growth in the expansion of the translation field, and it is currently also a central issue in translation studies.

As a result of the "iconographical turn" in contemporary literary creation, the original writing method that mainly uses words to convey meaning has been challenged by popular culture and Internet writing, and thus the textual writing is also challenged by image writing. The original translation style that was restricted to conversion in language and text has also been challenged by image translation and interpretation. Facing the impact of this trend, traditional translation based on the conversion of language and text has gradually turned to the translation and interpretation that involve images as well.

As scholars engaged in translation studies, we are faced with two questions: if there is indeed such a "turn" in contemporary literary and art criticism, how is it different from earlier text-based creation and criticism? Moreover, how do we translate "texts" expressed through images into text expressed by language? If the translation of an image described in words of the same language into written text is still an intralingual translation, then the translation of an image described in another language into Chinese is obviously an interlingual translation or intersemiotic translation. In this way, the territory of translation is naturally expanded, and higher demands are made on the translator's knowledge reservoir and interpretation skills. This is also seen in the construction and dissemination of national images.

In the era of globalization today, profound changes in our lives and the order of work have occurred with the rapid development of high technology. While creating all kinds of new machines, human beings are not always in control of their fate, nor the destiny of the planet we live on. The myth of "Man" with a capital M was disintegrated, and Man became "posthuman". Traditional humanism has also transformed into "post-humanism". No matter in which direction post-humanism develops, it cannot imply that it will completely replace the role and function of human beings. Human beings have survived long-term struggles and compromises with nature and continue to make their lives more comfortable and convenient. In addition to having tenacious vitality, human beings are undoubtedly also supported by certain emotions. For example, literature is a way for people to express emotions and subtle feelings.

In the era of post-humanism, many tasks formerly performed by humans are taken over by machines. Machines may indeed take over many tasks that humans performed in the past, this is especially proven by the recent rise of artificial intelligence (AI). AI engages in not only literary writing, but also translation. Therefore, some people predict that with the popularization of AI traditional translation will perish, but I beg to differ. There is no denying that the use of AI translation relieves translators from their heavy task of language conversion, but it also gives rise to a loss of job opportunities for a large number of translators who earn a living by translating.

As a result, some people over-exaggerate the role of AI, and argue that if AI can create excellent literary works, then why can't it replace literary translation? Indeed, it is entirely possible for AI to translate ordinary documents into another language comparatively accurately. After all, the intelligence represented by AI is slightly higher than the intelligence of the average person. However, when it comes to more complex tasks and delicate emotions, machines or AI cannot be compared with humans. It is not surprising that in cross-cultural communication, machine translation or AI translation will become increasingly common, and sooner or later it will even replace human translation. Admittedly, this view is not without reason.

With the development of AI translation, human translators have begun to face serious challenges. However, anyone familiar with the capabilities of translation software knows that when it comes to the translation of literary or theoretical works that contain rich, complex, and multiple imagery, translation software always makes mistakes. This proves that outstanding literary works and monographs in the humanities are created by authors with rich imagination or scholars with profound knowledge, so they cannot be replaced by any other reproduction and translation tools including, of course, machine and AI translation, because only those with an extraordinary ability and wisdom can appreciate refined culture and art, including literature. Similarly, only those literary geniuses can create outstanding literary works of permanent value, and their works cannot be created by others who are less talented, which is evident in the history of Chinese and foreign literature. There is truth in the ancient Chinese saying: "The writing mirrors the writer" (or: "The style is the man"), or in other words, one writer's literary talent cannot be imitated by anyone else. This is like a topic in the postgraduate examination of modern Chinese literature: identify a passage written by Lu Xun. Readers familiar with Lu Xun can immediately recognize from the half-classical, half-colloquial language style that the passage was written by Lu Xun, even if they have never read it before. This is also evidenced by the literary talent of Mao Zedong. During the revolutionary war, Mao often wrote editorials for Xinhua News Agency and even wrote commentator's articles in the name of a Xinhua reporter. Mao's elevated literary talent and broadmindedness even scared his enemy Chiang Kai-shek, because the latter could tell from the unique style and content that the essay was written by Mao. It is clear that the work of an author with a unique writing style cannot be imitated by others whose talents are slightly inferior, let alone AI translation.

Likewise, the speech and the writing style of an outstanding leader cannot be replaced by others, let alone those cold machines and AI. Therefore, on this point, we can fully draw the following conclusion: only excellent translators with extensive knowledge, outstanding literary talents and aesthetic cultivation can translate literary works with rich and complex contents into their own mother tongue. The same is true for the translation of theories. Great theorists such as Kant, Hegel, Nietzsche, Freud, Heidegger, and Derrida cannot be copied, and their theories are even untranslatable in the absolute sense. Brilliant translators can only translate the basic meaning of their theory at a relatively accurate level, but its subtle and controversial deep meaning cannot be accurately reproduced in another language. If literary translation is a kind of cross-cultural and cross-linguistic reproduction, then the translation of theories is, in a sense, a kind of cross-cultural interpretation and construction of theory.

10.2 The vision of translation studies in the age of globalization

It is beyond doubt that we live in an era of globalization, and whether we acknowledge it or not, we cannot escape from its shadow. Since the late 1990s, discussions about globalization and cultural issues have been growing, not only in Western academic circles but also in the humanities and social sciences in China. Almost all scholars in the humanities who are sensitive to theories have been actively or passively involved in this discussion or the discussion of topics related to globalization and culture. Although the phenomenon of globalization first emerged in the field of economics, it has become one of the most important topics of cutting-edge theories for scholars in the entire humanities and social sciences. Many people believe that the emergence of the phenomenon of globalization actually heralds a certain degree of Westernization, while in the view of Europeans, globalization is more a form of Americanization. This is particularly evident in the worldwide promotion of American-style democracy and the popularization of American English, and McDonalds and Coca Cola which represent American culture. However, it has always been my belief that in the field of the humanities and social sciences, Marx and Engels were the first thinkers and theorists to explore the phenomenon of globalization and its role in cultural production and literary criticism. Therefore, those engaged in the study of globalization and cultural issues should start by carefully reading the original works of the founders of Marxism. Only based on this can we put forward our own innovative ideas in the context of contemporary practices. Of course, we cannot deny that globalization is a traveling concept, moving from the economic field to the entire humanities and social sciences, and increasingly affecting our cultural studies and translation studies. The discussion of globalization in today's cross-cultural context has also become a key issue in the circles of cultural studies and translation studies. Therefore, when we reread *The Communist Manifesto* in the context of globalization, it is easy for us to see that as early as 1848, when capitalism was still a rising force in a period of development, Marx and Engels already had seen the many contradictions hidden inside, and when describing the impact of unlimited expansion of capital on the production of spiritual culture, they pointed out with foresight:

> And as in material, so also in intellectual production. The intellectual creations of individual nations become common property. National one-sidedness and narrow-mindedness become more and more impossible, and from the numerous national and local literatures, there arises a world literature.[10]

It should be said that the transition from economic globalization to the globalization of culture and the emergence of world literature is another important contribution of the founders of Marxism to the entire humanities and social sciences. The discovery of the laws that govern the operation of globalization by the founders of Marxism, like their discovery of the laws of surplus value in capitalist society, has made important contributions to the advancement of human history, and is also a valuable legacy for our current study into culture and literature and their translation in the era of globalization.

Although the above passage has been quoted on various occasions by Marxist researchers in the East and in the West, it is easy to see that globalization as a historical process has indeed manifested itself on two levels in Western history: one is the discovery of the Americas by Columbus who came all the way from Europe in 1492, which started the expansion of Western capital from the center to the periphery, namely, the grand project of capitalist modernity. Under this grand project, many economically underdeveloped and small countries either followed the European and American model or became an ordinary player in their grand project of modernity. The other is the situation where "from the numerous national and local literatures, there arises a world literature" as predicted by Marx and Engels which in fact forecast the possibility of a globalization trend in culture. Of course, people have different perceptions of the phenomenon of cultural globalization: some think it is impossible to exist at all, and the so-called "globalization of culture" is just a phenomenon fabricated by a group of intellectuals in the humanities; others believe it has already become an indisputable fact, such as the popularity of English, the establishment and adaptation of McDonalds around the world, the impact of Hollywood movies on culture and movies of other weak nations, the omnipresent impact of mass media and the Internet, etc. All these facts show that cultural globalization is approaching and it forces us to come up with some active countermeasures. On the other hand, it is easy to go from one extreme to the other for those who think that the globalization trend only shows a tendency to become similar while ignoring its diversity and differences. Therefore, it is better to adopt a dialectical attitude toward the phenomenon.

For the discussion of the survival value and future prospects of literature and culture in the context of globalization, we should take world literature (*Weltliteratur*) as the starting point. As we all know, the concept of "world literature" was formally introduced by Goethe for the first time in 1827. After reading some non-Western literary works including Chinese literature, Goethe who was in his seventies back then, concluded:

> ... poetry is the universal possession of mankind, revealing itself everywhere and at all times in hundreds and hundreds of men. ... I therefore like to look about me in foreign nations, and advise everyone to do the same. National literature is now a rather unmeaning term: the epoch of world literature is at hand, and everyone must strive to hasten its approach.[11]

Yet in fact, the literature of different nations in the world had already begun to exchange and communicate through translation before Goethe. During the Age of Enlightenment in Europe, a development in the direction of world literature had emerged.[12] However, at the time it was a Utopian illusion to call for the advent of world literature. Later, in *The Communist Manifesto* (1848), Marx and Engels used the term to describe the "cosmopolitan characteristics" that were a direct consequence of global capitalization on literary production of the capitalist class. Obviously, the founders of Marxism clearly indicated here that a kind of global literature had emerged alongside the accelerated pace of economic globalization and the expansion of the world market. From the perspective of our discipline today, world literature is in fact the early stage of comparative literature which in a way arose from the process of economic and financial globalization. In order to highlight the role of literary and cultural studies in the current era of globalization, we should as a matter of fact have a comparative and international outlook, so that it is possible to make progress in literary studies. This is perhaps the important reason why we should place literary studies in the broad context of global culture and world literature.

The new concept of "world literature" proposed by the founders of Marxism contributed to the emergence of the new discipline of comparative literature in the second half of the nineteenth century and its development in the twentieth century.

However, how do we interpret the concept of "world literature"?[13] In my view, from the dialectical point of view of cultural differences and pluralistic development, the term "world literature" does not imply that there is only one model of literature in the world. Rather, in the macroscopic, international, and even global context, there is a kind of world literature that still retains the original style and characteristics of each nation, but at the same time represents the world's most advanced aesthetic trend and direction of development. On the other hand, world literature acts as the universal benchmark for evaluating literature from various nations and makes it possible for literature of all nations to be evaluated in a large global context. In other words, a rather uniformly recognized standard is needed to evaluate whether an excellent literary work has a lasting impact and achieves an absolute sense of innovation in the world or in a particular national culture. In this regard, again we cannot do without the medium of translation.[14] There are many languages in the world, and Western languages, especially English, have always been in a hegemonic position, so it is difficult for any literary work or theory from any nation to have a worldwide impact if it is not translated and disseminated in English. This is exemplified by the global influence of thinkers and translation theorists such as Benjamin and Derrida discussed in this book, and especially the success of postcolonial theorists who were born in Third World countries and gradually moved from the periphery to the center, and finally gained high positions in the United States, the center of world academia. Unlike the economic route from the West to the East, the process of cultural globalization has two directions: one is the expansion of capital from the center to the periphery and the infiltration of (colonial) cultural values and ethos into the area; but then comes a second direction, namely the struggle and interaction between (colonized) marginal cultures with the mainstream cultures, which gives rise to the phenomenon of the marginal culture infiltrating into the main body of the mainstream culture and eliminating the hegemony of the latter. The second phenomenon can be fully illustrated by the infiltration and deconstruction of the original colonial culture into the host country, as well as by the process of westward advancement in the history of Chinese culture.[15] The mutual influence and infiltration between Eastern and Western cultures is becoming increasingly obvious today. The strategy of cultural translation proposed by postcolonial theorist Homi Bhabha has actually gone beyond the narrow scope of traditional translation and has reached the point of spreading one culture into another and relocating it. Therefore, in our view it is impossible for the phenomenon of cultural globalization not to be resisted by another force—cultural localization—and in the long run, the future development of world culture will depend to a large extent on the interaction between globalization and localization, or perhaps the tendency of "glocalization". We increasingly feel the indispensability of translation when we look at cultural issues from the perspective of "glocalization".

As mentioned above, Western Marxists and left-wing scholars have made considerable contributions even though the theory of globalization was constructed from cultural perspectives. Arjun Appadurai, American anthropologist who has done in-depth research into globalization, pointed out that when interpreting the phenomenon of globalization from the perspective of cultural modernity, the global cultural system has already experienced some kind of "disjuncture":

> [...] an elementary framework for exploring such disjunctures is to look at the relationship among five dimensions of global cultural flows that can be termed (a) ethnoscapes, (b) mediascapes, (c) technoscapes, (d) financescapes, and (e) ideoscapes.[16]

At least four out of these five aspects are inseparable from direct intervention of translation. Fredric Jameson, a representative of contemporary neo-Marxism, has also studied in depth the relationship between globalization and culture and he advocates discussing the phenomenon of globalization in terms of five other aspects, or rather five levels of impact when he speaks about the all-encompassing effects of globalization: (1) the pure technological aspect; (2) the political consequences of globalization; (3) the cultural forms of globalization; (4) the economy of globalization; (5) the social dimension of globalization.[17] This suggests that all five levels of globalization cannot go without translation. Although the views of these two scholars somewhat overlap, they still provide inspiration for us to take further steps to construct a theory that takes China's specific practices into account. Given that the international academic community has been conducting research on the phenomenon of globalization for over 20 years and has achieved considerable results, the theoretical construction that I propose here is largely based on their findings though of course my starting point is the cultural knowledge practice of China. It has always been my belief that we should broaden our horizons because the aspects that globalization involves have gone beyond the economic and financial fields long ago. Therefore, we might as well carefully examine the phenomenon of globalization from the following seven aspects in a comprehensive manner:

(1) globalization as a form of economic integration; (2) globalization as a historical process; (3) globalization as a process of financial marketization and political democratization; (4) globalization as a concept of criticism; (5) globalization as a narrative category; (6) globalization as a cultural construction; and (7) globalization as a theoretical discourse.

Of course, Jameson once proposed that globalization is also a philosophical discourse,[18] which naturally inspired my further theoretical constructions. Based on the research of my predecessors and contemporary international colleagues, I myself attempt to further carry out the theoretical construction of globalization from a contemporary Marxist perspective, taking into account the discussion of globalization in the Chinese context. In my view, only by examining the phenomenon of globalization as a whole from the above-mentioned seven aspects, can we fully and accurately understand the essential features of globalization in all its dimensions, and actively participate in international research and discussion of theories of globalization by starting from its specific practice and development status in China, so as to produce a strong voice of Chinese scholars.

It is beyond doubt that the emergence of globalization has had a profound impact on our literary theory and comparative literature studies. It makes us consciously place it against the broad background of world literature when we investigate and study the phenomena of national literatures, and when evaluating a writer or a work we must also compare it with their predecessors or contemporaries in the international context. When we review the theoretical concept of "world literature" in the context of globalization today, I believe that we should also consider the co-existence of cultural homogeneity and cultural difference: when we apply them to literary criticism we can draw the conclusion that because literature has certain things in common, we should place the literature of each nation in the broad context of world literature to evaluate its inherent literary forms and aesthetic styles, and the conclusions drawn will be of a more universal nature and have a certain sense of guidance for the development of different national literatures. On the other hand, the content expressed by the literature of each nation also has a strong national spirit and cultural identity, which is carried through the medium of different languages, so we must also consider the national literature's inherent characteristics and specific Zeitgeist. Overemphasizing one of the aspects mentioned above, at the expense of another is not, to say the least, a realistic attitude, or attitude of seeking truth from facts. Therefore, we should be fully aware of the fact that globalization shows more cultural differences than similarities, and that even expressions in the same literary genre are very different in different languages and cultures. Otherwise, we will be like some naive people who wonder what the use of translation is when most people around the world can speak English. However, since the great development of translation around the world in the last one or two decades, we have come to the opposite conclusion that translation has become increasingly indispensable and the study of translation has become a "prominent subject" in the humanities and social sciences today. Not only scholars in linguistics and literary studies study translation, but also art theorists and anthropologists pay special attention to translation, even scholars in law and sociology regard translation as their object of research, and so on. From this perspective, it seems that the popularization of English worldwide is not the end of translation, but rather translation is even more flourishing. Even literature written in English in the UK and that in the USA are quite different, not to mention those postcolonial "English" works with their distinctly local dialects and grammatical rules. Since translation is indispensable for the deeper communication between national literatures, cultural translation, which focuses on the phenomenon of literary translation, is inevitably on the agenda of scholars in the humanities and social sciences in the era of globalization.

Early back at the beginning of this century, Bassnett expressed her optimistic views about the status of contemporary translation studies by pointing out in her revised edition of *Translation Studies:*

> The apparent division between cultural and linguistic approaches to translation that characterized much translation research until the 1980s is disappearing, partly because of shifts in linguistics that have seen that discipline take a more overtly cultural turn, partly because those who advocated an approach to translation rooted in cultural history have become less defensive about their position.[19]

Her collaborator Edwin Gentzler also noted in the final chapter "The Future of Translation Studies" in his *Contemporary Translation Theories* (Second Edition):

> Additionally, translation of recent has enjoyed a renaissance in many parts of the world not included in the above chapters, such as Spain, Italy, Canada, Brazil, China, and especially in those nations in which borders have been opened, including countries in central and eastern Europe. In this age of globalization, "lesser known languages" are particularly threatened, and translation and the study of translation become of increasing importance. New studies on translation in smaller countries and new nations continue to inform theory; I suggest that we are just scratching the surface and that in the coming years more studies from a variety of perspectives, cultures and languages will emerge.[20]

As a Western scholar in translation studies and comparative literature, Gentzler's keen interest in translation studies in China is quite rare indeed. Over the past ten years, he has been following translation studies in China, either by publishing articles in Chinese journals in China through translation or writing articles for edited volumes edited by Chinese scholars, and he speaks highly of translation studies in China. In an article that he published more than ten years ago, he reviewed the status of translation studies in Europe, the USA, and China and then publicly appealed to the reader, "Here, I suggest, United States translation studies scholars can learn much from their colleagues around the world, especially from China, where such historical and descriptive work is well underway".[21] About the development of translation studies in the twenty-first century, he looked forward optimistically and said:

> I am not sure exactly where the field of translation studies is heading, but I like the feel of the energy and commitment. Such a global view and interdisciplinary connections cannot but help scholars gain new insights into the nature of translation and how it impacts everyday lives.[22]

Although Gentzler has no knowledge of Chinese, he understands the situation of translation studies in China based on direct exchange with Chinese scholars and by reading articles written in English by Chinese scholars, thanks to the intermediary and help of translation itself, of course. At the same time, this also inspired us with the following fact: in the past few decades, we spared no effort to introduce foreign, especially Western, cultural theories and translation theories into China, greatly promoting the emergence and development of the discipline of translation studies in China, but on the other hand, our publications in the international academic world, mainly the English-speaking world, are unsatisfactory in terms of quantity and quality. If scholars in other disciplinary fields of the humanities wish to reach out to the world, they often have to resort to translation because of the language barrier, so should we, as scholars in translation studies who are proficient in at least two languages and cultures, also beg others to help us translate our own Chinese-language works into foreign languages to be published internationally? The answer is obviously negative. If we as translators can only translate foreign works into our own native language but cannot translate works written by ourselves or others in our native language into foreign languages and reach a publishable level, then we are not really good translators. Therefore, in the era of globalization, the expectations and demands of translators and translation scholars have increased.

However, in the face of the unprecedentedly favorable situation of translation and translation studies, we cannot shut our eyes to the awkward situation that translation studies is now in: on the one hand, translation has drawn the attention of scholars from more and more disciplines, whose research into translation each from their own perspectives undoubtedly has greatly inspired scholars in translation studies; but on the other hand, the disciplinary status of translation studies itself has yet to be recognized, especially in schools where traditional disciplines are extremely powerful. Therefore, the strategy, as proposed in this book, to develop translation studies, as a frontier discipline between the humanities and social sciences on the one hand and natural sciences on the other is at least for now an expedient measure. Similar to the rise and all-round development of cultural studies many years ago, it has led to an increasing number of people discussing translation, and as a result, scholars in translation studies have increasingly become aware of the ambiguity and uncertainty of the status of their discipline. They even think that since so many people are concerned about translation it might imply that the discipline of translation does not involve any specialized and sophisticated learning. In my view, there is no need to worry about this, because both Jakobson the structuralist and Derrida the deconstructionalist have classified the phenomenon of translation into categories: in Jakobson's view only interlingual translation is true translation, though he did not deny the value inherent in intralingual translation and intersemiotic translation leaving wide space for future development for the latter two. In Derrida's view, there is translation in the narrow sense and that in the metaphorical sense. The former remains the domain of exploration for the experts of translation studies, while the latter is the channel for scholars outside the discipline of translation to enter translation studies. Only when this channel is unimpeded may scholars in translation studies carry out fruitful exchange and dialogue with colleagues in other disciplines within the humanities, social sciences and even natural sciences.

In the past, scholars in translation studies followed the frontiers of other related disciplines in an attempt to introduce new theories and research methods. Today, when we engage in equal exchanges and dialogues on a shared platform of globalization, isn't it true that we also consider developing our own theories in order to "export" them to other disciplines? If not, scientific translation studies that was once pushed to the extreme by structuralist linguists will become increasingly isolated, and its field will become increasingly narrow, and the price it will have to pay is that the status of translation studies as a discipline will decline, and the achievements of translation studies will not be valued. Therefore, there is no need to worry about the phenomenon of "overgeneralization of translation" in the field of translation studies, let alone worry about outsiders occupying the field of translation studies. Only with active participation of scholars outside the discipline will translation studies be able to consolidate its status as a discipline and will researchers in the field of translation studies have the opportunity to exchange views and carry out dialogues with their counterparts in the entire field of the humanities and social sciences.

Before concluding our discussions in this book, I would like to emphasize again that the cultural turn in translation studies does not represent the entirety of translation studies. It just represents a once dominant tendency or trend in contemporary translation studies. Its limitations are as obvious as its strengths: some people who lack basic language training and translation practice justify their inability to translate academic works accurately or their willful rewriting of literary masterpieces, under the pretext of "cultural translation". Therefore, we should continue to make the fundamental distinction between "mistranslation" and "creative interpretation": the former is the inevitable result of limited linguistic skills and superficial knowledge, while the latter is out of an excellent translator's need to actively explore and interpret the deep meaning of the original based on an accurate understanding of the work. Therefore, when we argue that absolute faithfulness is impossible from the cultural perspective, it is just an attempt to explain the difficulty of a successful translation, but it is never meant to advocate an unfaithful and indiscriminately creative "translation" which in fact is a "pseudo-translation" and is not discussed by researchers of translation studies. Practice has proved that authentic results of translation studies will have more and more prominent value as history advances and the discipline develops, while the results of pseudo-translation or superficial research will eventually be eliminated by history. Therefore, I am fully confident that translation studies will have a healthy development and maturity, and I am also willing to make my own modest contribution to its future development. This is also the reason why I have chosen "the cultural turn" as my special focus from among the many translation studies topics.

Notes

1 It should be especially mentioned here that at the International Conference on Cultural Translation (1–3 May 2008) held at the University of Cambridge, UK, Susan Bassnett was invited to deliver the keynote speech "Translation as Cultural Mediation", while the topics of the other participants were mostly related to the three themes of the conference: translating culture, translating modernity and translating China.
2 At the symposium "Translation of Global Culture: Towards Interdisciplinary Theoretical Construction" held in Beijing on 11–15 August 2006, a large number of scholars from outside the discipline of translation or the field of translation studies have submitted papers covering a wide range of interdisciplinary and cross-artistic translation issues, including literary and cultural translation, translation and art history, gender in translation, legal translation, translation and diaspora writing, the politics of translation, translation and music. For the conference proceedings, see Wang, N. & Early, G. (eds.). 2008. *Translating Global Cultures: Toward Interdisciplinary (Re)Constructions*. Beijing: Foreign Language Teaching and Research Press.
3 Translators' note: There are two ways to translate the term *xin wenke* (新文科) in the Chinese original—"new humanities" or "new liberal arts", with the former being a subset of the latter. We consulted the original author and he approved of both translations. New

liberal arts embody intersection and mutual penetration of arts and science. Even though the author is from the humanities, he wants to absorb useful methods and concepts from mathematics and science and strengthen the discipline that he is in. Meanwhile, he also hopes that mathematics and science can learn something from the humanities and social sciences. The reason why we choose "new humanities" here is to show its contrast with traditional humanities.

4 See Wang, N. 2020. The construction of the discipline of foreign languages from the perspective of the new humanities. *Zhongguo Waiyu* [Foreign Languages in China], (3): 4–10.
5 For the concept of global humanities, see Wang, N. 2018. The specter of derrida: Towards the construction of the global humanities. *Tansuo Yu Zhengming* [Exploration and Free Views], (6): 15–22.
6 For articles on cosmopolitanism published by Chinese scholars in international academic circles, see Pan, D. 2017. Cosmopolitanism, tianxia, and Walter Benjamin's "The Task of the Translator". *Telos, 180*: 26–46; Wang, N. 2017. From Shanghai Modern to Shanghai Postmodern: A Cosmopolitan View of China's Modernization. *Telos, 180*: 87–103; Xie, S. 2017. Chinese Beginnings of Cosmopolitanism: A Genealogical Critique of *Tianxia Guan*. *Telos, 180*: 8–25; Zhao, T. 2006. Rethinking Empire from a Chinese Concept "All-under-heaven (Tian-xia, 天下)". *Social Identities, 12*(1): 29–41; and Zhao, T. 2009. A political world philosophy in terms of all-under-heaven (Tian-xia). *Diogenes, 221*: 5–18.
7 Wang, N. 2019. The Historical Role of Translation in the New Culture Movement and Its Future Prospect. *Zhongguo Fanyi* [Chinese Translators Journal], (3): 13–21.
8 Ibid.
9 I once gave a new definition of translation at an academic conference, which was later revised and published as a written talk. See Wang N. 2015. Redefining translation: An interdisciplinary and visual cultural perspective. *Zhongguo Fanyi* [Chinese Translators Journal], (3): 12–13.
10 Marx, K. & Engels, F. 1966. *The Communist Manifesto*. Beijing: People's Publishing House, 30. Translators' note: This English version is quoted on the dedication page of Damrosch, D. 2003. *What Is World Literature?* Princeton, NJ & Oxford: Princeton University Press.
11 Goethe, quoted in Damrosch, D. 2003. *What Is World Literature?* Princeton, NJ & Oxford: Princeton University Press, 1.
12 Cf. Fokkema, D. 2007. World literature. In R. Robertson & J. A. Scholte (eds.), *Encyclopedia of Globalization*. Vol. 4. London & New York: Routledge, 1290.
13 For the term "world literature" coined by Goethe and its historical change, see Damrosch, D. 2003. *What Is World Literature?* Princeton, NJ & Oxford: Princeton University Press, 1–36.
14 For a detailed discussion of the relation between world literature and translation see Wang, N. 2009. "World literature" and translation. *Wenyi Yanjiu* [Literary Studies], (3): 24–33.
15 Translators' note: For example, Chinese tea and ceramics moved west. In the Ming dynasty, navigator Zheng He (1371–1433) went on expedition to the west and reached East Africa.
16 Appadurai, A. 1996. *Modernity at Large: Cultural Dimensions of Globalization*. Minneapolis & London: University of Minnesota Press, 33.
17 Jameson, F. 2002. Cultures of globalization. In N. Wang (ed.), *Globalization and Culture: The West and China*. Beijing: Peking University Press, 105–121. For English source, see Jameson, F. 2000. Globalization and political strategy. *New Left Review, 4*: 49.
18 Jameson, F. 1998. Notes on globalization as a philosophical issue. In F. Jameson & M. Miyoshi (eds.), *The Cultures of Globalization*. Durham, NC: Duke University Press, 54–77.

19 Bassnett, S. 2002. *Translation Studies* (3rd ed.). London & New York: Routledge, 3.
20 Gentzler, E. 1993. *Contemporary Translation Theories*. London & New York: Routledge, 187.
21 Gentzler, E. 2008. A global view of translation studies: Towards an interdisciplinary field. In N. Wang & Y. Sun (eds.), *Translation, Globalisation and Localisation: A Chinese Perspective*. Clevedon: Multilingual Matters Ltd., 117.
22 Ibid., p. 126.

Bibliography

Albrow, M. 1997. *The Global Age: State and Society Beyond Modernity*. Stanford, CA: Stanford University Press.
Appadurai, A. 1996. *Modernity at Large: Cultural Dimensions of Globalization*. Minneapolis: University of Minnesota Press.
Appiah, K. A. & Gates Jr., H. L. (eds.). 1995. *Identities*. Chicago, IL & London: The University of Chicago Press.
Arac, J. 1997. Postmodernism and postmodernity in China: An agenda for inquiry. *New Literary History, 28*(1): 135–145.
Arnold, D. 2004. *Art History: A Very Short Introduction*. Oxford & New York: Oxford University Press.
Ashcroft, B., Griffiths, G. & Tiffin, H. 1989. *The Empire Writes Back: Theory and Practice in Post-colonial Literatures*. London & New York: Routledge.
Ashcroft, B., Griffiths, G. & Tiffin, H. (eds.). 1995. *The Postcolonial Studies Reader*. London & New York: Routledge.
Baker, M. (ed.). 1998. *Routledge Encyclopedia of Translation Studies*. London & New York: Routledge.
Barthes, R. 1977. *Image–Music–Text*. S. Heath (ed.). London: Collins.
Bassnett, S. 1993. *Comparative Literature: A Critical Introduction*. Oxford: Wiley-Blackwell.
Bassnett, S. 2002. *Translation Studies* (3rd ed.). London & New York: Routledge.
Bassnett, S. & Lefevere, A. (eds.). 1990. *Translation, History and Culture*. London & New York: Pinter.
Bassnett, S. & Lefevere, A. 1998. *Constructing Cultures: Essays on Literary Translation*. Clevdon & London: Multilingual Matters Ltd.
Baudrillard, J. 1988. *Selected Writings*. M. Poster (ed. & intro.). Stanford, CA: Stanford University Press.
Beebee, T. O. 1994. *The Ideology of Genre: A Comparative Study of Generic Instability*. University Park, PA: The Pennsylvania State University Press.
Benjamin, W. 1968. The work of art in the age of mechanical reproduction. *Illuminations*. Harry, Z. (trans.) New York: Schocken.
Benjamin, W. 1992. The task of the translator. In R. Schulte & J. Biguenet (eds.), *Theories of Translation: An Anthology of Essays from Dryden to Derrida*. Chicago, IL & London: The University of Chicago Press, 71–82.
Berheimer, C. (ed.). 1995. *Comparative Literature in the Age of Multiculturalism*. Baltimore, MD & London: The Johns Hopkins University Press.

Bertens, H. & Fokkema, D. (eds.). 1997. *International Postmodernism: Theory and Literary Practice*. Amsterdam & Philadelphia: John Benjamins.

Bhabha, H. 1992. Postcolonial criticism. In S. Greenblatt & G. Gunn (eds.), *Redrawing the Boundaries: The Transformation of English and American Literary Studies*. New York: The Modern Language Association of America, 437–465.

Bhabha, H. K. (ed.). 1990. *Nation and Narration*. London & New York: Routledge.

Bhabha, H. K. 1994. *The Location of Culture*. London & New York: Routledge.

Butler, J. 2003. Values of difficulty. In C. Jonathan & K. Lamb (eds.), *Just Being Difficult? Academic Writing in the Public Arena*. Stanford, CA: Stanford University Press, 199–215.

Calinescu, M. 1987. *Five Faces of Modernity: Modernism, Avant–Garde, Decadence, Kitsch, Postmodernism*. Durham, NC: Duke University Press.

Chan, S. 2009. *A Chronology of Translation in China and the West: From the Legendary Period to 2004*. Hong Kong: The Chinese University Press.

Chen, X. 1995. *Occidentalism: A Theory of Counter-Discourse in Post-Mao China*. Oxford: Oxford University Press.

Chow, R. 1993. *Writing Diaspora: Tactics of Intervention in Contemporary Cultural Studies*. Bloomington & Indianapolis: Indiana University Press.

Cronin, M. 2003. *Translation and Globalization*. London & New York: Routledge.

Culler, J. 1983. *On Deconstruction: Theory and Criticism after Structuralism*. Ithaca, NY: Cornell University Press.

Culler, J. 2007. *The Literary in Theory*. Stanford, CA: Stanford University Press.

Damrosch, D. 2003. *What Is World Literature?* Princeton, NJ & Oxford: Princeton University Press.

Damrosch, D. 2009. *How to Read World Literature*. Oxford: Wiley-Blackwell.

De Man, P. 1986. Conclusions: Walter Benjamin's "The task of the translator". In *The Resistance to Theory*. Minneapolis: University of Minnesota Press, 73–105.

Delisle, J. & Woodsworth, J. (eds.). 1995. *Translators Through History*. Amsterdam & Philadelphia: John Benjamins.

Dentith, S. 1995. *Bakhtinian Thought: An Introductory Reader*. London & New York: Routledge.

Derrida, J. 1972. *Positions*. Paris: Minuit.

Derrida, J. 1976. *Of Grammatology*. G. C. Spivak (trans.). Baltimore, MD: Johns Hopkins University Press.

Derrida, J. 1978. *Writing and Difference*. A. Bass (trans.). Chicago, IL: University of Chicago Press.

Derrida, J. 1984. Deconstruction and the other. In R. Kearney (ed.), *Dialogues with Contemporary Continental Thinkers: The Phenomenological Heritage*. Manchester: Manchester University Press, 107–126.

Derrida, J. 1985. Des Tours de Babel. J. F. Graham (trans.). In J. F. Graham (ed.), *Difference in Translation*. Ithaca, NY & New York: Cornell University Press, 165–248.

Derrida, J. 1998. *Monolingualism of the Other; or, The Prothesis of Origen*. P. Mensah (trans.). Stanford, CA: Stanford University Press.

Derrida, J. 2001.What is a "relevant" translation? *Critical Inquiry*, *27*(2): 174–200.

Dirlik, A. & Zhang, X. (eds.). 2000. *Postmodernism and China*. Durham, NC & London: Duke University Press.

Dollerup, C. 1997. Translation as loan vs. translation as imposition. In M. Snell-Hornby, Z. Jettmarová & K. Kaindl (eds.), *Translation as Intercultural Communication*. Amsterdam & Philadelphia: John Benjamins, 45–56.

Dollerup, C. & Grun, M. 2007. *Basics of Translation Studies*. Shanghai: Shanghai Foreign Language Education Press.
Duing, S. (ed.). 1993. *The Cultural Studies Reader*. London & New York: Routledge.
Eagleton, T. 1997. The contradictions of postmodernism. *New Literary History, 28*(1): 1–6.
Eagleton, T. 2003. *After Theory*. London: Penguin Books.
Eagleton, T. 2004. The fate of the arts. *The Hedgehog Review, 6*(2): 7–14.
Eco, U. 1992. *Interpretation and Overinterpretation*. Cambridge: Cambridge University Press.
Esselink, B. 2000. *A Practical Guide to Localization*. Amsterdam & Philadelphia: John Benjamins.
Even-Zohar, I. 1978a. The position of translated literature within the literary polysystem. In J. S. Holmes, J. Lambert, & R. van den Broeck (eds.), *Literature and Translation*. Leuven: ACCO, 117–127.
Even-Zohar, I. 1978b. *Papers in Historical Poetics*. Tel Aviv: University Publishing Projects.
Even-Zohar, I. 1990. Polysystems studies. *Poetics Today, 11*(1): 1–94.
Fiedler, L. 1972. *Cross the Border—Close the Gap*. New York: Stein and Day.
Fiske, J. 1989. *Understanding Popular Culture*. London & New York: Routledge.
Foucault, M. 1972. *The Archaeology of Knowledge and the Discourse on Language*. Sheridan–Smith, A. M. (trans.) New York: Harper and Row.
Franco, B. 2016. *La Littérature Comparée: Histoire, Domains, Methods*. Malakoff: Amanda Colin.
Gentzler, E. 1993. *Contemporary Translation Theories*. London & New York: Routledge.
Gentzler, E. 1996. Translation, counter-culture, and *The Fifties* in the USA. In R. Álvarez & M. Carmen–África Vidal (eds.), *Translation, Power, Subversion*. Clevedon: Multilingual Matters, 116–137.
Gentzler, E. 2001. *Contemporary Translation Theories* (2nd ed.). Clevedon: Multilingual Matters.
Gentzler, E. 2003. Interdisciplinary connections. *Perspectives: Studies in Translatology, 11*(1): 11–24.
Giddens, A. 1984. *The Constitution of Society: Outline of the Theory of Structuration*. Cambridge: Polity Press.
Giddens, A. 1990. *The Consequences of Modernity*. Stanford, CA: Stanford University Press.
Gombrich, E. H. 1979. *Ideals and Idols: Essays on Values in History and in Art*. London: Phaidon.
Graddol, D. 2006. *English Next*. London: British Council.
Gutt, E. A. 1991. *Translation and Relevance: Cognition and Context*. Oxford: Oxford University Press.
Hardt, M. & Negri, A. 2000. *Empire*. Cambridge, MA: Harvard University Press.
Harpham, G. G. 2011. *The Humanities and the Dream of America*. Chicago, IL & London: The University of Chicago Press.
Hayles, N. K. 2012. *How We Think: Digital Media and Contemporary Technologies*. Chicago, IL & London: The University of Chicago Press.
Heidegger, M. 1977. The age of the world picture (1938). In Lovitt W. (trans. & ed.), *The Question Concerning Technology and Other Essays*. New York: Harper Torchobooks, 115–154.
Hermans, T. 1999. *Translation in Systems: Descriptions and System–Oriented Approaches Explained*. Manchester: St. Jerome.

Heylen, R. 1993. *Translation, Poetics & the Stage: Six French Hamlets*. London & New York: Routledge.
Holmes, J. 1988. The name and nature of translation studies. In *Translated! Papers on Literary Translation and Translation Studies*. Amsterdam: Rodopi, 67–80.
Hung, E. 1999. The role of the foreign translator in the Chinese translation tradition, 2nd to 19th century. *Target*, *11*(2): 223–244.
Hutcheon, L. 1985. *A Theory of Parody: The Teachings of Twentieth-Century Art Forms*. New York: Methuen.
Hutcheon, L. 1989. *The Politics of Postmodernism*. London & New York: Routledge.
Hutcheon, L. & Valdés, M. (eds.). 2002. *Rethinking Literary History: A Dialogue on Theory*. Oxford & New York: Oxford University Press.
Iser, W. 2000. *The Range of Interpretation*. New York: Columbia University Press.
Jakobson, R. 1992. On linguistic aspects of translation. In R. Schulte & J. Biguenet (eds.), *Theories of Translation: An Anthology of Essays from Dryden to Derrida*. Chicago, IL & London: The University of Chicago Press, 144–151.
Jameson, F. 1983. Postmodernism and consumer society. In H. Foster (ed.), *The Anti–Aesthetic: Essays on Postmodern Culture*. Seattle: Bay Press, 124–125.
Jameson, F. 1984. Postmodernism, or, the cultural logic of late capitalism. *New Left Review*, *146* (July–August): 59–92.
Jameson, F. 1991. *Postmodernism, or, the Cultural Logic of Late Capitalism*. Durham, NC: Duke University Press.
Jameson, F. 1998. Notes on globalization as a philosophical issue. In F. Jameson & M. Miyoshi (eds.), *The Cultures of Globalization*. Durham, NC: Duke University Press, 54–77.
Jameson, F. & Miyoshi, M. (eds.). 1998. *The Cultures of Globalization*. Durham, NC: Duke University Press.
Jauss, H. R. 1982. *Toward an Aesthetic of Reception*. T. Bahti (trans.). Minneapolis: University of Minnesota Press.
Jay, P. 2001. Beyond discipline? Globalization and the future of English. *PMLA*, *116*(1): 32–47.
Johansen, J. D. 1993. *Dialogic Semiosis: An Essay on Signs and Meaning*. Bloomington & Indianapolis: Indiana University Press.
Jusdanis, G. 1991. *Belated Modernity and Aesthetic Culture: Inventing National Literature*. Minneapolis: University of Minnesota Press.
Kachru, B. B. (ed.). 1982. *The Other Tongue: English Across Culture*. Urbana: University of Illinois Press.
Katan, D. 1999. *Translating Cultures: An Introduction for Translators, Interpreters and Mediators*. Manchester: St. Jerome Publishing.
Kingscott, G. 2003. Technical translation and related disciplines. *Perspectives: Studies in Translatology*, *10*(4): 247–255.
Kuhn, T. 1970. *The Structure of Scientific Revolution* (2nd ed.). Chicago, IL: University of Chicago Press.
Lefevere, A. 1992a. *Translation, Rewriting and the Manipulation of Literary Fame*. London & New York: Routledge.
Lefevere, A. (trans. & ed.). 1992b. *Translation/History/Culture: A Sourcebook*. London & New York: Routledge.
Lefevere, A. 1992c. *Translating Literature: Practice and Theory in a Comparative Literature Context*. New York: The Modern Language Association of America.
Leppert, R. 1996. *Art and the Committed Eye: The Cultural Functions of Imagery*. Boulder, CO: Westview Press.

Levenson, J. R. 1971. *Revolution and Cosmopolitanism: The Western Stage and the Chinese Stages*. Berkeley: University of California Press.
Lévi–Strauss, C. 1973. *Tristes Tropiques*. Weightman, J. & Weightman, D. (trans.) New York: Atheneum.
Liu, L. H. (ed.). 1999. *Tokens of Exchange: The Problem of Translation in Global Circulations*. Durham, NC & London: Duke University Press.
Lu, S. 2007. *Chinese Modernity and Global Biopolitics: Studies in Literature and Visual Culture*. Honolulu: University of Hawaii Press.
Lyotard, J.-F. 1984. *The Postmodern Condition: A Report on Knowledge*. Geoff, B. & B. Massumi (trans.) Minneapolis: University of Minnesota Press.
McHale, B. & Platt, L. (eds.). 2016. *The Cambridge History of Postmodern Literature*. New York: Cambridge University Press.
Meissner, W. 1990. *Philosophy and Politics in China: The Controversy over Dialectical Materialism in the 1930s*. Mann R. (trans.) London: Hurst & Company.
Miller, J. H. 1993. *New Starts: Performative Topographies in Literature and Criticism*. Taipei: Academia Sinica.
Miller, J. H. 2007. A defense of literature and literary study in a time of globalization and the new tele–technologies. *Neohelicon*, *34*(2): 13–22.
Mims, J. T. & Elizabeth, M. N. 2000. *Mirror on America: Short Essays and Images from Popular Culture*. Boston & New York: Bedford/St. Martin's.
Mitchell, W. J. T. 1986. *Iconology: Image, Text, Ideology*. Chicago, IL & London: The University of Chicago Press.
Mitchell, W. J. T. 1994. *Picture Theory*. Chicago, IL & London: The University of Chicago Press.
Mitchell, W. J. T. 2007. World pictures: Globalization and visual culture. *Neohelicon*, *34*(2): 49–59.
Munday, J. 2001. *Introducing Translation Studies; Theories and Applications*. London & New York: Routledge.
Nida, E. 1964. *Towards a Science of Translating, with Special Reference to Principles and Procedures Involved in Bible Translating*. Leiden: E. J. Brill.
Nida, E. 1984. *Signs, Sense, Translation*. Cape Town: Bible Society of South Africa.
Nida, E. A. 1993. *Language, Culture and Translating*. Shanghai: Shanghai Foreign Language Education Press.
Nida, E. A. & William, D. R. 1981. *Meaning Across Cultures*. Maryknoll: Orbis Books.
Niranjana, T. 1992. *Siting Translation: History, Post–structuralism, and the Colonial Context*. Berkeley: University of California Press.
Pollard, D. A. (ed.). 1998. *Translation and Creation: Readings of Western Literature in Early Modern China 1840–1918*. Amsterdam & Philadelphia: John Benjamins.
Poster, M. (ed.). 1993. *Politics, Theory, and Contemporary Culture*. New York: Columbia University Press.
Remak, H. 1961. Comparative literature, its definition and function. In N. Stallknecht & H. Frenz (eds.), *Comparative Literature: Method and Perspective*. Carbondale: Southern Illinois University Press.
Richards, I. A. 1968. *So Much Nearer: Essays Toward a World English*. New York: Harcourt, Brace & World.
Ricoeur, P. 1981. *Hermeneutics and the Human Sciences: Essays on Language, Action, and Interpretation*. John B. T. (trans.). Cambridge: Cambridge University Press.
Robertson, R. 1992. *Globalization: Social Theory and Global Culture*. London: Sage Publications.

Robertson, R. 1995. Glocalization: Time–space and homogeneity–heterogeneity. In M. Featherstone et al. (eds.), *Global Modernities*. London: Sage Publications, 25–44.

Robertson, R. & Scholte, J. (eds.). 2006. *Encyclopedia of Globalization*. Vols. 1–4. London & New York: Routledge.

Robertson, R. & White, K. (eds.). 2003. *Globalization: The Critical Concepts in Sociology*. Vols. 1–6. London & New York: Routledge.

Rossi, I. (ed.). 2020. *Challenges of Globalization and Prospects for an Inter–Civilizational World Order*. Switzerland AG: Springer Nature.

Rubel, P. G. & Rosman, A. (eds.). 2003. *Translating Cultures: Perspectives on Translation and Anthropology*. Oxford & New York: Berg.

Said, E. 1979. *Orientalism*. New York: Doubleday Books.

Said, E. 1982. Traveling theory. *Raritan*, *1*(3): 41–67.

Said, E. 1983. *The World, the Text, and the Critic*. Cambridge, MA: Harvard University Press.

Said, E. 2000. *Reflections on Exile and Other Essays*. Cambridge, MA: Harvard University Press.

Said, E. 2001. Globalizing literary study. *PMLA*, *116*(1): 64–68.

Saussy, H. (ed.). 2006. *Comparative Literature in an Age of Globalization*. Baltimore, MD & London: The Johns Hopkins University Press.

Schäfner, C. & Holmes, H. K. (eds.). 1995. *Cultural Functions of Translation*. Clevedon: Multilingual Matters Ltd.

Schulte, R. & Biguenet, J. (eds.). 1992. *Theories of Translation: An Anthology of Essays from Dryden to Derrida*. Chicago, IL & London: University of Chicago Press.

Shuttleworth, M. & Cowie, M. (eds.). 1997. *Dictionary of Translation Studies*. Manchester: St. Jerome.

Simon, S. 1996. *Gender in Translation: Cultural Identity and the Politics of Transmission*. London & New York: Routledge.

Singh, M., Kell, P. & Pandian, A. 2002. *Appropriating English: Innovation in the Global Business of English Language Teaching*. New York: Peter Lang.

Slack, J. D. 1996. The theory and method of articulation in cultural studies. In D. Morley & K. Chen (eds.), *Stuart Hall: Critical Dialogues in Cultural Studies*. London & New York: Routledge, 113–129.

Snell–Hornby, M. 1995. *Translation Studies: An Integrated Approach* (rev. ed.). Amsterdam & Philadelphia: John Benjamins.

Spivak, G. C. 1974. Translator's preface. In J. Derrida (ed.), *Of Grammatology*. Baltimore, MD: The Johns Hopkins University Press, 9–87.

Spivak, G. C. 1987. *In Other Worlds: Essays in Cultural Politics*. London & New York: Routledge.

Spivak, G. C. 1990. *The Post-colonial Critic: Interviews, Strategies, Dialogues*. S. Harasym (ed.). London & New York: Routledge.

Spivak, G. C. 1993. The politics of translation. In *Outside in the Teaching Machine*. London & New York: Routledge, 179–200.

Spivak, G. C. 1996. *The Spivak Reader*. D. Landry & G. MacLean (eds.). London & New York: Routledge.

Spivak, G. C. 1999. *A Critique of Postcolonial Reason: Toward a History of the Vanishing Present*. Cambridge, MA: Harvard University Press.

Spivak, G. C. 2000. Translation as culture. *Parallax*, *6*(1): 13–24.

Spivak, G. C. 2001. Questioned on translation: Adrift. *Public Culture*, *13*(1): 13–22.

Spivak, G. C. 2003. *Death of a Discipline*. New York: Columbia University Press.

Stallknecht, N. & Frenz, H. (eds.). 1961. *Comparative Literature: Method and Perspective*. Carbondale: Southern Illinois University Press.

Sternberg, M. 1981. Polylingualism as reality and translation as mimesis. *Poetics Today*, 2(4): 221–239.
Storey, J. (ed.). 1996. *What Is Cultural Studies? A Reader*. London: Arnold.
Sun, Y. 2003. Translating cultural differences. *Perspectives: Studies in Translatology*, 11(1): 25–36.
Tallmadge, J. & Harrington, H. (eds.). 2000. *Reading under the Sign of Nature: New Essays in Ecocriticism*. Salt Lake City: The University of Utah Press.
Tao, D. & Jin, Y. (eds.). 2005. *Cultural Studies in China*. Singapore: Marshall Cavendish Academic.
Thussu, D. K., De Burgh, H. & Shi, A. (eds.). 2018. *China's Media Go Global*. London & New York: Routledge.
Toury, G. 1980. *In Search of a Theory of Translation*. Tel Aviv: The Porter Institute.
Tudor, A. 1999. *Decoding Culture: Theory and Method in Cultural Studies*. London: Sage Publications.
Turner, B. S. 1994. *Orientalism, Postmodernism & Globalism*. London & New York: Routledge.
Van den Broeck, R. 1988. Translation theory after deconstruction. *Linguistica Antverpiensia*, 22: 266–288.
Veeser, H. A. (ed.). 1989. *The New Historicism*. London & New York: Routledge.
Venuti, L. (ed.). 1995a. *Rethinking Translation: Discourse, Subjectivity, Ideology*. London & New York: Routledge.
Venuti, L. 1995b. *The Translator's Invisibility: A History of Translation*. London & New York: Routledge.
Venuti, L. 1998. *The Scandals of Translation: Towards an Ethics of Difference*. London & New York: Routledge.
Venuti, L. (ed.). 2000. *The Translation Studies Reader*. London & New York: Routledge.
Venuti, L. 2001. Introduction to Derrida's "What is a 'relevant' translation?" *Critical Inquiry*, 27(2): 169–173.
Venuti, L. 2013. *Translation Changes Everything: Theory and Practice*. London & New York: Routledge.
Wang, J. 2007. *The Iron Curtain of Language: Maxine Hong Kingston and American Orientalism*. Shanghai: Fudan University Press.
Wang, N. 2000. The popularization of English and the "decolonization" of Chinese critical discourse. *ARIEL*, 31(1–2): 411–424.
Wang, N. 2001. Translatology: Toward a scientific discipline. *China Translators Journal*, 22(6): 2–7.
Wang, N. 2002. Translation as cultural "(de)colonisation". *Perspectives: Studies in Translatology*, 10(4): 283–292.
Wang, N. (ed.). 2003. Translation studies: Interdisciplinary approaches, a special issue on translation studies in China. *Perspectives: Studies in Translatology*, 11(1): 7–10.
Wang, N. 2004. *Globalization and Cultural Translation*. Singapore: Marshall Cavendish Academic.
Wang, N. & Early, G. (eds.). 2008. *Translating Global Cultures: Toward Interdisciplinary (Re)constructions*. Beijing: Foreign Language Teaching and Research Press.
Wang, N. & Sun, Y. (eds.). 2008. *Translation, Globalisation and Localisation: A Chinese Perspective*. Clevedon: Multilingual Matters.
Wu, D. D. (ed.). 2008. *Discourses of Cultural China in the Globalizing Age*. Hong Kong: Hong Kong University Press.
Young, R. J. C. 2003. *Postcolonialism: A Very Short Introduction*. Oxford: Oxford University Press.

Chinese references

Benjamin, W. 2006. *A Short History of Photography + The Work of Art in the Age of Mechanical Reproduction*. C. Wang (trans.). Nanjing: Jiangsu People's publishing house. [瓦尔特·本雅明. 2006. 摄影小史+ 机械复制时代的艺术作品. 王才勇译. 南京：江苏人民出版社.]

Brodsen, M. 2000. *Walter Benjamin: A Biography*. R. Guo, Y. Tang, & Z. Song (trans.). Lanzhou: Dunhuang Literature and Art Publishing House. [毛姆·布罗德森. 2000. 本雅明传. 国容等译. 兰州：敦煌文艺出版社.]

Cai, X. 2007. *The Relevance of Relevance: Derrida's Ideas on "Relevant" Translation and Beyond*. Beijing: China Social Sciences Press. [蔡新乐. 2007. 相关的相关：德里达"相关的"翻译思想及其他. 北京：中国社会科学出版社.]

Chen, C. & Yin, X. 2007. A lecture and academic transformation in the new era: An interview with Wang Ning and Wang Fengzhen. *China Book Review*, (1): 76–79. [陈晨，尹星. 2007. 一场演讲与新时期学术转型——王宁、王逢振访谈录. 中国图书评论, (1): 76–79.]

Chen, F. 2000. *Manuscript on the History of Chinese Translation Theory* (rev. ed.). Shanghai: Shanghai Foreign Language Education Press. [陈福康. 2000. 中国译学理论史稿 (修订本). 上海：上海外语教育出版社.]

Chen, Y. (ed.). 2005. *Translation and Postmodernity*. Beijing: China Renmin University Press. [陈永国. 2005. 翻译与后现代性. 北京：中国人民大学出版社.]

Derek, A. 2007. The critique of modernity in contemporary perspective. *Journal of Nanjing University*, (6): 50–59. [阿里夫·德里克. 2007. 当代视野中的现代性批判. 南京大学学报, (6): 50–59.]

Feng, Y. 2006. On Lawrence Venuti's deconstructive translation strategy. *Literary and Art Studies*, (3): 39–44. [封一函. 2006. 论劳伦斯·韦努蒂的解构主义翻译策略. 文艺研究, (3): 39–44.]

Fu, L. 1997. *Twenty Lectures on Masterpieces of World Art* (2nd ed.). Beijing: SDX Joint Publishing Company. [傅雷. 1997. 世界美术名作二十讲. 第2版. 北京：生活·读书·新知三联书店.]

Gombrich, E. H. 1989. *The Image and the Eye: Further Studies in the Psychology of Pictorial Representation*. J. Fan, S. Yang, Y. Xu, & C. Lao (trans.). Hangzhou: Zhejiang Photography Publishing House. [E. H. 贡布里希. 1989. 图像与眼睛：图画再现心理学的再研究. 范景中等译. 杭州：浙江摄影出版社.]

Jiang, X. & Zhang, J. 2007. Reinterpreting Venuti's theory of alienated translation—debating with Professor Guo Jianzhong. *Chinese Translators Journal*, (3): 39–44. [蒋骁华, 张景华. 2007. 重新解读韦努蒂的异化翻译理论——兼与郭建中教授商榷. 中国翻译, (3): 39–44.]

Lu Xun. 1981. *The Complete Works of Lu Xun*. Vol. 4. Beijing: People's Literature Publishing House. [鲁迅. 1981. 鲁迅全集. 第四卷. 北京：人民文学出版社.]

Lu, Y. (ed.). 2008. *An Introduction to Cultural Studies*, Shanghai: Fudan University Press. [陆扬编. 2008. 文化研究概论. 上海：复旦大学出版社.]

Marx, K. & Engels, F. 1966. *Communist Manifesto*. Beijing: People's Publishing House. [马克思, 恩格斯. 1966. 共产党宣言. 北京：人民出版社.]

Ma, Z. 1999. *A History of Chinese Translation*. Vol. 1. Wuhan: Hubei Education Press. [马祖毅. 1999. 中国翻译史. 上卷. 武汉：湖北教育出版社.]

McRobbie, A. 2007. *The Uses of Cultural Studies*. Q. Li (trans.). Beijing: Peking University Press. [安吉拉·麦克罗比. 2007. 文化研究的用途. 李庆本译. 北京：北京大学出版社.]

Meng, J. & Li, Y. (eds.). 2003. *Conflict-Harmony: Globalization and Asian Film and Television*. Shanghai: Fudan University Press. [孟建，李亦中等. 2003. 冲突·和谐：全球化与亚洲影视. 上海：复旦大学出版社.]

Ning, Y. 1999. Miller on the translation of literary theory. *Foreign Languages and Their Teaching*, (5): 37–39. [宁一中. 1999. 米勒论文学理论的翻译. 外语与外语教学, (5): 37–39.]

Qian, Z. 1981. *The Translation of Lin Shu*. Beijing: The Commercial Press. [钱锺书. 1981. 林纾的翻译. 北京：商务印书馆.]

Qin, X. 2019. *Critique of Contemporary Translation*. Beijing: Tsinghua University Press. [覃学岚. 2019. 当代译学批判. 北京：清华大学出版社.]

Sheng, A. 2008. The travel and variation of theory: Postcolonial theory in China. In N. Wang (ed.), *Frontiers of Literary Theory*. Vol. 5. Beijing: Peking University Press, 121–164. [生安锋. 2008. 理论的旅行与变异：后殖民理论在中国. 载王宁主编，《文学理论前沿》第五辑. 北京：北京大学出版社, 121–164.]

Sun, Y. 2004. *Perspective-Interpretation-Culture: Literary Translation and Translation Theory* (rev. ed.). Beijing: Tsinghua University Press. [孙艺风. 2004. 视角·阐释·文化：文学翻译与翻译理论. 北京：清华大学出版社.]

Tan, Z. 2004. *A Short History of Western Translation* (rev. ed.). Beijing: The Commercial Press. [谭载喜. 2004. 西方翻译简史（增订版）. 北京：商务印书馆.]

Turner, G. 1998. *British Cultural Studies: An Introduction*. W. Tang (trans.). Taipei: Asia Pacific Book Press. [戈莱梅·透纳. 1998. 英国文化研究导论. 唐维敏译. 台北：亚太图书出版社.]

Wang, D. 2008. A comparison of Venuti's and Lu Xun's views on foreignization in translation. *Chinese Translators Journal*, (2): 5–10. [王东风. 2008. 韦努蒂与鲁迅异化翻译观比较. 中国翻译, (2): 5–10.]

Wang, N. 2002a. *Beyond Postmodernism*. Beijing: People's Literature Publishing House. [王宁. 2002a. 超越后现代主义. 北京：人民文学出版社.]

Wang, N. (ed.). 2002b. *Globalization and Culture: The West and China*. Beijing: Peking University Press. [王宁编. 2002b. 全球化与文化：西方与中国. 北京大学出版社.]

Wang, N. 2006/2021. *Cultural Translation and Classical Interpretation* (rev. ed.). Beijing: Zhonghua Book Company. [王宁. 2006/2021. 文化翻译与经典阐释. 北京：中华书局.]

Wang, N. 2009. World literature' and translation. *Literary Studies*, (3): 24–33. [王宁. 2009". 世界文学"与翻译. 文艺研究, (3): 24–33.]

Wang, N. 2014. *Comparative Literature, World Literature and Translation Studies*. Shanghai: Fudan University Press. [王宁. 2014. 比较文学、世界文学与翻译研究. 上海：复旦大学出版社.]

Wang, N. 2019. *The History of Foreign Literary Criticism in Contemporary China*. Beijing: China Social Sciences Press. [王宁. 2019. 当代中国外国文学批评史. 北京：中国社会科学出版社.]

Xie, T. 1999. *Translation Studies*. Shanghai: Shanghai Foreign Language Education Press. [谢天振. 1999. 译介学. 上海：上海外语教育出版社.]

Xie, T. (ed.). 2003. *New Horizons in Translation Studies*. Qingdao: Qingdao Publishing Group. [谢天振. 2003. 翻译研究新视野. 青岛：青岛出版社.]

Xie, T. (ed.). 2008. *Introduction to Contemporary Foreign Translation Theory*. Tianjin: Nankai University Press. [谢天振. 2008. 当代外国翻译理论导读. 天津：南开大学出版社.]

Xie, T. & Cha, M. (eds.). 2004. *A History of Modern Chinese Literature in Translation*. Shanghai: Shanghai Foreign Language Education Press. [谢天振，查明建编. 2004. 中国现代翻译文学史. 上海：上海外语教育出版社.]

Xu, J. & Song, X. (eds.). 2008. *Into the World of Fu Lei's Translation*. Beijing: Higher Education Press. [许钧，宋学智编. 2008. 走进傅雷的翻译世界. 北京：高等教育出版社.]

Zhang, B. & Xu, J. (eds.). 2002. *Translation Studies for the 21st Century*. Beijing: The Commercial Press. [张柏然，许钧编. 2002. 面向21世纪的译学研究. 北京：商务印书馆.]

Zhang, J. & Zhang, N. 2005. *Principles of Literary Translation* (rev. ed.). Beijing: Tsinghua University Press. [张今，张宁. 2005. 文学翻译原理 (修订版). 北京：清华大学出版社.]

Zhang, N. 2004. *Criticism of Chinese and Western Translation*. Beijing: Tsinghua University Press. [张南峰. 2004. 中西译学批评. 北京：清华大学出版社.]

Index

Note: Page numbers followed by "n" denote endnotes.

A Critique of Postcolonial Reason: Towards a History of the Vanishing Present (Spivak) 87
adaptation 3, 16, 18, 43, 197, 201
Adorno, Theodor W. 30
Aesthetics (Hegel) 75
African postcolonial literature 110
Age of Enlightenment in Europe 201
"The age of the world picture" (Heidegger) 158
À la recherche du temps perdu see *Remembrance of Things Past* (Proust)
"alternative" modernity 5
America Confucius Institutes 169
American: comparative literature 108, 117; culture 23, 72, 109, 200; literary criticism 90, 107; literary theory 50, 95, 98; translation theory circles 77
American Comparative Literature Association 108
Americanization 185, 200
American New Criticism 44
American-style democracy 200
de Angelis, Milo 64, 68
Anglocentrism 4
Anglophone world 7, 9, 54, 55, 61, 63, 73, 77, 95, 190
antagonistic relationship 108
anthropocentrism 149
anthropological turn 112
anthropology 8, 17, 25, 38, 156
"anti-aesthetic" nature 7
anti-classical Chinese 179
anti-Confucianism movement 179
anti-suppression strategy 66
anti-tradition movement 179

aphasia phenomenon 11, 61
Aristotle 188
art: "art for art's sake" concept 139; in Chinese language 161; criticism 30, 197; psychology 158; translation of 157
artificial intelligence (AI) 9, 21, 198
artistic criticism 142–143
Asian literature 109
authenticity 19, 20, 42, 45, 46, 50, 99, 101
autocratic rule 179

Bakhtin, Mikhail 110, 113
de Balzac, Honoré 73
Barthes, Roland 152
Bassnett, Susan 1, 2, 4, 6, 12, 26, 27, 103, 117, 122, 124, 126, 127, 129, 130, 132
Baudelaire, Charles 30–32, 76
Baudrillard, Jean 140, 141
Beebee, Thomas 2
Beijing Xinzhi Shushe 182
Being and Time (Heidegger) 89
Bell, Daniel A. 177n10
Benjamin, W. 8, 18, 19, 29, 30, 34, 35, 36, 42, 61, 76, 91, 92, 93, 152, 153, 157
Bergson, Henri 185
Beyond Translation (Bassnett) 124
Bhabha, H. K. 2, 7, 20, 69, 81, 82, 98, 100, 104, 104n38, 165, 166
Bible 19, 34, 59–60
Biguenet, John 39
Black Holes (Miller and Asensi) 55
Bloom, Harold 54
"border-crossing" feature 145
"Border Crossings: Translating Theory" 56

British and American cultural studies 112
British Romantic poetry 54
broad cross-cultural context 3, 108, 193
broad multidisciplinary knowledge 126
Buddhist Scriptures in China 17

"cage of language" 26, 32, 150
Cai, Yuanpei 179
Calligraphy 161
Can Xue 170
Catford, John C. 122
Centre for Contemporary Cultural Studies (CCCS) 6
Centre for Translation and Comparative Culture Studies 124
Chan, Sinwai 189
Charles Dickens: The World of His Novels (Miller) 55
Chen, Anna Gustafsson 175, 177, 191
Chen, Duxiu 179, 180
China Information journal 173
Chinese: academic community 192; characters 160–161; context 184, 193; cultural modernity 5; cultural scholarship 11; global characteristics of 166; international academic circles 169–174; language and culture 3, 169; language and script 160; literary criticism 5, 10, 61; literary language 35; literary works 70; literature and culture 11, 117, 170, 184; reform and opening-up policy 178; as regional-global language 169; religious culture 179; revolution 178, 179, 195; translation community 43
Chinese Academic Translation Project 70
Chinese Academy of Social Sciences 109
Chinese American literature 109
"Chinese" American writers 168
Chinese Communist Party (CCP) 179, 195
Chinese culture 3, 5, 8, 10–12, 23, 34, 69, 159, 168, 202; aphasia phenomenon 11; colonizing, process of 190; globalization of 160; long-standing deficit in 116; soft power of 157; total Westernization of 165, 167; values and aesthetic sentiments of 168
Chinese fever 166, 169
Chinese language: Calligraphy 161; with Chinese characters 160; Europeanization 5; into foreign languages 206; May Fourth Movement 85; modernization of 67
Chinese literature 9, 61, 110, 186; academic works, in English context 9; cultural criticism of 113; internationalization of 176
Chinese-to-foreign translation 23
Chomsky, Noam 20
Cicero, Marcus Tullius 17
classical Chinese literature 5, 35, 180, 185, 186
classical European literary text 125
Cohen, Ralph 112
Collège International de Philosophie 37
colonialism 89, 92, 95
colonial translators 94, 96
colonization 76, 106, 167, 181
commodity economy 140
communication 16, 18, 19, 40, 47
The Communist Manifesto (Marx and Engels) 182, 200, 201
community culture 6
comparative literature 1, 16, 17, 25, 106, 107, 110, 111, 112, 113, 124, 125, 126, 127, 128, 146; authenticity of 108; definition of 112; Pan-cultural tendency 108; perspective of 109; postmodernism and postmodernist issues 109; Western-centrism 125
Comparative Literature: A Critical Introduction (Bassnett) 124
Comparative Literature: Facing the Choice Again (Bassnett) 112
Comparative Literature in the Age of Globalization (Saussy) 108
comparative literature studies 115, 123
comprehensive knowledge 18
computer-updated machine translation 21
Concept of Art Criticism in German Romanticism 30
Confucian concepts 160
Confucianism 183
Confucius Institutes 166, 169, 188
Constructing Cultures: Essays on Literary Translation (Bassnett) 1, 12, 103, 117
consumer culture 6, 107, 140; aesthetic features of 136–142; aesthetic value of 141; characteristics of 139, 141; ornamental value 141; packaging 141; performativity 141;

postmodernism 138; timeliness of 141
consumer society 66, 135–143, 147
contemporary Chinese literary criticism 67, 107, 112
contemporary Chinese literature 34, 76, 113, 142–143, 145, 185, 197
contemporary culture: iconographical turn 142–145; scholarship 128; visual culture 142–145
contemporary neo-Marxism 203
contemporary translation studies 1, 18, 20
Contemporary Translation Studies 103
Contemporary Translation Theories (Gentzler) 77, 78n2, 205
"The contradictions of postmodernism" (Eagleton) 136
contrastive linguistics 16, 17, 106
copyright law 74
corpus-based analysis 25
correspondence theory 128
cosmopolitan characteristics 201
cosmopolitanism 194
countless relative truths 20
Cowie, M. 17, 179
creative interpretation 207
creative treason 7
critical inquiry 45, 143
"Critical Inquiry: The End of Theory?" conference 144
criticism 56, 86, 98, 99, 114
Critique of the Gotha Program (Marx) 182
cross-artistic approach 144
cross-cultural communication 198
cross-cultural comparisons 115
cross-cultural context 200
cross-cultural intersemiotic translation 22, 149–158, 150, 152, 156, 161–162
cross-cultural studies 1
cross-cultural translation 150, 197
cross-linguistic translation 197
Culler, J. 39
cultural-political criticism 82
Cultural Revolution 184, 185
Cultural School 2, 131
Cultural Sciences 13n12
cultural studies 1, 106, 107; Anglocentric model of 1; "anti-aesthetic" nature of 7; anti-elite and massoriented characteristics of 7; contemporary development of 7; definition of 6; dilemma of 6; non-elite academic discourse and research method 7; theoretical methods of 113; translation based on 2; translation turn in 4, 9, 18
cultural translation 2, 4, 20, 71, 86, 100, 165, 207; concept of 84, 98; "foreignness" of 102; performative process of 102
cultural translation strategy 69, 98–104
cultural translation theory 8
cultural transmission 14n13, 114
cultural turn 8, 9, 77, 178, 195, 196
culture/cultural: academic thoughts 69; in age of globalization 165; anthropology 17; authenticity 19; "borderline" theory 101; capital 76; communication 24, 169; concepts 61; construction 104; controversial concept 16; criticism 7, 10, 45, 62, 71, 77, 113, 139, 146; dimension 4; Enlightenment 179–181; fast food 147; globalization 18, 23, 114, 116, 187; identity 109; infiltration 101; interpretation 25; landscapes 23; modernity 203; and political strategies 91–97; proliferation 136; reproduction 84; transformation 14n13, 60

da (expressiveness) 3
Damrosch, David 27n1
Das Kapital 182
da Vinci, Leonardo 154–156
Death of a Discipline (Spivak) 87, 125
Deconstruction and Postcolonial Translation 103
deconstruction principles 47, 60
deconstruction theory 29, 36, 62, 88
deconstructive criticism 54, 55, 87
deconstructive methods 54, 131
deconstructive philosophy 44
deconstructive translation 57, 86–91, 101; forerunner of 29–36; intervention and influence 36–39; issue of untranslatability 40–45; principle 90; "relevant" translation 45–51
deconstructive translation theory 29, 36, 40, 54, 61, 89, 122
deconstructive turn 50
deep-rooted epistemological system 83
De la grammatologie (Derrida) 20, 38
de Man, Paul 54, 78n1
demarginalization 83
democratic revolutions 180

Deng, Xiaoping 178
Denham, John Sir. 63
"depovertization" process 178, 189
Derrida, Jacques 2, 7, 19, 20, 21, 22, 29, 33, 36, 37, 42, 45, 47, 48, 54, 62, 67, 75, 88, 90, 93, 104, 122, 138, 148, 196; cultural and theoretical interpretation 89; cultural translation 91; deconstruction theory 90; linguistic translation 91; in translation studies 88; view of translation 90
"de-third-worldization" process 178, 189
Devi, Mahasweta 86, 94, 95
Die literarische Welt journal 35
différance 39, 49, 50, 89
The Disappearance of God: Five Nineteenth-Century Writers (Miller) 55
discursive world concept 120
Dissemination (Derrida) 37, 89
Dollerup, Cay 2, 16, 27
domestication 61, 63, 67, 68
Dream of the Red Chamber novel 56
Dryden, John 63
"dual reader," role of 89
dubbing and subtitling 25
Du Droit a la philosophie see The Law of Philosophy (Derrida)
Du, Fu 188
dynamic cultural interpretation 21
dynamic equivalence 19

Eagleton, T. 7, 98, 113, 136
The Ear of the Other (Derrida) 37
Eastern and Western cultures 112
East-West cross-cultural theoretical perspective 3
ecocriticism 149
École Normale Supérieure (ENS) 37
economic development 178
economic globalization 23, 107, 116, 200
Elective Affinities (Goethe) 30
Eliot, T. S. 185, 188
elite culture 135
Engels 184
Engineering Citation Index (EI) 14n15
English 10, 11, 171, 176; "English-centric" research mode 8; English-centrism 8; as hegemonic language 2; literature and culture 98
Englund, Peter 175
Eoyang, Eugene Chen 2, 3

Essentialism 99
The Ethics of Reading: Kant, de Man, Eliot, Trollope, James, and Benjamin (Miller) 55
ethnocentrism 62
ethno-national boundaries 169
Eurocentric comparative literature 128
Eurocentrism 15, 125
Europeanization 5, 167
Even-Zohar, Itamar 108, 122
exotic cultures 21
"external study of translation" 171

faithfulness 5, 19, 21, 31, 41, 149, 157
fashion and film culture 6
Faulkner, William 175, 185, 188
feminism 17, 92
Feminist Experiences: The Women's Movement in Four Cultures (Bassnett) 124
feminist movements 86
Feng, Zhi 120
feudal dynasties 179
Fiction and Repetition: Seven English Novels (Miller) 55
foreignization 61, 63
foreignization strategy 55, 69
foreignizing translation strategy 64
foreign languages 15, 194, 206
foreign literature 5, 10
"foreignness" concept 102
foreign-to-Chinese translation 23
formalism 129
Foucault, M. 71, 77, 99, 119, 138
frequent practice 18
Freudianism 173
Freud, Sigmund 67, 185
Frye, Northrop 113
Fu, Lei 73, 149, 153, 160, 190

The Gadfly (Voynich) 184
Gao, Xingjian 170, 190
general culture 137
Gentzler, Edwin 20, 26, 27n1, 29, 49, 77, 97, 205
Glas (Derrida) 37, 87
global culture 21, 188–191
global English(es) to global Chinese(s) 165–169
global humanities concept 194
globalization 2, 4, 8, 11, 16, 23, 24, 59, 100, 110, 113, 131, 143, 159, 160, 185; cultural perspective 192;

of culture 201; impact of 166; phenomenon of 203; world cultures 167
global language systems 23, 160
"glocalization" strategy 110
Goethe 181, 184, 188
Goldblatt, Howard 175, 177, 191
Gombrich, Ernst 152, 153, 158
Gorky, Maxim 184
grabbism 5, 13n8
Gu, Hongming 190
Guo, Moruo 5, 181

half-colloquial language style 199
Hartman, Geoffrey 54
Hawthorne and History: Defacing It (Miller) 55
Heaney, Seamus 72–73
hegemonic power 167
Heidegger, Martin 29, 67, 87, 158, 185
Hemingway, Ernest 185, 188
Herberts, Richard 30
Hermans, Theo 2
hermeneutic theories 17, 111
History of the International Labor Alliance (Marx) 182
How Steel Was Tempered (Ostrovsky) 184
Hugo, Victor 187
Hu, Shi 5, 179, 181
Husserl, Edmund 37, 75, 89, 90
hybridity, cultural strategy of 98–104, 99

Ibsen, Henrik 181
iconographical criticism 144, 145
iconographical turn 142, 197
iconographical writing 136, 145, 148, 161
Illuminationen (Illuminations) 30
image criticism 144
image translation 152
Imaginary Maps (Devi) 86, 95
imperialism 89, 148
independent discipline 16
In Other Worlds: Essays in Cultural Politics (Spivak) 87
instrument of ideology 182–185
intercultural communication translation 128
intercultural dimension 25
intercultural research 3
intercultural translation 4
interdisciplinary 83, 144, 194
interlingual translation 22
international academic community 3, 10, 11, 203

International Conference on Cultural Translation 207n1
international English literature 127
international translation community 17
international translation studies 116
international translation symposium 15
Internet 18, 116, 197; culture 6; literature 67; writing 147
interpretation 86–91
intersemiotic translation 22, 25, 100, 135, 145
intralingual translation 22, 41
irreproducibility 50
Iser, Wolfgang 2, 7, 77, 151, 152

Jakobson, R. 22, 40, 41, 135, 144, 150, 197
Jameson, F. 7, 100, 109, 113, 138, 139, 141, 187, 203
Jauss, Hans Robert 76, 77
Jia, Pingwa 170
Johansen 162
John Christophe (Roland) 155
Joyce, James 185, 188

Kant, Immanuel 87–88
Kingdom of Poetry 67
Klein, Melanie 96
Knives and Angels: Latin American Women's Writing (Bassnett) 124
Kuang, Mohan 182
Kundera, Milan 185

La Carte postale see The Post Card (Derrida)
La Dissémination see Dissemination (Derrida)
Lambert, José 2, 12n1
Laocoon (Lessing) 149
La Société de consummation (Baudrillard) 140
La voix et le phénomène see Speech and Phenomenon (Derrida)
The Law of Philosophy (Derrida) 37
Leavis, F. R. 6, 113
L'écriture et la différence see Writing and Difference (Derrida)
20 Lectures on World Masterpieces of Art (Fu Lei) 153, 154
Lee, Mabel 170, 190
Lefevere, André 1, 2, 4, 6, 12, 26, 27, 103, 117, 119, 120, 122, 123, 124
Le Spleen de Paris (Paris Spleen) poem 30
Lessing, Gotthold E. 149

Lévi-Strauss, Claude 37–38
Li, Bai 188
Li, Dazhao 179, 182
Ling Shan (Gao) 170
linguistic adjustments 71
linguistic and cultural context 58
linguistic conversion 91
linguistic faithfulness 32
linguistic knowledge 36
linguistic turn 112
"linguo-centric" translation, definition of 197
linguo-centrism stigma 144, 196
linguo-symbolic text 151
Lin, Shu 43, 52n29, 187, 190
Lin, Yutang 190
literal language, faithfulness of 21
literal translation 21, 46, 65
literary creation 17, 75, 142, 144, 145, 189, 197
literary criticism 39, 55, 59, 113, 135
"Literary History as a Challenge to Literary Theory" (Jauss) 76
Literary Knowledge: A Polemical and Programmatic Essay on its Nature, Growth, Relevance and Transmission (Lefevere) 117
literary theory 37, 113, 114, 142, 197
literary translation 18, 21, 30, 32, 61, 78, 118, 149
Literature and Translation (Bassnett) 124
literature-as-universal-civilizing-force approach 126
literature knowledge 107
Liu, Zhenyun 170
The Location of Culture (Bhabha) 99, 100
logocentrism 88–89, 98
L'Oreille de l'autre see The Ear of the Other (Derrida)
Lukács, Georg 83, 86
Lu Xun 5, 13n8, 34, 35, 78, 167, 179, 180, 187, 188, 199

MacGaffey, Wyatt 157
machine translation 198
macro-theoretical perspective 100
Malmqvist, Göran 175
de Man, Paul 8, 33
Mao, Zedong 178, 182, 183, 199
"Mao Zedong Thought" 183
Marges de la philosophie see Margins of Philosophy (Derrida)
"marginal" discipline 22
Margins of Philosophy (Derrida) 37, 89
Márquez, Gabriel García 185
Marxism 61, 137, 180, 182, 183, 195, 200
Marxist philosophy 44
Marxist Socialism (Marx) 182
Marx, K. 184
Master of Translation and Interpreting programs 16
May Fourth Movement 5, 61, 67, 85, 181, 190; cultural academic thoughts 69; Western literature 69
May Fourth New Culture Movement 153
media culture 6
metaphysical interpretation 90
Michelangelo 154
Middle Kingdom 167, 179
Miller, J. Hillis 2, 7, 27, 54, 55, 85, 113, 170
mimicry 98–104
Ming Dong Gu 188
minoritization 103, 167
"minority" studies 82
misreading 60
mistranslation 207
Mitchell, W. J. T. 143, 144, 159
modern Chinese literature 5, 67, 120, 170, 173, 186, 199
Modern English 72
modernism, traditional sense of 137
modernist art 141
modernist culture, characteristics of 139
modernist elite culture 138
modernist poetry 30
modernity 109
Modern Language Association of America 121
Mona Lisa (Da Vinci) 154–155
monographs 16
Morrison, Donald 175
Mo Yan 170, 174, 175, 189, 190
multi-disciplinary knowledge 56, 87
mutual infiltration 66
"My View on Marxism" (Li) 182

Naipaul, V. S. 185
national culture, decolonization of 68
National Social Science Fund of China 192, 194
Nation and Narration (Bhabha) 99
neocolonialism 85
New Culture Movement 179, 180, 195
New Literary History journal 76, 111
Newmark, Peter 122

New Starts: Performative Topographies in Literature and Criticism (Miller) 56
Nida, Eugene 19, 20, 122
Nietzsche, Friedrich 67, 87, 179, 185
Niranjana, Tejaswini 103
non-authenticity 99
non-elitist culture 8
non-literary translation 25
non-marginalization movement 117

Occidentalism 116
Of Grammatology (Derrida) 9, 14n14, 42, 86, 87, 89, 93
On Deconstruction: Theory and Criticism after Structuralism (Culler) 39
One-Way Street (Benjamin) 30
online writing 6
On Literature (Miller) 55
Opium War 167
oral interpreting 25
ordinary people 57
Orientalism 81–86, 82, 83, 99; concept of 84; construction and criticism of 83; definition of 83
Oriental myth 82
original source language 58
Origin of Geometry (Husserl) 37, 75, 89
The Origin of German Tragic Drama (Benjamin) 30
ornamental value 141
Ostrovsky, Nicolas Alexyevitch 184
Others (Miller) 55
Outside in the Teaching Machine (Spivak) 87, 91
outsiders 2
"overgeneralization of translation" phenomenon 206

Pan-cultural tendency 107, 108
paradoxical crisis 126
Paris's Sights (Baudelair) 76
People's Republic of China 178
performativity 141
Perspectives: Studies in Translatology (Dollerup) 16, 27n3
philosophical translation 43
pictorial turn 142, 197
picture theory 143
Plato 188
pluralism 38
pluralistic symbiosis 106
Poets of Reality: Six Twentieth-Century Writers (Miller) 55

political modernity 61
"The Politics of Translation" 86
polysystem theory 108, 129, 131
popular culture 6, 138
post-Babelian 41
The Post Card (Derrida) 37
postcolonial criticism 99
postcolonial cultural criticism 70
postcolonial cultural translation 101
postcolonial female authors 93
postcolonial "interaction" 66
postcolonialism 17, 85, 113; characteristics of 87; critical theory of 86; "three musketeers" of 87
postcolonial translation theory 20, 81, 86, 98, 101, 103; cultural and political strategies 91–97; cultural translation strategy 98–104; deconstructive translation 86–91; interpretation 86–91; mimicry, hybridity, the third space 98–104; Orientalism 81–86; principle of 89; traveling theory 81–86
Post-Colonial Translation: Theory and Practice (Bassnett) 124
post-enlightenment 116
post-humanism 198
postmodern age 145
postmodern consumer society 140–141
postmodernism 100, 108, 109, 113, 138, 188; characteristics of 138, 139; Western Marxist studies 139
poststructuralism 17, 138
Pound, Ezra 63
power politics 82
previous literary *vs.* linguistic translation 130
proposition 44, 71
Proust, Marcel 30, 32, 36, 185
pseudo-translation 3, 9, 207

Qian, Xuantong 179
Qian, Zhongshu 43–44, 52n30, 188
Qing Dynasty 5, 13n7, 69
Qu, Yuan 188

Race and Class issue 83
Raritan Quarterly 83
Reading Narrative (Miller) 55
reading strategy 59
Red Sorghum (Mo Yan) 175
"Reflection on Comparative Literature in the Twenty-First Century" 132

Reflections on Exile and Other Essays (Said) 83, 86
relevant translation 20–21, 47
Remak, Henry 112
Rembrandt 154
Remembrance of Things Past (Proust) 35, 76
"reproduction-style" cultural translation 83
Rethinking Translation: Discourse, Subjectivity, Ideology (Venuti) 62
"retranslating" literary 114
revolutionary ideas 64
Reynolds, Joshua 154
Robertson, Roland 27n2
Roland, Roman 155
romantic literature 87
Rothenberg, Anne F. 99
The Rout (Fadeyev) 183
Rubens, Peter Paul 154
Ruo Fei 182
Russian formalist criticism 111

Said, Edward 81, 82, 83, 86, 99, 104, 113
Sartre, Jean-Paul 67, 185
Saussy, Haun 108
The Scandals of Translation: Towards an Ethics of Difference (Venuti) 62
Schleiermacher, Friedrich 63, 64–65
Schneider, Axel 177n10
Scholte, Jan Aart 27n2
"school of translation studies" 117
Schopenhauer, Arthur 185
Schulte, Rainer 39
Science Citation Index (SCI) 14n15
scientific literature 21
scientism impact 111
secondary elaboration 101
Second World War 125
self-Orientalization 84
sense-for-sense translation 20
Shakespeare 184, 188
Shanghai Academy of Art 153
Shuttleworth, M. 17, 179
"singular" (monolithic) modernity 186
Sino-foreign cooperation approach 70, 174
Sixth Triannual Congress of the Chinese Comparative Literature Association and International Congress 112
Snell-Hornby, Mary 122
Social Sciences in China 75
socio-cultural phenomena 24
Soul Mountain (Xingjian) 190
Soviet literary thought 184

specific culture 137
Specters of Marx (Derrida) 37
Spectres de Marx see *Specters of Marx* (Derrida)
Speech Acts in Literature (Miller) 55
Speech and Phenomenon (Derrida) 37, 89
Spivak, Gayatri 2, 7, 20, 27, 27n1, 49, 69, 75, 81, 86, 87, 88, 89, 99, 103, 113, 125, 130, 146, 171; gender and racial characteristics 92; translation theory and practice 97; Translator's Preface 90
Steiner, George 122
structural anthropology 38
structuralism 17, 38, 50
structuralist turn 50
structural linguistics 20, 206
Subaltern Studies 94
sub-discipline 113
subjective consciousness 70
subjective initiative 43
subjective interpretation 43
subjectivity 33, 119
superficial faithfulness 32
Su, Shi 188
Sylvia Plath (Bassnett) 124

Tableaux Parisiens see *Paris's Sights* (Baudelair)
Taine, Hippolyte 154
"Talks at the Yan'an Forum on Literature and Art" 183
Tao, Yuanming 188
Tarchetti, Iginio Ugo 63
target language 62, 96
The Task of the Translator (Benjamin) 18, 30
textual criticism 144
textual translation 135
theoretical criticism 144
Theories of Translation: An Anthology of Essays from Dryden to Derrida (Schulte and Biguenet) 39
thinking, "Western-centric" mode of 115
third space 98–104
Third World texts 82, 93–94, 99
time and space concept 141
Topographies (Miller) 55
totality, modernist conception of 138
Toury, Gideon 50, 122
Tower of Babel (Derrida) 18, 39–41, 44, 45, 96

traditional Chinese art 153
traditional Chinese culture 3, 34, 35
traditional comparative literature studies 112
traditional linguistic translation studies 88
traditional "orthodox" disciplines 17
traditional sense, core principles in 50
traditional textual criticism 142
traditional translation 152
transcending colonialism 85
transformational-generative grammar 20
translatability 32, 41, 47, 96, 120, 128
Translating Cultures (Spivak) 96
Translating Literature: Practice and Theory in a Comparative Literature Context (Lefevere) 117, 121
Translating Literature: The German Tradition: From Luther to Rosenzweig (Lefevere) 117
Translating Poetry: Seven Strategies and a Blueprint (Lefevere) 117
translation: Buddhist Scriptures 17; as communication skill 16; concept of 18; cross-cultural translation 197; cross-linguistic translation 197; as cultural enlightenment 179–181; cultural turn in 193; as culture 96; definition of 2, 4, 122, 196; dynamic and manipulative role of 118; faithfulness of 157; as global culture and world literature 188–191; independent discipline of 17; as instrument of ideology 182–185; linguistic-centralism in 196; linguistic faithfulness 32; multi-disciplinary to 20; multi-perspective approach to 20; paradox of 41; "resistant" foreignizing-style of 68; traditional definition of 18; as way of opening up to the world 185–188; Western cultural contexts 152; word-for-word language-based type of 151
Translation Changes Everything: Theory and Practice (Venuti) 62
translation concept 6
translation criticism 123
Translation/History/Culture: A Source Book (Lefevere) 117
"Translation of Global Culture: Towards Interdisciplinary Theoretical Construction" 207n2
translation "proper" 41

Translation, Rewriting and the Manipulation of Literary Fame (Lefevere) 117, 118
translation studies 109, 115; achievements 17; construction of 18–22; cultural studies 18; cultural turn in 122, 129, 192; development of 128; discipline of 87; legitimizing 16–18; vision of 199–200
Translation Studies (Bassnett) 124, 128
Translation Studies Colloquium in Leuven 6
The Translation Studies Reader (Venuti) 62
translation studies turn 9, 22–27
translation theory 2, 17, 18, 20, 21, 29, 30, 33, 39, 46, 50, 55, 70, 77
translation turn 1, 113
translatology 16
translators: subjective consciousness 70; task of 42; translation and interpretation 34
The Translator's Invisibility: A History of Translation (Venuti) 61, 62, 71
Translator's Preface (Spivak) 9, 86, 89, 90
transnational capitalism 100
transparency 66
traveling theory 56, 81–86, 84, 85
Tripp, Chester D. 99
Turk, Horst 2
Turner, Graeme 113
Twain, Mark 188

universal philosophical thought 59
untranslatability 41, 45, 47, 50, 60, 96, 120, 128

Venuti, Lawrence 20, 42, 45, 61–62, 63, 64, 66, 68, 69, 71, 78, 78n2
Versions of Pygmalion (Miller) 55
"very prescriptive" theory 50
Victorian Subjects (Miller) 55
virtual cyberspace 145, 147
visual culture 136, 138, 142, 197
visual culture criticism 144
Voynich, Ethel Lilian 184

Waiting for Godot (Beckett) 191
Wang, Anyi 170
Wang, Yangming 188
Wenxin Diaolong 135
Wenyi Yanjiu (Literary and Art Studies) 13n4
Western Age of Enlightenment 149

"Western-centric" research mode 8
Western-centric vision 127
Western-centrism 15, 125
Western cultural contexts 93, 152
Western cultural modernity 5
Western culture and literature 5
Western imperialist cultural hegemonism 82
Westernization 5, 185, 187
Western literary studies 111
Western literary theories 67
Western literature 5, 44, 69
Western Marxism 7, 139, 187
Western metaphysics 88
Western postmodern theory 138
Williams, Raymond 7, 113
Wong, Laurence K. P. 189
"word-by-word" translation 46
The Work of Art in the Age of Mechanical Reproduction (Benjamin) 30, 157
world language system 167
world literature 188–191
"World Literature and Translation Studies" (Venuti) 78
"world literature" concept 201–202, 204
"world picture" era 159

The World, the Text and the Critic (Said) 83
Writing and Difference (Derrida) 37, 89

xin (faithfulness) 3
Xinhua News Agency 199
Xin Qingnian magazine 180
Xiong, Deshan 182

ya (elegance) 3
"Yale Critics" 54
Yale University 54
Yan, Fu 3, 190
Yang, Gladys 170
Yang, Xianyi 170, 190
Yan, Lianke 170
Yu, Hua 35, 170, 187

Zhang, Jiang 56
Zhang, Longxi 177n10
Zhang, Yimou 160
Zhongguo Bijiao Wenxue (Comparative Literature in China) 13n4
Zhongguo Fanyi (Chinese Translators Journal) 13n4
"Zhu Guangqian's translation" 75
Zhu, Zhixin 182

For Product Safety Concerns and Information please contact our EU representative GPSR@taylorandfrancis.com
Taylor & Francis Verlag GmbH, Kaufingerstraße 24, 80331 München, Germany

www.ingramcontent.com/pod-product-compliance
Lightning Source LLC
Chambersburg PA
CBHW061346300426
44116CB00011B/2015